Byron and Italy

Manchester University Press

Byron and Italy

EDITED BY
ALAN RAWES AND DIEGO SAGLIA

Manchester University Press

Copyright © Manchester University Press 2017

While copyright in the volume as a whole is vested in Manchester University Press, copyright in individual chapters belongs to their respective authors, and no chapter may be reproduced wholly or in part without the express permission in writing of both author and publisher.

Published by Manchester University Press
Altrincham Street, Manchester M1 7JA
www.manchesteruniversitypress.co.uk

British Library Cataloguing-in-Publication Data is available

ISBN 978 1 5261 0055 9 hardback
ISBN 978 1 5261 4352 5 paperback

First published by Manchester University Press in hardback 2017

This edition first published 2020

The publisher has no responsibility for the persistence or accuracy of URLs for any external or third-party internet websites referred to in this book, and does not guarantee that any content on such websites is, or will remain, accurate or appropriate.

Typeset by Out of House Publishing

Contents

	Notes on contributors	*page* vii
	Abbreviations	x
	Byron in Italy: a chronology	xi
	Introduction: 'Un paese tutto poetico' – Byron in Italy, Italy in Byron ALAN RAWES AND DIEGO SAGLIA	1
1	The literature of Italy in Byron's poems of 1817–20 NICHOLAS HALMI	23
2	Byron's ethnographic eye: the poet among the Italians GIOIA ANGELETTI	44
3	From Lord Nelvil to Dugald Dalgetty: Byron's Scottish identity in Italy JONATHAN GROSS	61
4	The garden of the world: Byron and the geography of Italy MAURO PALA	77
5	'Something I have seen or think it possible to see': Byron and Italian art in Ravenna JANE STABLER	94
6	'Something sensible to grasp at': Byron and Italian Catholicism BERNARD BEATTY	112

CONTENTS

7 The politics of the unities: tragedy and the
   Risorgimento in Byron and Manzoni   130
   ARNOLD ANTHONY SCHMIDT

8 *Parisina*, *Mazeppa* and Anglo-Italian displacement 149
   PETER W. GRAHAM

9 This 'still exhaustless mine': de Staël, Goethe and
   Byron's Roman lyricism   166
   ALAN RAWES

10 Playing with history: Byron's Italian dramas   188
   MIRKA HOROVÁ

11 'Where shall I turn me?': Italy and irony in *Beppo* and
   Don Juan   208
   DIEGO SAGLIA

   Select bibliography   227
   Index   241

Contributors

Gioia Angeletti is Associate Professor of English Literature at the University of Parma. Her research focuses mainly on late-eighteenth- and nineteenth-century English and Scottish poetry and theatre and, more recently, contemporary Scottish women playwrights. She is the author of *Eccentric Scotland: Three Victorian Poets* (2004) and *Lord Byron and Discourses of Otherness: Scotland, Italy, and Femininity* (2012), and is the editor of *Emancipation, Liberation, and Freedom: Romantic Drama and Theatre in Britain, 1760–1830* (2010). She is working on a monograph on eighteenth- and nineteenth-century diasporic Scottish writers.

Bernard Beatty is Senior Fellow in the School of English at the University of Liverpool and Associate Fellow in the School of Divinity at the University of St Andrews. He is the author of two books and has edited three collections of essays on Byron. He has written on Romanticism, the Bible, many major authors and aspects of literary theory. He was editor of *The Byron Journal* from 1986 to 2004. Recent publications have been about Shelley and the theatre; Byron, Pope and Newman; Browning and Newman; Romantic decadence; and Byron's temperament. Pending ones are on Byron and Pope, and Byron's 'dramatic monologues'.

Peter W. Graham is Professor of English at Virginia Tech and Director of International Relations for the Messolonghi Byron Research Center. His publications on Byron and his circle include *Byron's Bulldog: The Letters of John Cam Hobhouse to Lord Byron* (1984), *Don Juan and Regency England* (1990) and various essays.

Jonathan Gross is Professor of English at DePaul University. He is the author of *Byron: The Erotic Liberal* (2000) and the editor of *Byron's 'Corbeau Blanc': The Life and Letters of Lady Melbourne* (1997).

Nicholas Halmi is Professor of English and Comparative Literature at the University of Oxford and Margaret Candfield Fellow of University College, Oxford. He is the author of *The Genealogy of the Romantic Symbol* (2007) and the editor, most recently, of the *Norton Critical Edition of Wordsworth's Poetry and Prose* (2013). In 2015 he was awarded a Leverhulme Trust Major Research Fellowship to write a book on aesthetic historicism in the Romantic period.

Mirka Horová teaches English literature in the Department of Anglophone Literatures and Cultures at Charles University in Prague. With her research focus predominantly on Byron, her academic work includes British Romanticism in general, contemporary Romantic legacies and Scandinavian literature. Her publications on Byron include special issues of *The Byron Journal* (2015) and *Litteraria Pragensia* (2013), and chapters in numerous books, most recently in R. Beaton and C. Kenyon Jones (eds.), *Byron: The Politics of Poetry and the Poetry of Politics* (2016). She is currently working on a monograph on Byron's drama and a co-edited collection of essays in honour of Peter Cochran.

Mauro Pala is Professor of Comparative Literature at the University of Cagliari. He has been a Fulbright distinguished lecturer at the University of Notre Dame, a visiting professor at the University of Limoges and a visiting scholar at Trinity College Dublin. Since 2011 he has also been a lecturer at the Writing the Mediterranean Summer School at the University of Malta. He has published extensively on European Romanticism, critical theory and Postcolonial Studies. He is a member of the scientific board of the Palermo European PhD programme in Cultural Studies and, since 2014, has sat on the ruling Board of COMPALIT, Italy's leading association for Comparative Literature Studies. He is currently working on a book on forms of subalternity in Joyce.

Alan Rawes teaches at the University of Manchester. His publications include *Byron's Poetic Experimentation* (2000), *English Romanticism and the Celtic World* (co-ed., 2003), *Romantic Biography* (co-ed., 2003), *Romanticism and Form* (ed., 2007), *Reading, Writing* *and the Influence of Harold Bloom* (co-ed., 2010) and a special issue of *Litteraria Pragensia – Tears, and Tortures, and the Touch of Joy: Byron in Italy* (co-ed., 2013). He is a past editor of *The Byron Journal* (2005–12) and a current joint president of the International Association of Byron Societies.

Diego Saglia teaches at the University of Parma. He is the author of several essays on Byron and of the monographs *Byron and Spain: Itinerary in the Place of Writing* (1996) and *Lord Byron e le maschere della scrittura* (2009). His edited book *Byron e il segno plurale: tracce del sé, percorsi di scrittura* (2011) won the 2012 Elma Dangerfield Prize. He is also a member of the scientific advisory committee for the 'Museo Byron' project at Palazzo Guiccioli in Ravenna.

Arnold Anthony Schmidt teaches at California State University Stanislaus. His essays have appeared in *The Byron Journal*, the *Journal of Anglo-Italian Studies*, *Nineteenth-Century Contexts* and *The Wordsworth Circle*, as well as in essay collections such as B. Klein (ed.), *Fictions of the Sea* (2002) and W. Krajka (ed.), *Beyond the Roots: Conrad's Ideology & Art* (2005, also republished in a Polish translation). His *Byron and the Rhetoric of Italian Nationalism* was published in 2010. With support from the Andrew W. Mellon Foundation for research at the Huntington Library, he is currently editing a twenty-four-play anthology of *British Nautical Melodramas, 1820–1850*.

Jane Stabler teaches English literature at the University of St Andrews. Her books include *Byron, Poetics and History* (2002), which was awarded the Elma Dangerfield Prize and the British Academy's Crawshay Prize in 2003, and *The Artistry of Exile: Romantic and Victorian Writers in Italy* (2013). She currently holds a Major Leverhulme fellowship to complete work on a new edition of *Don Juan* for the Longman Annotated English Poets edition of Lord Byron's poetry.

Abbreviations

BLJ *Byron's Letters and Journals*, 12 vols, ed. L. A. Marchand (London: John Murray, 1973–94). All quotations from Byron's letters are taken from this edition.
CHP *Childe Harold's Pilgrimage* (in *CPW*).
CMP *Byron's Complete Miscellaneous Prose*, ed. A. Nicholson (Oxford: Clarendon Press, 1991).
CPW Lord Byron, *The Complete Poetical Works*, 7 vols, ed. J. J. McGann (Oxford: Clarendon Press, 1980–93). All quotations from Byron's poetry and drama are taken from this edition.
DJ   *Don Juan* (in *CPW*).

Byron in Italy: a chronology

1816

5 October: Byron and Hobhouse leave Villa Diodati for Italy, via the Rhone Valley and Simplon Pass.
10 October: They pass through Domodossola and stop at Ornavasso for the night.
11 October: On Lake Maggiore, they row to Isola Bella.
12 October: They reach Milan and take rooms at the 'Ancien Hotel de S. Marco'; over the following days they go to La Scala, visit the Biblioteca Ambrosiana twice, meet the Milanese intelligentsia (and Stendhal) and see Tommaso Sgricci at La Scala.
3 November: They leave Milan for Venice, visiting Verona, Vicenza and Padua on the way.
10 November: They arrive in Venice, and Byron takes lodgings above the shop of Signor Segati; Byron then begins studying Armenian at the monastery on San Lazzaro and embarks on a love affair with Marianna Segati.
12 November: Visits the Biblioteca Marciana.
5 December: Hobhouse departs on a tour of Italy.
26 December: Begins to attend the *conversazione* of Countess Albrizzi.

1817

12 January: Daughter Allegra born in Bath.
January–February: Byron's first Venetian *Carnevale*.
13 April: Visits the Manfrini Palace.

17 April: Leaves Venice for Rome, stopping at Padua, Ferrara, Bologna and Florence.
29 April: Arrives in Rome, stays at 66 Piazza di Spagna, visits the sights, sees an execution, sits for a bust by Thorvaldsen, finishes *Manfred* and *The Lament of Tasso*.
20 May: Leaves Rome for Venice, stopping again at Florence.
28 May: Arrives back at Venice.
14 June: Moves to Villa Foscarini at La Mira, outside Venice.
16 June: *Manfred* published.
26 June: Begins *Childe Harold* IV.
1 July: 'Monk' Lewis visiting Byron.
29 July: Finishes first draft of *Childe Harold* IV.
31 July: Hobhouse, Lewis and Marianna all with Byron at Villa Foscarini.
5 August: Begins affair with Margarita Cogni (while still with Marianna).
29 August: Signor Segati tells Byron and Hobhouse the anecdote that inspires *Beppo*.
September: Douglas Kinnaird and W. S. Rose visit Venice, Byron meets R. B. Hoppner.
11 October: Byron and Hobhouse visit Arquà.
23 October: Finishes *Beppo*.
1 November: Visits Este.
13 November: Leaves Villa Foscarini and moves back to Venice.

1818

January–February: Byron's second Venetian *Carnevale*.
8 January: Hobhouse leaves Venice for England, with the manuscript of *Childe Harold* IV.
19 January: Sends *Beppo* to John Murray.
22 January: Meets Teresa Guiccioli.
28 February: *Beppo* published.
28 April: *Childe Harold* IV published.
2 May: Allegra brought to Venice, staying with the Hoppner family.
Early June: Moves to the Palazzo Mocenigo on the Grand Canal, with Allegra.
25 June: Wins swimming race from the Lido to the far end of the Grand Canal.

3 July: Begins *Don Juan*.
July: Margarita moves into the Palazzo Mocenigo.
22 August: P. B. Shelley and Claire Clairmont arrive in Venice.
23 August: Shelley visits Byron, and they ride along the sands of the Lido.
26 August: Tells Murray he has finished his memoirs.
August: Allegra sent to Este.
19 September: Finishes Canto I of *Don Juan*.
24–29 September: The Shelleys visit Byron, who reads Canto I of *Don Juan* to Percy.
11–19 November: Byron's lawyer, Hanson, visits; Byron occupied with the sale of Newstead, and his will.
13 December: Begins Canto II of *Don Juan*.

1819

January–February: Byron's last Venetian *Carnevale*.
3 April: Sends Murray Canto II of *Don Juan*.
6 April: Informs Hobhouse he has fallen in love with Teresa Guiccioli.
13 April: The Guicciolis leave Venice for Ravenna.
15 May: Sends Murray *Don Juan* I and II, to be published anonymously.
1 June: Leaves Venice for Ravenna.
2–10 June: Travels to Ravenna via Padua, Ferrara and Bologna.
10 June: Arrives in Ravenna to find Teresa ill after a miscarriage.
21 June: Writes dedicatory sonnet to *Prophecy of Dante*.
28 June: *Mazeppa* and 'Ode to Venice' published.
15 July: *Don Juan* I and II published anonymously.
9 August: The Guicciolis leave Ravenna for Bologna.
10 August: Leaves Ravenna for Bologna.
11 August: Sees Alfieri's *Mirra* at the Arena del Sole theatre.
End of August: Allegra arrives to stay with Byron in Bologna.
September: Begins Cantos III–IV of *Don Juan*.
12 September: Leaves for Venice with Teresa; they stay at Villa Foscarini.
7–10 October: Thomas Moore visits Byron.
11 October: Gives Moore his memoirs.
28 October: Back at Palazzo Mocenigo.
1 November: Count Guiccioli arrives at Palazzo Mocenigo to take Teresa back; they depart ten days later.

8 November: Tells Murray he has written 110 stanzas of *Don Juan* III and 500 lines of *The Prophecy of Dante*.
30 November: Finishes Cantos III–IV of *Don Juan*.
21 December: Leaves Venice for Ravenna to join Teresa.
23 December: Stops in Bologna.
24 December: Arrives back in Ravenna, staying at the Albergo Imperiale.

1820

February: Moves into Palazzo Guiccioli.
19 February: Sends Cantos III and IV of *Don Juan* to Murray.
21 February: Finishes translation from Pulci's *Morgante Maggiore*.
14 March: Sends *The Prophecy of Dante* to Murray.
March: Writes 'Observations upon an Article in *Blackwood's Magazine*' and 'Francesca' (published 1830).
9 April: Tells Murray he has started writing *Marino Faliero*.
April: Carbonari activity increasing.
May: The Guicciolis' marriage in crisis.
2 July: Revolution breaks out in Naples.
13 July: Tells Moore that the pope has granted the Guicciolis a separation.
17 July: Finishes *Marino Faliero* (sends Act I to Murray on 25 July).
July/August: Joins the Carbonari, becoming *il Capo* of *I Cacciatori Americani*.
7–17 August: Sends remaining acts of *Marino Faliero* to Murray.
16 August: Visits Teresa at her father's house in Filetto.
14 October: Writes the dedication for *Marino Faliero*.
16 October: Begins Canto V of *Don Juan*.
November: Writes more material for his memoirs; Teresa moves to her father's house in Ravenna.
27 November: Finishes Canto V of *Don Juan*.
9 December: Death of local troop commander, Luigi dal Pinto, outside Byron's house.
28 December: Sends Canto V of *Don Juan* to Douglas Kinnaird.

1821

4 January: Begins 'Ravenna Journal'.
13 January: Begins *Sardanapalus*.
10 February: Writes first Bowles–Pope controversy letter.
14 February: Finishes Act I of *Sardanapalus*.
16 February: Has been buying arms for the Carbonari.
1 March: Allegra sent to the Capuchin convent in Bagnacavallo.
21 April: *Marino Faliero* and *The Prophecy of Dante* published.
25 April: *Marino Faliero* performed at Drury Lane by Robert William Elliston despite Murray's attempts to have it stopped.
27 May: Finishes *Sardanapalus*.
12 June: Begins *The Two Foscari*.
6 July: Tells Murray he has promised Teresa not to continue writing *Don Juan*.
10 July: Teresa's brother, Pietro Gamba, and father, Ruggero, are exiled to Florence.
16 July: Begins *Cain*.
25 July: Teresa leaves Ravenna for Florence.
August: Writes *The Blues*.
6–21 August: P. B. Shelley visits Byron in Ravenna.
8 August: Cantos III–V of *Don Juan* published.
September: Writes *The Vision of Judgment*.
10 September: Sends *Cain* to Murray.
4 October: Sends *The Vision of Judgment* to Murray.
9 October: Begins *Heaven and Earth*.
15 October: Begins 'Detached Thoughts'.
29 October: Leaves Ravenna for Pisa (stopping at Bologna) to join Teresa and the Shelleys.
1 November: Arrives at Casa Lanfranchi in Pisa.
5–20 November: P. B. Shelley introduces Byron to Edward Williams, Thomas Medwin and Prince Argiropolo; Byron meets John Taaffe.
14 December: Sends *Heaven and Earth* to Murray.
19 December: *Sardanapalus*, *The Two Foscari* and *Cain* published.
21 December: Begins *Werner*.

1822

3 January: First sitting for a bust by Lorenzo Bartolini.
15 January: Meets Edward Trelawney.
20 January: Finishes *Werner*.
28 January: Lady Noel dies (Byron adopts the name of 'Noel Byron' from 17 February).
24 March: Quarrel with Stefano Masi, a garrison sergeant major, outside Pisa; Masi stabbed by Byron's coachman.
14 April: Begins Canto VI of *Don Juan*.
20 April: Allegra dies.
26 April: P. B. Shelley and Williams leave Pisa for Lerici.
May: Moves to Villa Dupuy in Montenero.
29 June: The Gambas exiled from Tuscany and leave for Lucca.
Early July: Leigh Hunt and his family arrive and settle at Casa Lanfranchi, where Byron and Teresa are now settled.
8 July: P. B. Shelley and Williams sail from Livorno on the *Don Juan*, heading for Lerici.
12 July: Mary Shelley receives news that the boat has sunk.
18 July: P. B. Shelley's body found washed ashore.
End of July: Has finished Cantos VI–VIII of *Don Juan*.
15–16 August: Williams' and P. B. Shelley's bodies cremated on the beach at Viareggio.
Early September: Finishes Canto IX of *Don Juan*.
15–21 September: Hobhouse visits.
27 September: Leaves Pisa for Genoa.
3 October: Takes up residence at Casa Saluzzo in Albaro, Genoa, with Teresa, her father and her brother, Mary Shelley, Leigh Hunt and Hunt's family.
5 October: Finishes Canto X of *Don Juan*.
6 October: Begins Canto XI of *Don Juan*.
15 October: *The Vision of Judgment* published in the first issue of *The Liberal*.
31 October: Writes to John Hunt offering the unpublished six cantos of *Don Juan*, *Werner* and *Heaven and Earth* for publication in *The Liberal*.
14 November: Sends Mary Shelley sections of *The Deformed Transformed* for fair-copying.
18 November: Notifies Murray of his intention to change publisher.

23 November: Murray publishes *Werner*.
9 December: Has completed Canto XII of *Don Juan*.

1823

1 January: *Heaven and Earth* published in second issue of *The Liberal*.
10 January: Has finished *The Age of Bronze*.
February: Finishes *The Island*.
6 February: Sends corrected proofs of *Don Juan* VII to Kinnaird.
20 February: Sends corrected proofs of *Don Juan* VIII to Kinnaird.
24 February: Has finished Canto XIII of *Don Juan* (and sends this to Kinnaird by 8 March).
8 March: Has finished Canto XIV of *Don Juan*; sends *The Island* to Kinnaird.
15 March: Sends Canto XIV of *Don Juan* to Kinnaird.
31 March: Sends Canto XV of *Don Juan* to Kinnaird.
1 April: Earl and Lady Blessington, her sister Mary Ann Power and Count Alfred D'Orsay visit Byron, and then meet him regularly through April and May.
5 April: Edward Blaquiere, representative of the London Greek Committee, and Andreas Louriotis, delegate of the Greek government, visit Byron.
29 April: Elected as a member of the London Greek Committee.
6 May: Finishes Canto XVI of *Don Juan*.
8 May: Begins Canto XVII of *Don Juan*, writing fourteen stanzas before leaving for Greece.
18 June: Engages a ship, the *Hercules*, for two months and orders uniforms and helmets for himself and others.
26 June: *The Island* published by John Hunt.
16 July: Byron sets sail for Greece with Trelawney, Count Pietro Gamba, Dr Francesco Bruno, Constantine Skilitzy, various servants (Tita Falcieri, William Fletcher, Lega Zambelli and five or more others), five horses, his bulldog Moretto and the Newfoundland Lyon.

Introduction: 'Un paese tutto poetico' – Byron in Italy, Italy in Byron

Alan Rawes and Diego Saglia

The connection between Byron and Italy is one of the most familiar facts about British Romanticism.[1] The poet's many pronouncements about the country (where he lived between 1816 and 1823), its history, culture and people, as well as about his own experiences in Italy and among Italians, are well known and part of his legend. More particularly, Byron's debauchery in Venice and would-be heroics in Ravenna are often known even to those acquainted with the poet's biography only in its most simplified versions. In contrast, though the critical panorama has been changing in recent years, serious attention to Byron's literary engagement with Italy has tended to be discontinuous. Yet he wrote much of his greatest poetry in Italy, and under its influence, poetry that would have a profound bearing not only on the literature but also the wider culture, history and politics of the whole of Europe, and not least Italy itself.

As a result, Byron's relationship with Italy, and the poetry it produced, speaks to a much broader modern-day audience than simply a literary one. This book bears witness to this fundamental fact about Byron's Italian writings by relating the texts Byron wrote in Italy to numerous features of early nineteenth-century European (and particularly, of course, Italian) culture, and highlighting many of their hugely influential contributions to the histories of all kinds of literary and non-literary discourses concerning, for example, identity (personal, national and European), politics, ethnography, geography, religion – even tourism.

However, these contributions and their influence are rooted in an underlying dual phenomenon – Byron's 'Byronisation' of Italy and Italy's 'Italianisation' of Byron – and the principal aim of this book is to broaden and deepen our understanding of this complex two-way process and its implications for the ways in which we read the poetry – and other writings, particularly the letters – that Byron produced in, and on, Italy.

The process can still be seen working itself out in Italy, where plaques are present wherever Byron resided or visited. In some cases they appear where the building is no longer extant (as in Ravenna's Piazza San Francesco) or even where he never was. Possibly the best-known example of the latter is the notorious inscription on the 'Grotta Byron' ('Byron Grotto') in Portovenere, placed there in 1877, hymning Byron's swim from Portovenere to Lerici (defying 'the waves of the Ligurian sea') and memorialising the fact that this grotto inspired him 'in the sublime poem The Corsair'.[2] Byron's Italian years saw him produce a great deal of poetry, but, of course, not *The Corsair*, which was published in 1814. Though diverting, however, the mistake on the part of the Italian authors of the inscription is a telling one, for it demonstrates the extent to which Byron's relationship to Italy – and the influence of that relationship in areas well beyond literature – has become a blend of fact, invention and reinvention, fantasy, legend and myth.

The 'Byron Grotto' inscription, among many others, whether reliable or fanciful, is just one example of that kind of invention of tradition that draws upon celebrities and their aura in order to appropriate them for, to make them an integral part of, a culture, discourse or context to which they never belonged and which can transform them almost beyond recognition. Thus, inscriptions – literal, literary and more widely cultural – tend to interweave Byron's life, myth and writings, and Italy as their *locus*, in ways that obscure all of these things as much as they illuminate them. In many cases, they make manifest the appropriative intentions of the Italian scholars and authorities who put these plaques up.[3] They also bear witness to the lasting legacy of nineteenth-century perceptions of Byron as an Italian poet, or at least a profoundly Italianised one, which began to spread after his death. These perceptions too generated their own myths. As Byron's posthumous reputation evolved in the nineteenth century, the poet was increasingly linked to Italy – to the extent, for example, that 'the

British cultural consciousness' saw it as axiomatic that 'it had been first and foremost Italy which had provided the stage for the display of Byron's public image as mad, bad, and dangerous to know'.[4] This, of course, is not the case at all – Byron was 'mad, bad, and dangerous to know' long before he got to Italy.[5] But myths about 'immoral' Italy rubbed off on Byron, just as myths about Byron rubbed off on Italy. The 'Byronisation' of Italy went hand in hand with the 'Italianisation' of Byron – and to such an enormous extent that hordes of later travellers to Italy (think of Charles Dickens or the many tourists clutching their *Murray's Handbooks*) got to grips with the peninsula by first engaging with (agreeing or disagreeing with, revelling in or condemning) Byron's and Italy's constructions of each other.

Nevertheless, the deep-seated Italianness of Byron himself while in Italy, and of large and significant portions of his poetic output, is beyond dispute. In everything, from his love affairs in Venice to his relationship with Teresa Guiccioli, from his adoption of the *ottava rima* and the models of Alfieri and Casti to his translations of Dante and Pulci, from his Venetian satire, *Beppo*, to his dramatisations of Venetian history, we see Byron saturating himself and his work in the Italian culture surrounding him. Thus, Mary Shelley, in an 1826 review of three books on Italy for the *Westminster Review*, defines the 'Anglo-Italian' as a figure who 'understands Italian', 'attaches himself' to the locals and 'appreciates' their manners, and specifically posits Byron as the prototype of this figure and *Beppo* as the starting point of the 'Anglo-Italian literary tradition'.[6] And in Italy, almost a century later, a young Umberto Bosco, one of the major voices in twentieth-century Italian Studies, could still confidently claim that Byron was an 'almost Italian' poet: 'more than a foreigner full of affection for Italy', Byron 'becomes among [Italians] almost Italian; so feel our own contemporaries, so it will be sung hereafter'.[7]

It is with the real, historical 'Anglo-Italian' Byron, and his 'almost Italianness' as a poet – rather than the fantasies, myths and legends that later came to surround and obscure him – that this volume is primarily concerned. However, as soon as we identify this as our topic we run into other, typically Byronic, complications. As we throw the spotlight on Byron in Italy and Italy in Byron, the links connecting the writer and the country very quickly reveal themselves to be composed of a series of intersecting, interactive and constantly shifting planes: personal (the poet's love affairs and friendships, both British and Italian), situational (a chameleon-like poet adapting to very different localities and local cultures within a disunited and variegated country), cultural (the weight of Italy's heritage, its present-day artistic and literary vitality, Italy's lack of social, linguistic and cultural unity resonating with Byron's antipathy to systems) and political (the Holy Alliance and Italy's constitutional ambitions and aspirations to independence interweaving with Byron's Whiggish cult of liberty). And as we watch all of this become refracted through the prism of Byron's literary inventions, as well as through his constant, highly performative self-inventions and reinventions, in his letters as well as his poetry, we begin to recover just how unusually pervasive, astonishingly far-reaching and highly distinctive Byron's 'Byronisation' of Italy and Italy's 'Italianisation' of Byron were – and why Byron's engagement with Italian culture became so widely influential in the first place.

Byron's relation to Italy was neither stable nor consistent. It is much more fascinating than this from the very outset, and the chapters in this book stress this fact. The aim here is not to reduce Byron's interactions with Italy to a single trope, theme, idea or even ideology but to explore them in all their complex variety. Those interactions varied across genre, for example, but also across time, as Byron and Italy became more and more embedded in one another during the poet's seven-year stay. Byron's first sight of Italy from the Alps is inscribed in the final stanzas of *Childe Harold's Pilgrimage* III, where the clouds lead the poetic 'I' in the direction of the Alpine range and the land beyond it:

> The clouds above me to the white Alps tend,
> And I must pierce them, and survey whate'er
> May be permitted, as my steps I bend
> To their most great and growing region, where
> The Earth to her embrace compels the powers of air.
>
> Italia! too – Italia! looking on thee,
> Full flashes on the soul the light of ages,
> Since the fierce Carthaginian almost won thee,
> To the last halo of the chiefs and sages,
> Who glorify thy consecrated pages;
> Thou wert the throne and grave of empires; still,

> The fount at which the panting mind assuages
> Her thirst of knowledge, quaffing there her fill,
> Flows from the eternal source of Rome's imperial Hill.
>
> (109–10)

These stanzas mark Byron's initial poetic approach to, and crossing over into, Italy – his introduction to the land he had decided to visit as an extension of his tour through Belgium, Germany and Switzerland but which instead became his adoptive country until his departure for Greece in 1823. The lines are fully conventional in terms of imagery. They feature an assortment of well-established *topoi*: the crossing of the barrier of the Alps, a rite of passage for travellers and a 'must' in literary reworkings of the trip to Italy; the reference to Hannibal; the description of a land favoured by nature and art (going back to the classical *laus Italiae*); the apostrophe complete with exclamations (conveying overwhelming emotion in the face of the inexpressible); the evocation of the past cultural glories that find continuity in the present; imperial history and, eventually, Rome. Byron's poetic entrance into Italy is therefore 'canonical', his moves fully encoded and recognisable – he is going to tread on 'classic ground' and wants to make all the right gestures.[8] And the alliterative image of the light of past ages 'full flash[ing] on the soul' captures a typically Romantic visionary awareness of all the pluralities of the past, simultaneously – a kind of Italy-induced euphoria.

Filled with clichés as they are, however, these early lines on Italy pave the way for *Childe Harold's Pilgrimage* IV (1818) and, though conventional and formulaic themselves, anticipate the much more intricately conflicted lyricism of Canto IV, its complexities and contentiousness – its anti-imperial discourse, its reworking of the *topos* of the 'ruin', its engagement with the living forces of present-day Italy, its monumentalising of the self in place and time.

The Italy Byron encountered once he had crossed the Alps in 1816 was a divided country that had been deeply affected by recent revolutionary and Napoleonic upheavals and by the Restoration instigated by the Congress of Vienna. From the 1790s onwards, the north had been largely in the sphere of French influence, especially the territories of the Cisalpine Republic (1797–1802), later transformed into the Kingdom of Italy (1805–14). In particular, the 1797 Treaty of Campoformio between France and Austria brought about the cession of Venice, Istria and Dalmatia to Austria and the creation of an independent Ligurian state. After the mainland territories of the House of Savoy were occupied and then annexed by France, Sardinia became the seat of the Piedmontese monarchy until 1814. The State of the Church became the short-lived Roman Republic (1798–99), while the Parthenopean Republic lasted only a few months in 1799. The Kingdom of Naples was a Napoleonic client state between 1806 and 1814, while in the same period Sicily was under British occupation. With the return of the *ancien régimes* in 1814, a general state of unrest ensued, with secret societies forming (most famously that of the Carbonari), increased surveillance by local powers who were generally under the influence of Austria, and the interference of other powers, especially Russia, through networks of espionage. Politically, the state of the country was potentially explosive. Socially, different forms of disunity (political, economic and linguistic) divided the population, which oscillated between a rooted localism and nascent nationalism, or between resignation and acquiescence and an urge to rebel against Austrian-sponsored despotisms. Culturally, in music, literature and the arts, this field of tensions translated into a multifaceted and contradictory panorama in which nostalgia for past glories combined with the desire to embrace changes inspired by either foreign or home-grown impulses, as well the need to stop the process of cultural marginalisation on the international stage and return to playing a major international role.[9]

As Byron grappled with this culture of fragmentation, conflict and contradiction, the works he produced while in Italy were as impressive in their formal variety as they were astonishing in their content, for example: *The Lament of Tasso* (1817), *Beppo* (1818), *Childe Harold's Pilgrimage* IV (1818), *Mazeppa* (1819), *The Prophecy of Dante* (1821), *Marino Faliero* (1821), *Sardanapalus* (1821), *The Two Foscari* (1821), *Cain* (1821), *The Vision of Judgment* (1822), *Werner* (1822), a translation of the first canto of Pulci's *Morgante Maggiore* (1823), *Heaven and Earth* (1823), *The Age of Bronze* (1823), *The Blues* (1823), *The Island* (1823), *The Deformed Transformed* (1824) and, of course, *Don Juan* (1819–24). Many of these works, of course, also directly address Italy and Italian culture, and each does so in its own, distinctive and original way, as the chapters in this book seek to demonstrate.

However, Byron's literary Italy emerged not only from within its Italian contexts but also from within the context of many other Europe-wide engagements with Italy and its culture, from the late eighteenth century through to the 1820s. From the outset these variously draw upon Gothic and anti-Catholic demonisations, are tinged with Grand Tour-style aristocratic pleasure-seeking and revel in the multiplication of references to classical, medieval and Renaissance culture. After 1815 these become imbued with political reimaginings of the country in terms of what Marilyn Butler identified as a liberal, post-Waterloo 'Cult of the South', in contrast to the Germano-Slavic policies of the tyrannous Holy Alliance.[10] In addition, Italy was a staple component in the myth of the 'warm south', which, as Esther Schor reminds us, the Romantics made into an 'imaginary elsewhere of lemon trees and olive groves' and a 'sensuous landscape of desire'.[11] Byron's Italy emerges, then, in the context of – indeed, as a reaction to – what Maureen McCue has termed a 'post-Waterloo fever for Italy' that swept right across Europe, fuelled by Napoleon's final defeat and the reopening of the Continent to travel – and therefore by the fact that after 1815 travel to Italy became easier and cheaper.[12] Italy was no longer the prerogative of the aristocracy but available to middle-class tourists too.

Throughout the Romantic period, the presence of Italy in poems, novels and plays was pervasive, ubiquitous and multiform – and it only became more so in the post-Napoleonic period. Ann Radcliffe's *The Mysteries of Udolpho* (1794) and *The Italian* (1797), along with Charlotte Dacre's *Zofloya* (1806), are only a few of the most famous instances of Gothic Italy. Even more influential was Madame de Staël's *Corinne, ou l'Italie* (1807). Mary Shelley continued this female Italian tradition in her 1826 *Valperga*, linking Italian history to the contemporary liberal preoccupation with despotism and the politically representative polity, and Stendhal would turn to more recent, though equally politicised, Italian history in *La Chartreuse de Parme* (1839). Some of the most popular stage plays in Britain in the aftermath of Waterloo – Henry Hart Milman's *Fazio* (1818), Richard Lalor Sheil's *Evadne* (1819) and Barry Cornwall's *Mirandola* (1821) – reworked in various ways the Renaissance *topos* of the Italian court as a hotbed of intrigue, as did Shelley in *The Cenci* (1819). At the same time, Leigh Hunt promoted an Italianised poetics in *The Story of Rimini* (1816), and Keats, Barry Cornwall and John Hamilton Reynolds followed him in offering their versions of Cockney Italianism in metrical tales on Italian themes. And then, of course, there were Italian histories – key examples being Gibbon's *Decline and Fall of the Roman Empire* (1776–88), Roscoe's lives of Lorenzo de' Medici (1796) and Leo

X (1805), Sismondi's *Histoire des républiques italiennes du moyen âge* (1807–17) and Daru's *Histoire de la République de Venise* (1819) – and travel books such as Hester Piozzi's *Observations and Reflections Made in the Course of a Journey through France, Italy, and Germany* (1789), Eustace's tours of Italy (1813, 1815), Lady Morgan's *Italy* (1821) and Goethe's *Italienische Reise* (1816–29), with their enormous shaping power over all kinds of representations of Italy. The figurative arts and music played their role, too, as did the several waves of political exiles looking for asylum abroad from the failed Italian uprisings of the early 1820s, who crucially contributed to the increasing popularity of their country's culture in Britain and elsewhere. Translations of, and guides to, Italian literature also flourished: Pierre-Louis Ginguené's *Histoire littéraire d'Italie* (1811–19) was an especially formative example in Byron's case.[13]

This Europe-wide Italomania informs Byron's Italy at every turn, as he variously draws on, challenges and develops what had become an enormous body of writing on Italy by the time he lived there. He also shared with other contemporary writers on Italy a wide-ranging textual knowledge of the country and its literature, developed through his readings in both Britain and Italy. He claimed to have 'perused either in the original, or Translations', 'Tasso, Ariosto, Petrarch, Dante, Bembo [and] Metastasio' in his 1807 'Reading List',[14] and the catalogues for the sales of his books in 1813 and 1816 indicate that by then he had acquired two copies of Ariosto's *Orlando furioso*, three of Tasso's *Gerusalemme liberata*, at least two copies of Dante's *Divina Commedia*, three different editions of Petrarch's poetry, a thirteen-volume edition of Machiavelli's works, Bandello's *Novelle*, Goldoni's *Memoirs* and John Black's 1810 *Life of Tasso*.[15] He first read Ugo Foscolo's *Ultime lettere di Jacopo Ortis* in 1813,[16] and lists Alfieri's works among '*my* Italian books' in an 1813 letter to Lady Melbourne.[17] Stendhal tells us he read 'Buratti's works' and 'Goldoni's comedies' in Milan in 1816,[18] in anticipation of going to Venice, and his letters, as well as the notes, prefaces, advertisements and dedications to his poetry – and, of course, the poetry itself – attest to a knowledge of many more Italian writers including Casti, Filicaja, Forteguerri, Guarini, Monti and Parini. But he also prided himself on his direct knowledge of the country and its culture. In his correspondence, some of which he wrote in Italian,[19] he never tired of stressing the fact that he was in Italy and that he was writing from there: 'I have lived in their houses and in the heart of their families', he famously tells John Murray in a letter of 1820.[20] Informed by all kinds of reading, Byron's Italy is also a very personal one.

Yet his personal relation to the country is complicated by a pervasive dialectic between familiarity and distance. The Italy Byron encountered and wrote about was simultaneously a land already known, from his reading and his own experience, and an always new and surprising adventure. This ambivalent attitude becomes a central component of his vision and interpretation of Italian culture, geography and people. For Byron, being in Italy is irreducibly dual. He is both inside Italy and Italian life, and self-consciously outside it, as an English lord, a Scottish mercenary, a cosmopolitan poet, a European celebrity or even just 'a broken Dandy' on his 'travels' (*Beppo*, 52). This, of course, has political as well as experiential and literary implications: being in Milan or Venice means being aware of the Austrians; being in Ravenna of the authority of the papal legate and of the overall supervision of the Austrians; being in Tuscany (Pisa and Leghorn in particular) means knowingly taking advantage of a regime (temporarily) tolerant of liberal ideas. Byron's direct and personal relation to Italian society is thus also strongly geopolitical, as well as geocultural, but here, as always, intimacy and distance go hand in hand, for he is both embedded in historical and political realities and viewing them from afar.

As a consequence, his involvement in Italy generally is participative and emotional yet also fascinatingly ironic and, at times, even aloof. This doubleness emerges in many episodes and anecdotes recounted in his letters. A revealing instance is his journal account of an encounter in the countryside near Ravenna with a young woman, Rosa Benini, the wife of the local *vetturino* (coachman), who unexpectedly asks him who the pope is.[21] Byron explains as best he can, mildly amused by the situation (having to explain the pope to a Catholic woman) and probably also scandalised by the ignorance in which the people are kept. But his account of the meeting most pointedly dramatises his relation to Italy as simultaneously that of an insider and an outsider. He is here encountering, and playing a part in, the 'real' life of Italy, as well as explaining Italian culture, in Italian, to an Italian. Yet he marks out his distance from *her* Italian culture – it is as if Rosa Benini hailed from another land entirely. As an insurmountable barrier rises between them, Byron is surprised and does not entirely understand what is going on: Italy has suddenly become illegible. The doubleness enshrined in this episode will return again and again in the chapters of this book, as their readings of Byron's life, poems and letters situate their texts within – and between – a range of historical (inter)national, literary and personal contexts.

The volume as a whole inevitably draws on a long history of scholarly work on the topic of 'Byron and Italy'. In the anglophone world of the nineteenth century and the first half of the twentieth century, this work was primarily biographical. Landmark studies here – still very useful today – include Peter Quennell's *Byron in Italy* (1935), Iris Origo's *The Last Attachment* (1949) and Doris Langley Moore's *The Late Lord Byron* (1961). Literary criticism was for a long time limited to a few scattered chapters and journal articles, though important work on Byron appeared in book-length studies of 'Romantic' Italy generally such as C. P. Brand's *Italy and the English Imagination* (1957). However, as Alan Rawes and Mirka Horová maintain, even these few studies of Byron and Italy tended to be lost within 'an increasing volume of critical work on Byron that, on the whole, treated Byron's writing while in Italy as engaged with British, rather than Italian, concerns, or read Byron's poetry in glorious isolation'.[22] For a long time – into this century – the only English-language critical book wholly focused on Byron and Italy was Peter Vassallo's *Byron and the Italian Literary Influence* (1984), a comparative study that offers plentiful information on the poet's borrowings from recent Italian literature (Casti in particular), especially in relation to his *ottava rima* work, as well as exploring his knowledge of Italian classics and more general connections with Italian culture. In Italy, the first half of the twentieth century saw the publication of works on the impact of Byron and Byronism in Italy,[23] as well as a number of studies of Byron's influence on nineteenth-century Italian writers, his 'local presence' (in Venice, Ravenna and Bologna, among other places) and a number of biographical works, often mixing fact with fiction.[24] The most important early twentieth-century Italian critical work on Byron was by Mario Praz, in a number of essays on the poet published between 1924 and 1966 and books such as *La fortuna di Byron in Inghilterra* (1925) and *La carne, la morte e il diavolo nella letteratura romanica* (1930). In the wake of Praz's early work on the poet, 'Byron scholarship in Italy became more mature and critically aware', but the question of the poet's engagement with Italy and its culture was still largely treated, in Italy as in the anglophone world, in an exclusively biographical key, or, sometimes, as an episode in the larger sweep of cultural history.[25] Indeed, while there was a steady stream of Byron scholarship in Italy during the twentieth century, most studies of Byron's relationship to the country and its culture were decidedly narrative and descriptive rather than critical, with occasionally outstanding contributions such as the essays published by Giorgio Melchiori between 1958 and 1981, though even these mostly focused on Byron's impact on Italian literary and political discourse, rather than on Italy's impact on Byron and his literary recreations of it.[26]

The twentieth-first century has seen all this change, both in English-speaking countries and in Italy. Indeed, with Italian scholars increasingly publishing in English, and in the climate of global critical conversations made possible by digital technologies, it makes little sense any more to talk about two separate critical traditions, which have come dramatically together around the topic of 'Romantic Italy' generally, and Byron and Italy in particular, in recent years. The books, chapters, essays and special journal issues that have been published this century testify not only to the swell of international scholarly interest in Byron's relationship to Italy but also to a number of new directions within the field.[27] Emphasis is now being placed on the intersections between biography and writing in Byron's Italian poetry, issues of intertextual relations between Byron's texts and Italian ones, the historical and political questions Byron's texts raise about Italy during the early Risorgimento and Byron's 'Italian' self-constructions and the questions of identity, cultural geography, otherness, language and cosmopolitanism that these constructions raise.

Some broad themes emerge across this contemporary body of work on Byron and Italy. One is Italy as a construct in Byron's work, an object viewed through a variety of filters, from reading and from lived experience, that bring with them a plurality of discourses about the country and its culture – historical and literary, sociological, economic, political and so on. A second is Byron's Italy as a place for performance, and not merely a space of writing: the poet himself, as he appears in both his letters and his verse, is here read as a literary spectacle, performed for an international audience, in the context of a peculiarly spectacular country and society. A third theme is that of Byron's social experience of Italy – his participation in several groups and networks such as the coterie of Milanese intellectuals, the Pisan circle, his life and work with Leigh Hunt and his family, his relationships with Mary and Percy Shelley, Thomas Medwin and others, or his links to the Gambas and their revolutionary and liberal friends. Yet another theme is Byron's very different constructions of Italy through different genres of writing – lyric, dramatic, epic, mock-epic, romance, satire, etc. – which lend themselves to what we may tentatively call a 'new formalist' investigation of the ways in which the choice of genre and metrical structure is conditioned by contextual historical, political and cultural forces.

Perhaps, though, the most prominent and most widely shared preoccupation among the new generation of writers about Byron and Italy centres on location and locatedness. Two monographs that read Byron's relationship to Italy as a complex exercise in self-location, as well as cross-cultural and transnational identification, have led the way here. On the one hand, Stephen Cheeke's *Byron and Place* (2003) explores the intersection in Byron's thinking about place between 'being there, being in-between, having been there' and finds that the experience of Italy offered the poet an opportunity to produce another original reconfiguration of this triad in the 'hope that belonging nowhere may represent a freedom to belong anywhere and to speak any language, to cease to be a stranger, [...] a hope that had come under sharp pressures post-1816 for Byron, and yet [...] a hope that *Childe Harold* canto four re-asserts'.[28] On the other hand, Maria Schoina's *Romantic 'Anglo-Italians'* (2009) attends to Byron's displacement to and acclimatisation in post-Napoleonic Italy, as part of a wider phenomenon – found also in the Shelleys and Leigh Hunt – that aimed at the creation of a 'hyphenated identity and displayed varying degrees of identification with Italianness in an attempt to establish a bicultural identity', a process evidently fraught with ambivalences and contradictions.[29]

From these and other perspectives, current scholars across national and international traditions have been turning to the topic of Byron and Italy with unprecedented enthusiasm and a new spectrum of critical approaches. This volume brings many of these scholars and their perspectives together to take the pulse of current debates, contribute to them and open up new lines of enquiry for the future. As it does so, it also raises a series of questions that are central to Byron Studies more generally and especially pertinent to the transnational and intercultural aspects of the poet's figure and output. Thus, if the focus of the volume is on Byron 'writing Italy', its implications are much wider. How did Italy affect, change and inform Byron's thinking about matters far beyond Italy? 'Being there' certainly affected his sense of his own individual identity and of the labile nature of the self. It affected his politics – both in theory and in practice. And, of course, it profoundly affected his whole development as a writer – of lyrics, dramas, satires and more. Byron did not just become rather 'un-English' as a man in Italy (Moore describes him looking not like a British aristocrat but like a decadent Continental fop in Genoa).[30] He also started to be seen, especially by detractors, as rather un-English as a poet: Southey, from his highly hostile standpoint and aware that Byron would be reading him, called *Don Juan* 'an act of high treason on English poetry'.[31] In fact, the chapters in this book, addressing the multiplicity and plurality of Byron *and* Italy, explore some of the ways in which the poet turned the country and its culture into an essential element of what Peter Manning calls 'the ensemble of life and work we call "Byron"'.[32] They examine constitutive tensions within this Italianised ensemble at both a textual and an experiential level. They consider the deep-lying interaction of fact and fiction, the ambivalent points of view, Byron's being in Italy but also imagining himself as belonging elsewhere, the spirituality and material experience of Italy at a particular moment in its history, and the web of connections and gaps between these dimensions, as all fundamentally constitutive of Byron's Italy. Accordingly, they help this book to return its topic to the centre of critical debates not just about Byron but British and European Romanticism much more widely – at a moment in our own history that is once again forcing Britain to think deeply about its relationship with the rest of Europe and forcing Europe to rethink its understanding of the British.

The first two chapters of the volume, by Nicholas Halmi and Gioia Angeletti, announce the book's two broad thematic approaches to 'Byron and Italy': via Byron's engagement with Italian culture (here poetry, but elsewhere art, drama and history) and via his engagement with Italy as a living society, a real place and an active, urgent, human reality. Both chapters also introduce a central aspect of Byron's engagement with Italy that later chapters will return to again and again: his constant 'Italian' self-invention and reinvention, in both his poetry and his letters. Our understanding of Byron's complex, contradictory reimagining – and reimaging – of himself in Italy is then further enriched by the third chapter, by Jonathan Gross, on Byron's 'Italian' Britishness, in contrast to his 'Anglo-Italianness'. The Italian Byron was deeply rooted in, but also endlessly fluctuated between, 'two worlds' (*DJ*, XV, 99), and at every turn Byron's engagement with Italy throws into sharp relief questions of national, personal and public identity.

Focusing on *The Lament of Tasso*, *The Prophecy of Dante* alongside Byron's translations of Filicaja in the fourth canto of *Childe Harold's Pilgrimage* and Pulci's *Morgante Maggiore*, Halmi first explores the ways in which Byron 'exploited both the writings and the figures of Italian writers (especially the exiled Dante and imprisoned Tasso) to construct his own cosmopolitan poetic identity', reinventing himself as simultaneously – and ambiguously – an English and an Italian poet. Championing the cause of Italian freedom and unification in his poems on Dante and Tasso and the translation of Filicaja, Byron presents himself as the modern culmination of an Italian, nationalist poetic tradition he helped to invent – for Italian as much as for British consumption. In the translation of Pulci, however, Byron stresses his foreignness to both British and Italian poetic traditions, cutting a cosmopolitan figure not through identity but through difference. While in his letters – and, of course, many of his poems – Byron is both British and Italian, Italian literature could also offer the poet a way of being neither.

Where Halmi focuses on Byron's poetry, Angeletti gives her attention to Byron's 'idiosyncratic letters and journals' to British correspondents and their 'ethnographic observation of the human and cultural geography of Italy'. Insisting on the contingent reality of the country, rather than an idealised 'Italy', these letters show Byron as a cultural mediator between Italy and Britain as he immerses himself in, and offers an insider's view of, Italy's quotidian life, its 'anthropological and ethnographic *marginalia* or *minutiae*'. Yet, as Angeletti shows, Byron's letters home also perform a delicate balancing act between immersion and difference, as he retains his Britishness even as he acquires Italianness. This Anglo-Italian doubleness, already foregrounded as a key element of Byron's poetry by Halmi, here becomes a fundamental feature of Byron's life in and letters from Italy as well – and will resurface again in a number of other chapters too.

In typical Byron fashion, however, the doubleness of his identity in relation to Italian life and culture is not a matter of blurring distinct selves into one another but of the coexistence, side by side, of sharply defined singularities. Jonathan Gross's chapter thus stays with the letters to discuss some of the ways in which Byron's Italianisation actually intensified his sense of his own Britishness, which everywhere underpins and complicates his relationship to Italy: even as the British poet was 'rebranding' himself as almost but never entirely Italian, the Italianised British aristocrat was reimagining himself as a Scottish mercenary in the midst of Italian revolution. As Gross shows, under the influence of Madame de Staël's Lord Nelvil and Walter Scott's novels (which he avidly read while in Italy), Byron depicted himself in his letters home as an aristocratic Scottish lord leading a band of troops or as serving the Italian cause 'like Dugald Dalgetty' in Scott's *A Legend of Montrose*. As Gross puts it, Byron 'never felt himself more Scottish than when residing in Ravenna, Venice, Genoa and Pisa'.

A sequence of four essays follows, each focusing on Byron's relationship to one crucial aspect of early nineteenth-century Italian culture: its geography (Mauro Pala), its visual artistic inheritance (Jane Stabler), its Catholicism (Bernard Beatty) and its early Risorgimento politics (Arnold Anthony Schmidt).

Pala's chapter on the geographies of Italy foregrounds another key theme of the volume, first introduced by Angeletti and returned to by other contributors: while reading Byron's poetry confronts us repeatedly with the poet's digressive, fluid *mobilité*, studying his relationship to Italy in particular repeatedly confronts us with his capacity for sustained attention to the given. However, as Pala demonstrates, focusing on Canto IV of *Childe Harold's Pilgrimage*, attending to the given is not simply a matter of 'seizing' the 'colouring of the scenes which fleet along' (*CHP*, III, 112) for Byron. The poet's depictions of Italy's landscapes and cityscapes are, rather, 'complex, heterogeneous and personal negotiations' not just with 'real places' but also 'their attendant histories' – negotiations that 'not only make place an essential element of the consciousness observing it but also make that observing consciousness an essential element of place'.

Stabler's chapter turns from Italian landscape to Italian art, offering us a 'way of reading Byron's response to' the art of Italy 'beyond well-known classical and Renaissance paintings and sculptures' by concentrating on 'the relationship between Byron's *Cain* and the church art of Ravenna'. Stabler's method here is openly speculative, and this allows her to suggest a whole range of ways in which 'the visual art of Ravenna might have shaped the creativity' of *Cain*: for Stabler, 'the form of *Cain* departs from all Byron's previously stated aesthetic preferences, but not from what he could see around him in Ravenna's religious art'. Her speculative method also allows her to raise some important and fundamental questions about Byron's possible absorption of all sorts of Italian artworks that he never mentions but certainly saw, the creative role of memory in Byron's response to the art he encountered in Italy, and the poet's 'fascination' not just with the art he did see, but, through that art, with 'ways of seeing and knowing'.

Beatty documents the evolution of Byron's personal and poetic relationship with Catholicism from what was presumably his first real encounter with it at Newstead Abbey in 1798 through to the final cantos of *Don Juan* and the figure of Aurora Raby. Detailing and exploring Byron's experience of Italian friars, priests, cardinal legates, a pope and, most importantly, Italian Catholic women, Beatty suggests that, in Catholic Italy, 'spiritually, Byron found something sensible to grasp at'. Ranging across Byron's poetic career, Beatty sees the poet begin as a John Knox in response to Catholicism but progressively become not only a thinker of 'theological precision' but also a 'sympathetic outsider and even insider' to Italian Catholic experience.

Rather than approaching Byron's much-discussed engagement with the early Risorgimento through biography, Schmidt throws new light on Byron's Italian politics from a formalist perspective. Taking *The Two Foscari* as his case study, and rooting his discussion in the highly politicised contemporary Italian critical debates about the dramatic unities, Schmidt teases out the political implications of Byron's adherence to the unities by comparing his play to Alessandro Manzoni's *Il conte di Carmagnola*, which programmatically violates them. Focusing specifically on the playwrights' representations of the fifteenth-century mercenary leader, Francesco Bussone da Carmagnola, Schmidt shows how these writers' use or abuse of the unity of time in particular reveal Manzoni's Risorgimento agenda on the one hand and Byron's 'general scepticism about leadership' and 'uncertainty about social and political change' on the other.

The last four chapters together offer an extended study of the major literary works Byron wrote in Italy and/or on Italian topics. Byron's 'Italian' works are here grouped generically and set against various biographical, historical and literary contexts – British, Italian and more widely European – in order to allow us to think about Byron's literary investment in Italy in broader terms than those offered by the study of individual works alone, though, naturally, individual works are discussed in detail. As a result, new perspectives emerge on Byron's narrative, lyric, dramatic and satirical poetry per se – most especially on the ways in which each offered Byron its own distinctive way of entering, exploring, absorbing, processing and deploying Italian culture. The ways in which Byron engaged with Italy are never reducible to any kind of singularity, and his use of multiple genres when writing about the Italian world foregrounds this very clearly.

We begin with Byron's Italian narrative poems. Peter Graham singles out *Parisina* (written in England but on an Italian topic) and *Mazeppa* (written in Italy but on a non-Italian topic). 'Considered separately and together', Graham argues, these two poems 'can help readers understand the intricate fabrication of Byron's Anglo-Italian identity', while considering them 'in dialogue' and in relation to Italy 'throws new light on these two tales generally sidelined in the Byron canon'. In *Parisina*, Graham shows us, Italy offers a 'cautionary tale' to Regency England and offers Byron a place to 'imagine and poetically release' things in his own life that he had to publicly suppress in England. In *Mazeppa*, Byron explores key aspects of his life in Italy in an imagined location 'displaced from Italy rather than to it'. Both demonstrate, in surprising ways and in contradiction to much critical thinking about Byron, the importance of '*not* being on the spot' to both the poet's narrative method and his poetic self-fashioning.

Alan Rawes turns to Byron's Italian lyric mode, taking *Childe Harold* IV's description of the Palatine as an exemplary instance of the sustained poetic attentiveness highlighted by Pala. Rawes puts this description alongside the accounts of the Palatine in Goethe's *Italienische Reise* and de Staël's *Corinne, ou l'Italie*. Comparing these three texts, which together 'largely defined the Romantic reinvention of Italy and, in particular, Rome', Rawes draws out their very different ways of responding to the city, arguing that, 'while the fictional and autobiographical works of de Staël and Goethe appropriate the ruins of Rome for their own needs and purposes, *Childe Harold* IV presents us with an attentive responsiveness to the ruins of Rome per se'. Where Goethe seeks an education in Rome, and de Staël finds consolation, Byron creates a wholly original lyric mode and persona that are 'highly attentive to "all" the "treasures" of "eye", "ear", "heart" and "soul"', reinventing Rome as an 'exhaustless mine' (*CHP*, IV, 108, 128) of experiences that hosts of later tourists then came to explore, relish and revel in.

Byron's dramatic representations of Italian history – *Marino Faliero*, *The Two Foscari* and *The Deformed Transformed* – are the topic of Mirka Horová's chapter. Demonstrating the extent to which 'play' – in its 'performative' and 'sportive' but also 'competitive' and 'manipulative' senses – underpins Byron's dramatic rendering of Italy in these works, which combine the carnivalesque and the grotesque to paint a profoundly disturbing picture of Italy's past, Horová shows how Byron's Italian dramas use Italian history to think about the ways in which European historical 'progress' more generally, and the 'humanising' role of art in that progress, repeatedly, endlessly and inevitably descend into sheer violence. For in Byron's dramatic art, as Horová argues, Italy 'becomes *pars pro toto* for the Renaissance', Venice 'represents republicanism', and 'Rome stands for the entirety of human history'. Byron's Italian dramas give us a distinctive, coherent and relentless reading of Italian history through particular episodes of it, a reading that places 'Byron's ideas about the nature of, and the forces ruling, not just Italian but all history' centre stage.

Bringing together many of the themes of previous chapters, Diego Saglia's chapter focuses on Byron's 'Italian' satires – *Beppo*, *Don Juan* and the late prose fragment, 'An Italian Carnival'. Saglia foregrounds in particular Byron's 'parabasic "turn" to Italy' in these works, arguing that the poet's 'complex self-positioning in Italy lies behind' both their 'innovative poetics' and their 'delineation of an unprecedentedly multiform world view'. Saglia begins with the 'ambivalences and contradictions' embedded in *Don Juan*'s references to Pulci, Ariosto, Dante, Petrarch and Boccaccio, showing the extent to which Italy's literature serves 'to construct Byron's medley mode' even as that literature 'falls prey to the mode's own subversive discourse'. Turning to *Beppo*, Saglia teases out the ways in which the figure of the *cavalier servente* 'provides Byron with a fluid gestural and performative model for his Italian turn' and illuminates 'essential facets' of the 'inherently Italian, parabasic nature' of Byron's Italian satire. Finally, with 'An Italian Carnival', which 'reprises' the 'Janus-faced attitudes and approaches to Italy' that so deeply mark Byron's later poetic satires,

Saglia brings us back to the letter from Byron to John Murray already mentioned in this introduction:

> I have lived in their houses and in the heart of their families – sometimes merely as 'amico di casa' ['friend of the family'] and sometimes as 'Amico di cuore' ['friend of the heart'] of the Dama – and in neither case do I feel authorized in making a book of them. – – Their moral is not your moral – their life is not your life – you would not understand it.[33]

For Saglia, 'in a way, in the 1823 fragment, the poet seems to comply with Murray's request by drawing a picture of Italy, seen through the lens of Carnival', but this volume as a whole offers a bolder claim. Situating himself ambiguously and performatively somewhere between the 'them' of Italy and the 'you' of Britain, Byron did 'make a book of' Italy, in all the senses conjured up by that small phrase. And the chapters of that book – *The Prophecy of Dante*, *Childe Harold* IV, *Beppo*, *Marino Faliero* and *Don Juan*, to mention just a few – helped set the stage for the total reimagining of Italy, from the inside and the outside, that ran throughout the nineteenth century and beyond. As Italy Italianised Byron, so Byron Byronised Italy, leaving in his wake a land 'still impregnate with divinity', 'where the deep skies assume / Hues which have words, and speak to ye of heaven' (*CHP*, IV, 55, 129).

Notes

1 The Italian quotation in our title ('a country all poetic') is taken from Byron's dedication to *Childe Harold* IV, in *CPW*, vol. II, p. 123. The phrase was coined by the Piedmontese poet Diodata Saluzzo Roero (1774–1840) and quoted by Ludovico di Breme in *Intorno all'ingiustizia di alcuni giudizi letterari italiani* (1816). See A. Colombo, '*I lunghi affanni ed il perduto regno*': *cultura letteraria, filologia e politica nella Milano della Restaurazione* (Besançon: Presses Universitaires de Franche-Comté, 2007), pp. 126–9.

2 See M. Curreli, 'Golfo dei poeti, lapidi bugiarde e altri miti', *Soglie*, 6:2 (2004), 19–44.

3 On plaques and Byron's name and works in Italy, see B. Schaff, 'Italianised Byron – Byronised Italy', in M. Pfister and R. Hertel (eds.), *Performing National Identity: Anglo-Italian Cultural Transactions* (Amsterdam: Rodopi, 2008), pp. 103–21 (pp. 115–19).

4 Schaff, 'Italianised Byron – Byronised Italy', p. 110.
5 Lady Caroline Lamb coined this famous phrase in her diary on the day she met Byron for the first time in 1812. See E. Jenkins, *Lady Caroline Lamb* (London: Victor Gollancz, 1932), p. 95.
6 M. Shelley, 'The English in Italy', *The Westminster Review*, 6 (October 1826), 325–41 (p. 327). Shelley is reviewing Lord Normanby's *The English in Italy*, Charlotte Anne Eaton's *Continental Adventures* and Anna Jameson's *The Diary of an Ennuyée*. See also M. Schoina, *Romantic 'Anglo-Italians': Configurations of Identity in Byron, the Shelleys, and the Pisan Circle* (Farnham: Ashgate, 2009), pp. 65–72.
7 In Italian: 'più che straniero affezionato all'Italia, [Byron] diventa tra noi quasi italiano; tale lo avvertono i contemporanei, tale sarà cantato in seguito' (U. Bosco 'Byronismo italiano', *La Cultura*, 3:6 (1924), 252–64 [p. 262]).
8 On the notion of 'classic ground' and Italy as a paradigmatic instance of this concept, see C. Duffy, *The Landscapes of the Sublime, 1700–1830* (Basingstoke: Palgrave Macmillan, 2013), pp. 8–10.
9 For useful historical accounts of post-Napoleonic Italy, see D. Mack Smith, *The Making of Italy, 1796–1866* (Houndmills: Palgrave, 1988); L. Riall, *The Italian Risorgimento: State, Society and National Unification* (London and New York: Routledge, 1994); S. Woolf, *History of Italy, 1700–1860* (London: Methuen, 1979).
10 See M. Butler, *Romantics, Rebels and Reactionaries: English Literature and Its Background, 1760–1830* (Oxford: Oxford University Press, 1981), pp. 120–37.
11 E. Schor, 'The "warm south"', in J. Chandler (ed.), *The Cambridge History of English Romantic Literature* (Cambridge: Cambridge University Press, 2009), pp. 224–5 (p. 224).
12 M. McCue, *British Romanticism and the Reception of Italian Old Master Art, 1793–1840* (Farnham: Ashgate, 2014), p. 2.
13 Byron acquired a copy of Ginguené's *Histoire* while in Italy. See J. Stabler, *The Artistry of Exile: Romantic and Victorian Writers in Italy* (Oxford: Oxford University Press, 2013), p. 17.
14 *CMP*, pp. 3, 1.
15 P. Cochran, 'Byron's library', available at https://petercochran.files.wordpress.com/2014/12/byrons-library.pdf.
16 See Byron's marginalia in the copy of Foscolo's novel he read in 1820, in D. D. Fischer and D. Reiman (eds.), *Shelley and His Circle, 1773–1822*, 8 vols (Cambridge, Mass.: Harvard University Press, 1961–2002), vol. VIII, p. 1108.
17 Letter of 5 October 1813, in *BLJ*, vol. III, p. 133.

18 'Stendhal's account of Byron at Milan', in Lord Byron, *The Works of Lord Byron: Letters and Journals*, 6 vols, ed. R. E. Prothero (London: John Murray, 1902–4), vol. III, pp. 438–45 (p. 445).
19 See Carla Pomarè, '"I am now an Italoquist": Byron's correspondence in Italian', *The Byron Journal*, 44:2 (2016), 97–108.
20 Letter of 21 February 1820, in *BLJ*, vol. VII, p. 42.
21 See 'Detached thoughts', No. 117, in *BLJ*, vol. IX, p. 51.
22 A. Rawes and M. Horová, 'Introduction', *Tears, and Tortures, and the Touch of Joy: Byron in Italy*, *Litteraria Pragensia*, 23:46 (December 2013), 1–5 (p. 2).
23 See, for example: G. Muoni, *La fama del Byron e il byronismo in Italia* (Milan: Società Editrice Libraria, 1906); G. Muoni, *La leggenda del Byron in Italia* (Milan: Società Editrice, 1907); A. Porta, *Byronismo italiano* (Milan: Cogliati, 1923).
24 See G. Iamartino, 'Translations, biography, opera, film and literary criticism: Byron and Italy after 1870', in R. Cardwell (ed.), *The Reception of Byron in Europe*, 2 vols (London and New York: Thoemmes Continuum, 2004), vol. I, pp. 98–128.
25 Iamartino, 'Translations, biography', p. 125.
26 See Iamartino, 'Translations, biography', p. 126.
27 See, for example, and in addition to recent studies mentioned elsewhere in this introduction: G. Angeletti, *Lord Byron and Discourses of Otherness: Scotland, Italy and Femininity* (Kilkerran: Humming Earth, 2012); L. Bandiera and D. Saglia (eds.), *British Romanticism and Italian Literature: Translating, Reviewing, Rewriting* (Amsterdam: Rodopi, 2005); F. Burwick and P. Douglass (eds.), *Dante and Italy in British Romanticism* (Basingstoke: Palgrave Macmillan, 2011); L. Crisafulli (ed.), *Immaginando l'Italia: itinerari letterari del Romanticismo inglese* (Bologna: CLUEB, 2002); P. Cochran, *Byron and Italy* (Newcastle: Cambridge Scholars, 2012); J. Luzzi, *Romantic Europe and the Ghost of Italy* (New Haven, Conn.: Yale University Press, 2008); C. Pomarè, *Byron and the Discourses of History* (Farnham: Ashgate, 2013); J. Sachs, *Romantic Antiquity: Rome in the British Imagination, 1789–1832* (Oxford: Oxford University Press, 2010); D. Saglia, *Lord Byron e le maschere della scrittura* (Rome: Carocci, 2009); D. Saglia (ed.), *Byron e il segno plurale* (Bologna: Bononia University Press, 2011); A. A. Schmidt, *Byron and the Rhetoric of Italian Nationalism* (Basingstoke: Palgrave Macmillan, 2010); A. Yarrington, S. Villani and J. Kelly (eds.), *Travels and Translations: Anglo-Italian Cultural Transactions* (Amsterdam and New York: Rodopi, 2013).

28 Stephen Cheeke, *Byron and Place: History, Translation, Nostalgia* (Basingstoke: Palgrave Macmillan, 2003), pp. 14, 97.
29 Schoina, *Romantic 'Anglo-Italians'*, p. 5.
30 See D. Saglia, 'Touching Byron: masculinity and the celebrity body in the Romantic period', in R. Emig and A. Rowland (eds.), *Performing Masculinity* (Basingstoke: Palgrave Macmillan, 2010), pp. 13–27 (p. 21).
31 Letter to Walter Savage Landor of 20 February 1820, quoted in Andrew Rutherford (ed.), *Byron: The Critical Heritage* (London: Routledge & Kegan Paul, 1970), p. 179.
32 Quoted in C. Tuite, *Lord Byron and Scandalous Celebrity* (Cambridge: Cambridge University Press, 2015), p. xix.
33 *BLJ*, vol. VII, p. 42.

1

The literature of Italy in Byron's poems of 1817–20

Nicholas Halmi

Although travel to Italy was an almost obligatory rite of passage for young English aristocratic males in the eighteenth century, the interests of these tourists were typically restricted to seeing and acquiring antiquities. Earlier travellers, such as Thomas Coryat in 1608 and Milton in 1638, had been more interested in contemporary than in ancient Italy, for they had considered travel and an acquaintance with other nations to be beneficial to their participation in a shared humanistic culture. Coryat had observed Italian life keenly and recorded his impressions minutely, while Milton had frequented the learned academies (where he won approval for his Latin poetry) and met Italian intellectuals, including Galileo, then in his fourth year under house arrest. In the eighteenth century, however, the educational aim of Continental travel narrowed from the broadly humanistic to the more specifically aesthetic, centred on classical art; and often enough even that aim was little more than a pretext for the acquisition of a superficial worldliness on an extended holiday.[1] Johann Joachim Winckelmann complained privately about the philistinism of the nominally distinguished English visitors to whom he was expected, as keeper of the Vatican antiquities and Rome's most prominent antiquarian, to give guided tours of the city.[2] In this increasingly commodified experience of the Italian past, the living contemporary land largely ceased to be of interest to Grand Tourists except in so far as it assisted (or hindered) their sightseeing and collecting. The eighteenth-century Italian artists most familiar to the English were those who supplied visitors with pictures of themselves and the sights: the portraitist Pompeo Batoni, the view-painters Canaletto and Giovanni Paolo Panini and especially the engravers Giuseppe Vasi and Giovanni Battista Piranesi.

Thus the growth in the popularity of the Grand Tour across the first three quarters of the eighteenth century was not directly matched by an increased interest in Italian literature and history. It was an Italian expatriate, the critic Giuseppe Baretti, who began to revive British interest in Italian literature with his *Remarks on the Italian Language and Writers* and *Dissertation upon the Italian Poetry*, both published in 1753. Translations of Ariosto's *Orlando furioso* by Joseph Higgins and William Hoole followed in 1755 and 1783, while Hoole's 1747 translation of Tasso's *Gerusalemme liberata* was reprinted seven times between 1764 and 1803. Susannah Dobson's 1775 *Life of Petrarch* stimulated translations of his lyrics; two translations of Dante's *Inferno* – but not of the other canticles – were published in 1782; and Metastasio's poetry became a staple of young ladies' singing lessons. But only in the early nineteenth century, when travel to Italy was impeded by war, did study of the language and literature become more common. This development was motivated, C. P. Brand speculates, by British sympathy for the plight of Italy under foreign occupation and fostered by the presence of literarily active Italian exiles in London, most notably Ugo Foscolo and Antonio Panizzi.[3] Among British Romantic writers, J. H. Frere, Wordsworth, Scott, Coleridge, Southey, Landor, Thomas Campbell, Thomas Moore, Leigh Hunt, J. H. Reynolds, both Shelleys and Felicia Hemans read Italian literature in the original, while Blake, De Quincey and Keats acquired at least a basic knowledge of the language.

Byron's reception of the literature, however, was distinctive in its extent and its dual aspect: not only reading but actively appropriating. His letters and notes to his poems attest to an interest that extended beyond Dante, Petrarch, Ariosto and Tasso to Pulci, Machiavelli, Bandello and Guarini, among Renaissance writers, Filicaja in the seventeenth century, Forteguerri, Goldoni, Casti and Alfieri among eighteenth-century writers and Monti and Foscolo among his contemporaries. This interest had certainly developed before he travelled to Italy, for Italian-language editions of the *Furioso* and *Liberata*, Bandello's *Novelle*, Dante's *Commedia*, Machiavelli's *Opere* and Petrarch's lyrics, as well as several Italian dictionaries and grammars, were among the books that Byron was compelled to auction off in April 1816 to pay his debts.[4] But only after having visited Ferrara on

19 April 1817, a visit that prompted him to write *The Lament of Tasso*, did he begin to engage with Italian literature poetically.

Focusing on the poems Byron wrote in the years 1817–20, in particular *The Lament of Tasso*, *The Prophecy of Dante*, two stanzas of the fourth canto of *Childe Harold's Pilgrimage* and the translation of the first canto of Pulci's *Morgante Maggiore*, we can see how Byron exploited both the writings and the figures of Italian writers (especially the exiled Dante and imprisoned Tasso) to construct his own cosmopolitan poetic identity. In a famous essay written in 1839, the Italian revolutionary Giuseppe Mazzini described Byron as the exemplary poet of subjective life.[5] But Mazzini's understanding of subjectivity in Byron as the projection of a unitary self onto external reality is precisely what Byron's poetry contests. Indeed, its construction of the 'Byronic' self is a central element of its social engagement. Created in dialogue with the reading public and the larger world, the 'self' that emerges in his poems is a product of the poet's responses to others, past, present and future.[6] Byron himself insisted, in a journal entry of 1813: 'To withdraw *myself* from *myself* (oh that cursed selfishness!) has ever been my sole, my entire, my sincere motive in scribbling at all; and publishing is also the continuance of the same object, by the action it affords to the mind, which else recoils upon itself'.[7] However seriously we take this explanation of his reason for writing, as if anticipating T. S. Eliot's poetics of impersonality, it is a fair description of how he creates his poetic persona – Byron wearing the mask of Byron, so to speak. What is at issue here is not the correspondence (or lack of it) between representation and biographical fact, but the representation itself. And in the poetry Byron wrote between 1817 and 1820 we find him adopting the verse forms and narrative strategies of Italian poets, translating their verse directly, ventriloquising their sorrows and projecting their vindication into a future represented implicitly by the English poet himself.

Byron's transhistorical identification with these poets derived from a self-consciously historicised sense of alienation from his own time and native land. At the same time, by conjuring up a succession of poets who experienced and opposed tyranny of one kind or another, Byron sought equally to promote the idea of an Italian nation unified by its literary tradition and dedicated to the liberation of the peninsula from foreign domination. But to the extent that it elided the complexities of translating a cultural into a political nationalism,

Byron's *certaine idée* (to appropriate de Gaulle's famous phrase) was a wish-fulfilment, betraying an impatient ambition for Italians that they themselves, in their linguistic and cultural and political heterogeneity, could not have realised in the immediate post-Napoleonic years.

In *The Giaour*, *The Corsair* and *The Siege of Corinth*, relying on triangular plots centred on two men and a woman (or two women in *The Corsair*), Byron had used the manifest confrontation between Eastern and Western characters to suggest latent similarities based on the socio-political and gender hierarchies in both European and Eastern nations. This is particularly true of *The Giaour*, in which the Venetian Giaour and Turkish Hassan are drawn into a fatal conflict figured as personal resemblance and cultural self-estrangement. But in his Italian poems Byron implied an increasing detachment from his native land by presenting an identification and engagement with Italy – its language (including regional dialects), its literature, its history, its politics. Whereas in the Eastern tales he had confronted the West with itself through the exotic medium of the East, in the Italian poems of 1817–20 he confronted English readers with a defamiliarised representation of himself through the decidedly less exotic, though still foreign, medium of Italianness. The irony of Byron's well-known reference in stanza 51 of *Beppo* to selling the English public 'samples of the finest Orientalism' is deeper than many commentators have acknowledged, for these words are uttered not in the declarative mood by the poet *in propria persona* but in the optative by a 'nameless sort' of narrator, an English poet who must content himself with repeating an Italian anecdote in an Italian verse form precisely because he is unable to produce those 'pretty poems never known to fail' in the English market: 'Oh that I had the art of easy writing / What should be easy reading' (*Beppo*, 51–2). In other words, this figure mock-regretfully differentiates himself from the most popular contemporary author of Eastern tales. As the Byron of the fourth canto of *Childe Harold's Pilgrimage* claims, 'I've taught me other tongues, and in strange eyes / Have made me not a stranger' (*CHP*, IV, 8); but it is now in Italy that Byron 'rides out' on 'Autumn evenings', dines on 'becaficas', watches the 'Sun set, sure he'll rise tomorrow', loves (and speaks) 'the language, that soft bastard Latin' and likes 'the women too' (*Beppo*, 42–5). The poet is so thoroughly assimilated into his adopted land that it has ceased to be alien to him and he to it. Yet, of course, as the adjectives 'other' and 'strange', indicating a residual foreignness, qualify the confident negation of the noun 'stranger', so the poet Byron, writing in English to English readers about Italy and Italian writers, recognised that the Italianness of the persona 'Byron' consisted in an irresolvable dialectic of identity and alterity.

Byron insinuates a Byronic Italianness in three principal ways: by appropriating Italian texts, whether directly (as in epigraphs) or indirectly (as in translations); by assuming Italian voices, such as Tasso's in *The Lament of Tasso* and Dante's in *The Prophecy of Dante*; and by adopting attitudes or points of view identified as Italian, as in the untroubled elaboration of Venetian customs in *Beppo*. By way of introduction to the complexities of these processes, we might consider an extraordinary passage in the fourth canto of *Childe Harold's Pilgrimage*. Narrating retrospectively the poet's leisurely journey from Venice to Rome via Ferrara and Florence from April to June 1817, the canto offers an extended affirmation and elaboration (allowing for some geographical licence) of its epigraph from Ariosto's fourth *Satira*:

> Visto ho Toscana, Lombardia, Romagna,
> Quel Monte che divide, e quel che serra
> Italia, e un mare e l'altro, che la bagna.
> [I have seen Tuscany, Lombardy, Romagna, Those mountains (the Apennines) that divide and those (the Alps) that cut off Italy, and one sea and the other that bathe her.].

For the most part, the ensuing travelogue, with its frequent historical reflections (supplemented by extensive historical notes), offers the perspective of an admiring but not uncritical English observer. Yet Byron also dissolves the distinctions between Englishman and Italian, between foreigner and native, in stanzas 42–3, which are, as his note acknowledges, a translation of Vincenzo da Filicaja's patriotic sonnet, 'Italia, Italia, O tu coi feo la sorte'.[8] Updating the sonnet's reference to French advances along the Po at the start of the War of Spanish Succession in 1701 to the post-Napoleonic 'many-nation'd spoilers' – a change that acknowledges historical particularity within the general pattern of the nation's 'fatal charms' for foreign powers – Byron incorporates Filicaja's lament for occupied Italy into his own poem as if to declare himself an Italian patriot.[9]

Translated into English and transformed from a Petrarch sonnet into two Spenserian stanzas, its origin signalled only in the note, 'Italia, Italia' loses, however, its identity as an Italian poem: it has as it were been colonised by *Childe Harold's Pilgrimage*. Although Byron's commitment to Italian freedom was to manifest itself practically in 1820–1, when he assisted the Ravenna Carbonari in preparing for revolt against the Austrian occupiers, the idea of vicarious patriotism implied in his appropriation of Filicaja's poem is detached from the word's etymological and conventional sense of devotion to one's own land (from the Greek *patrios*, 'of one's fathers'). Byron thus denaturalises patriotism, like national identity itself, treating it as an elective affinity that need not be rooted in the nation or country to which it is directed (and his later Philhellenism demonstrated its transferability). Conceived as a political stance, patriotism is indeed an abstraction – as was, of course, the very 'Italy' apostrophised by Filicaja and Byron, a cultural fiction referring to a non-existent political state and an artificially created national language.

If the interpolated translation assumes Filicaja's voice by appropriating his verse directly, *The Lament of Tasso*, composed immediately after the visit to Ferrara recounted in stanzas 35–41 of *Childe Harold IV*, engages more complexly with the poet whose voice it assumes. Cast as Tasso's reflection on and during his long confinement in the Ospedale di Sant'Anna, ostensibly on account of his madness, by his erstwhile patron Alfonso II d'Este, the poem constitutes, given the liberties Byron takes with the historical record, an act of imaginative projection into the past. As Anna Jameson observed in 1829, while almost 'every sentiment there expressed' may be found in Tasso's minor poems, the figure of Tasso himself 'has been transfused with such a glowing impulse into its new mould, it never seems to have been adapted to another [...] and it has been stamped by a kindred and a master spirit'.[10] Although the extent of Byron's reading of Tasso's lyrics is unknown, the two poems with which Jerome McGann justly suggests *The Lament of Tasso* has the strongest parallels, 'O magnanimo figlio' (addressed to Alfonso) and 'O figlie di Renata' (addressed to the duke's sisters Lucretia and Leonora), were reprinted in an appendix to John Black's *Life of Tasso*, of which Byron had owned a copy in England.[11] Emphasising the contrast between Tasso's former status as an honoured guest and patronised poet and his current status as a prisoner, both of these poems from the years

1579–82 appeal not only to the individual siblings' sense of pity but equally to the aristocratic virtue of courtesy, of which, Tasso implies, his imprisonment is a violation. 'Per me pietade è spenta / e cortesia smarrita, / se 'n te, signor, non nasce e non si trova' ('For me pity is spent and courtesy lost if they do not spring from and exist in you'), he tells the duke, while he seeks to recall the sisters to themselves with the memory of their courtesies to him – 'in voi la memoria / di voi, di me rinnovo; / vostri effeti cortesi' ('In you I renew the memory of yourselves, [as well as] of me; of your courteous acts') – the juxtaposition of 'voi' and 'me' being pointedly paralleled three lines later by that of 'qual son, qual fui' ('what I am, what I was').[12]

Byron preserves the bitterness of these personal appeals and the starkness of their contrast between Tasso's freedom and imprisonment, the first stanza of *The Lament of Tasso* elaborating on the denial to the poet of light, exercise and the sociable pleasures of dining and conversation. Where Tasso himself, in 'O figlie di Renata', had enumerated these pleasures – 'studi, diporti ed agi, / mense, logge e palagi' ('study, diversion and leisure, meals, arcades and palaces', lines 48–9) – Byron's Tasso acknowledges the psychological effect of their deprivation:

> the mind's canker in its savage mood,
> When the impatient thirst of light and air
> Parches the heart [...].
>   [...] Captivity displayed
> Stands scoffing through the never-opened gate,
> Which nothing through its bars admits, save day
> And tasteless food, which I have eaten alone
> Till its unsocial bitterness is gone;
> And I can banquet like a beast of prey,
> Sullen and lonely.
>   (*Lament*, 5–7, 11–17)

Yet the difference between the original Tasso and Byron's is more pronounced than the similarity, for the latter is defiant even in his abjectness, attributing his imprisonment – in accordance with a legend that Byron would have known from Black's *Life* to be without historical foundation – to the social effrontery of his expressed love for Leonora d'Este. Adopting a variant of the triangular plot he had used in the Eastern tales, as well as of the wilfulness characteristic of the protagonists of those tales and that of the recently completed *Manfred*, Byron makes the conflict between 'Tasso' and 'Alfonso II' over 'Leonora' (I use inverted commas to emphasise their fictional status) the occasion to present the unfortunate poet as the victim of tyrannical persecution. Whereas the author of 'O figlie di Renata' refers self-abnegatingly to his 'weak words' and 'copious tears' ('Scarse son le parole, / lagrime larghe', lines 44–5), the speaker of *The Lament of Tasso* proudly recalls his poetic achievement in *Gerusalemme liberata*:

> For I have battled with mine agony,
> And made me wings wherewith to overfly
> The narrow circus of my dungeon wall,
> And freed the Holy Sepulchre from thrall,
> And revelled among men and things divine.
>   (21–5)

Uncertain of divine favour ('I thought mine enemies had been but man, / But spirits may be leagued with them – all Earth / Abandons – Heaven forgets me'), 'Tasso' appeals to history for his vindication, trusting in his poetic power to 'make / A future temple of my present cell, / Which nations yet shall visit for my sake' after the rule of the Este dynasty has ended and Ferrara itself fallen into decline (198–200, 219–27).

History is obliging, for the poet's prediction in *The Lament of Tasso* is confirmed by Byron's preface to the poem, which remarks that Tasso's preserved cell is more compelling to visitors to the 'decayed, and depopulated' city than either Ariosto's house or tomb.[13] But as with the translation of Filicaja's sonnet, the assumption of Tasso's voice entails the replacement of the historical figure with one of Byron's creation, even more mediated, indeed, than the Filicaja of *Childe Harold's Pilgrimage* since the speaker's verse so loosely resembles Tasso's appeals to the Este family. Only notionally Italian himself, this figure is posthumously defended by a foreigner, one of those very 'strangers' who, the lamenting poet warns from sixteenth-century Ferrara, will 'wonder o'er thy unpeopled walls' in the future (226). Estranged from his own courtly society, 'Tasso' is thus vindicated, if not by the Lord, then by a lord, and an English one at that.

More is at stake in *The Lament of Tasso*, however, than 'a poetical representation of Byron in a contemporary act of imagining himself as Tasso'.[14] The English poet's identification with the Italian presupposes a commonality between them, the insinuation of which is a concern not only of *The Lament of Tasso* itself but of the stanzas on Ferrara in *Childe Harold's Pilgrimage* and later of *The Prophecy of Dante*. Discounting Tasso's madness as merely 'imputed' by Alfonso (4) and endorsing the legend of his love for Leonora in order to bring into sharper focus the duke's antagonism towards the poet, Byron treats Tasso's imprisonment not as historically unique but as transhistorically exemplary of the conflictual relationship between poetic genius and contemporary society, particularly its ruling elite (a theme treated more ambivalently by Goethe in his 1790 verse play, *Torquato Tasso*, and more pathetically by Felicia Hemans in her 1828 poem, 'Tasso's Coronation'). Whereas the poet of 'O figlie di Renata' mourns his alienation from humanity – 'Da' nipoti d'Adamo, / oimè!, che mi divide?' ('From the descendants of Adam, / Alas! what divides me?', 53–4) – Byron's prophetic Tasso takes solace in the thought of fellowship with future pilgrims to 'this consecrated spot' (240), his empty cell.

That the genius, however despised or abused by his patrons and countrymen, is a member of an imaginary community recognisable only to later generations is reinforced in the stanzas of *Childe Harold's Pilgrimage* immediately preceding the translation from Filicaja. Observing, as in the preface to *The Lament of Tasso*, Ferrara's current desolation – 'a curse upon the seats / Of former sovereigns' – Byron in his guise as the narrator of *Childe Harold* IV emphasises the contrast between the pettiness of the Este dynasty and the greatness of its court poets:

> Patron or tyrant, as the changing mood
> Of petty power impell'd, of those who wore
> The wreath which Dante's brow alone had worn before.
> (*CHP*, IV, 35)

Neither the brutality of Alfonso d'Este nor the hostility of the sixteenth-century Cruscan poets and Boileau (recalled contemptuously in stanzas 36–8, with a long note by Hobhouse on the Cruscan Lionardo Salviati's motive of gaining favour with the Este family) could prevent Tasso from receiving his rightful, if posthumous, recognition as one of the trinity of supreme Italian writers, 'paralleled by those, / Thy countrymen, before thee born to shine, the Bards of Hell and Chivalry' (*CHP*, IV, 40). Abstracted from his historical particularities, Tasso joins the exiled Florentine Dante and the Emilian-born Ferrarese Ariosto in epitomising Italian poetry. But the stability of that national identity is immediately compromised by the assertion of another poetic parallel: between Ariosto and Walter Scott. If one is 'the southern Scott, the minstrel who call'd forth / A new creation with his magic line', the other is 'the Ariosto of the North', who sings 'ladye-love and war, romance and knightly worth' (*CHP*, IV, 40). Once again, therefore, Italianness proves separable from a specific nationality: while in the translation of Filicaja's sonnet the quality is equivalent to an attitude, in stanza 40 it is equivalent to a poetic practice. Although this is not strictly an 'Italy without Italians' – Joseph Luzzi's apt phrase for the pervasive northern European perception of Italy noted in my first paragraph, as a land inhabited more by monuments and relics than by people – it is certainly an exclusive community to which nationality is not the crucial condition of admission.[15]

Such a community is what Percy Shelley envisioned as the audience of *The Prophecy of Dante*, composed in 1819–20 but published (despite Byron's importuning of John Murray) only in April 1821: 'the subject, no less than the style, is addressed to the few, and [...] will only be *fully* appreciated by the select readers of many generations'.[16] Shelley's anticipation of a transhistorical readership perhaps responds to the temporal scheme of the poem itself, which, like *The Lament of Tasso*, employs a 'telescoping of history' (as Carla Pomarè calls it) whereby the speaker, a historical figure, makes predictions that the poem's reader, for whom the future envisaged by the speaker is now the past, knows to have been fulfilled – a technique that Dante himself had used in *La Divine Commedia*, as had Milton in the last two books of *Paradise Lost*.[17] Future readers, Shelley must have thought, would recall past readers of *The Prophecy of Dante*, just as 'Dante' in the poem looks forward to those successors 'who will not sing in vain', namely Petrarch and the 'two greater still than he', Ariosto and Tasso (*Prophecy*, I, 9, 107). But Byron evidently hoped for a larger contemporary readership, as much Italian as English, for he conceived the poem, as his letters and conversations about it attest, to be an intervention in Italian politics: 'The time for the *Dante* would be now', he wrote to Murray on 17 August 1820, 'as Italy is on the eve of great things.'[18] Since an Italian translation of the fourth canto of *Childe Harold's Pilgrimage* (mentioned by Byron in the preface to *The*

Prophecy of Dante) had been published within a year of the English edition, he could reasonably expect that this poem, too, once published, would be quickly translated and circulated in Italy. Hence the (slightly aggressive) apology in the preface for adopting *terza rima*, the verse form of the *Commedia*: 'I would request the Italian reader to remember that when I have failed in the imitation of his great "Padre Alighier," I have failed in imitating that which all study and few understand.'[19]

If that translation of *Childe Harold's Pilgrimage* was, as Byron claimed to Thomas Medwin, well received because Italians regarded it 'in a political light, and they indulged in [his] dream of liberty, and the resurrection of Italy', then *The Prophecy of Dante*, which Byron told Medwin 'was intended for the Italians and the Guiccioli', endorsed the cause of Italy's liberation from foreign rule more fully and explicitly.[20] Shifting focus as he proceeds from the personal in Canto I to the national in Canto II, Byron's Dante associates the condition of exile with a detachment from historicity: 'I am not of this people, nor this age' (I, 143). Though exiled, he is 'free' (I, 176); though mortal, he has composed a poem that will be read through the ages (I, 144–8); though no longer Tuscan, he is fully Italian (II, 19–20, 33). Estrangement from his 'native soil' (I, 41) – which Byron admitted to Medwin to be a basis of his own identification with the poet[21] – has given him 'an external life beyond [his] fate' (IV, 13), a position as it were outside history from which he acquires a vision of Italian history, not only from antiquity to the Middle Ages but beyond to the post-Napoleonic occupation: 'the veil of coming centuries / Is rent, – a thousand years which yet supine / Lie like the ocean waves ere winds arise, / [...] Float from eternity into these eyes' (II, 35–9). This vision, which is largely a litany of war and domination by foreign powers – 'The Goth hath been, – the German, Frank, and Hun / Are yet to come' (II, 70–1) – is unified both temporally, in encompassing the past and future, and politically, in subsuming the different peoples and states of the peninsula under the single name 'Italia'. Beginning Canto II by predicting his own role in unifying Italy linguistically – 'We can have but one country, and even yet / Thou'rt mine – my bones shall be within thy breast, / My soul within thy language' (II, 19–21), 'Dante' concludes the canto by addressing those to whom his predictive powers do not extend, Byron's contemporaries, with the warning that they shall not 'break the chain' of occupation and oppression unless they overcome 'Doubt and Discord' among themselves: 'we, / Her sons, may do this with *one* deed – Unite!' (IV, 138, 139, 144–5).

   Speaking a foreign tongue, given to him by a foreign poet in exile from his own nation, this Dante advises future Italians to escape from their past. The poetic self he fashions in *The Prophecy of Dante*, though obviously fictional, is a product of the historical poet's posthumous reception, a process culminating in Byron's identification with him and projection of a post-Napoleonic Italian nationalism onto him. The poem's combination, whose relative novelty Byron's preface avers, of *terza rima* with the English language is singularly appropriate, for the political programme adumbrated in the 'prophecy' is equally dependent on the exiled Florentine and the self-exiled Englishman. In contrast to *The Lament of Tasso*, which implicitly grants Byron himself the role of Tasso's posthumous liberator, fulfilling the poem's prophecy with his pilgrimage to the poet's preserved cell, *The Prophecy of Dante*, which articulates a political aspiration to be realised beyond the poem's own time of composition, conveys a less affirmative, more ambivalent sense of the poetic self. If Dante requires Byron's intervention to be turned into the advocate of a free and unified Italy, then Byron in turn requires Italian literary figures of incontestable eminence to enlist as points of reference in inculcating a sense of nationhood. The role that Byron assigns himself here is less of a liberator than of an interpreter, elaborating the political implications of a long literary tradition grounded in a shared language. It is a role whose success the 'prophecy' itself does not, because it cannot, vindicate.

   With his translation of the first canto of Pulci's *Morgante Maggiore*, Caroline Franklin has argued, Byron sought on the one hand to contribute to the effort of the Shelleys and Leigh Hunt to create 'a cosmopolitan canon of writers who championed liberty' as a counterweight to the politically conservative appropriation of Shakespeare and other Renaissance dramatists by Coleridge and William Gifford, and on the other hand to reclaim satiric comedy as a moral instrument from the 'pioneering anti-Jacobin wits Frere and William Stewart Rose' (one the author of a mock-heroic Arthurian adaptation of Pulci, the other a translator of Ariosto and Casti).[22] In *The Prophecy of Dante*, with an eye to an Italian as well as an English audience, Byron has Dante prophesy a canon established by the endurance of its poetry in public esteem through time and despite the suffering of the poets themselves and the hostility of their immediate contemporaries – Petrarch tormented by love (III, 202), Ariosto and Tasso subjected to 'penury and pain' (III, 151) and Dante himself, of course, ripped 'from all kindred, from all home, all things / That make communion sweet, and soften pain' (I, 164–5). What distinguishes these writers, the few who sing of liberty 'and soar upon that eagle's wing, / And look in the sun's face with eagle's gaze / All free and fearless as the feather'd king' (III, 70–2), from those whom the speaker consigns to the inferno of oblivion is a refusal to prostitute their genius to patrons and rulers with false praise (III, 73–97).[23] Thus 'Dante', having remained unattracted by 'the tyrannous fraction, and the bawling crowd' and unwilling to 'make men's fickle breath the wind that blows / [His] sail' (I, 35, 55–6), proclaims his intellectual freedom in lines recalling Byron's assertion, in Canto III of *Childe Harold's Pilgrimage*, that

> I have not loved the world, nor the world me;
> I have not flattered its rank breath, nor bow'd
> To its idolatries a patient knee.
> (*CHP*, III, 113)

Petrarch, Dante foresees, will receive the laureate's crown not only for his love poetry but for 'his higher song / Of Freedom' (III, 104–5).

In this way, but also in others, *The Prophecy of Dante* is more fully engaged than *The Lament of Tasso* with Italian literature and history. Written at Teresa Guiccioli's request (as the preface obliquely informs us) and possibly in response to Giuseppe Bossi's poetic appeal of 1817 to Byron to take up the cause of 'Italia oppressa' ('oppressed Italy'), as Peter Vassallo suggests, the poem makes numerous references to passages in Dante's writings (some noted by Byron himself).[24] The patriotic sentiment, 'I would have had my Florence great and free' (II, 59), for example, alludes to the famous *canzone* in which the personifications of divine and human justice and the law, having themselves been banished from the world, comfort Dante and prompt him to consider his exile an honour – 'l'essilio che m'è dato, onor mi tengo' ('the exile that is inflicted on me, I hold as an honour'). The rhetorical question, 'What have I done to thee, my people?' (IV, 141), is a direct translation from a letter attributed to Dante by his humanist biographer Leonardo Bruni. And the antepenultimate and penultimate tercets (IV, 145–50), in which the speaker anticipates never returning to Florence, are reminiscent of another letter expressing Dante's willingness to remain permanently in exile rather than pay for a pardon from the Florentine government.[25] Beyond its reliance on Dante's own works, *The Prophecy of Dante* adheres closely to Giulio Perticari's 1819 defence, in *Dell'Amor patrio di Dante*, of the poet as a patriot despite his bitter invectives against his fellow Florentines; and it implicitly aligns Alfieri (who had died in 1803) with a Dantean opposition to tyranny by alluding in the preface to the Piedmontese poet's sonnet on Dante's tomb ('O gran Padre Alighier') and in Canto III (lines 80–3) to his refusal, recounted in his autobiography, to meet the king of Sardinia in 1784 because 'one who enters a tyrant's house makes himself a slave'.[26] But for all its engagement with Italian texts and historical figures, the poem's prophecy does not include the realisation of the ideal on whose behalf it enlists the great national poets, Italy's self-liberation from foreign domination.

The disjunction between political vision and action is one of several that haunt the poem. 'Dante' anticipates a twofold compensation for his involuntary exile from Florence, one personal in the vindication of his cultural centrality, the other national in the establishment of an independent Italy. Although the former is affirmed (if through the agency of a foreign poet) in the literary vision at the centre of Canto III, its desired connection to the latter – the linguistically unifying poetry of Dante and his chosen successors inspiring the political unification of Italy – is questioned at both the beginning and the end of the canto. If the broader compensation, not being clearly foreseeable, must be deferred till the arrival of a 'being – and even yet he may be born – / The mortal saviour who shall set thee free' (III, 53–4), then how comforting can the narrower compensation be? Must a 'heritage enriching all who breathe / With the wealth of a genuine poet's soul' (III, 154–5) be its own 'recompense' (III, 165), because it is 'the whole / Of such men's destiny beneath the sun' (III, 159–60)? The canto ends without contradicting the melancholy thought that poetry makes nothing happen.

Canto III thus enacts within itself the disjunction between the hopeful exhortations of Canto II, which assume the imminent possibility of the expulsion of the Austrians from Italian territory, and the sober reflections of Canto IV, in which 'Dante', foreseeing Julius II's ill-treatment of Michelangelo, concedes the inability of art, even that created by geniuses, to inspire moral change in tyrants, 'who but take her for a toy' (VI, 85). The appearance in this canto of the Renaissance pope as a self-serving artistic patron makes more striking the omission in Canto II of the Catholic Church as a temporal power adamantly opposed to revolutionary movements on the peninsula – indeed, Romagna was one of the territories restored to papal rule by the Congress of Vienna, and Austrian troops were permitted to garrison in Ferrara and Comacchio to suppress any uprising in the papal territory.[27] Though it suited his propagandistic purposes to present Italy as a land oppressed by the puppet princes and occupying armies of foreign states, particularly Austria, Byron was scarcely unaware – especially given his role in 1820–1 as an unofficial intermediary between the Ravenna Carbonari and Count Giuseppe Alborghetti, the secretary to the papal legate of Romagna – that the national liberation he supported required rebellion also against the reactionary power at the country's very heart. And if the poem avoids implicating the church directly in Italy's post-Napoleonic condition, the appeal at the end of Canto II, quoted earlier, to overcome internal division still acknowledges the inadequacy of the dichotomy between Italians and foreigners asserted earlier in the canto's narrative of the country's history. When discord among Italians themselves, as in the civil strife characteristic of the city-states of Dante's time (which increased their vulnerability to foreign intervention) or the fractiousness of the Carboneria in Byron's time, constitutes a major obstacle to their constituting themselves as a nation, how stable a category is Italian nationality?

Unsurprisingly, *The Prophecy of Dante* concludes not with a triumphant vision of national unity but with the relatively modest hope that the poet himself will be acknowledged by a prophet long after his death, even if his prophecy itself has been ignored:

> I may not overleap the eternal bar
> Built up between us, and will die alone,
>   Beholding, with the dark eye of a seer,
>   The evil days to gifted souls foreshown,
> Foretelling them to those that will not hear,
>   As in the old time [i.e., Dante's own], till the hour be come
>   When Truth shall strike their eyes through many a tear,
> And make them own the Prophet in his tomb.
>   (IV, 148–54)

Stephen Cheeke has sensitively analysed the ambiguity in the last line of the verb 'own', which conveys a sense both of recognition – Italians identifying themselves as such in confirming Dante to be their national poet – and of possession.[28] From the perspective of the poem's speaker, such possession consists in a future generation's reclaiming of him from his exile by unifying Italy, but from Byron's perspective it consists in appropriating Dante and transforming him into an advocate for a political vision of which the Florentine was assuredly innocent. 'The dust she [Italy] dooms to scatter' (I, 75) is transferred to *The Prophecy of Dante* and, as it were, then thrown back in the faces of Dante's countrymen. On 7 September 1820, Byron wrote to Murray that 'the Huns [Austrians] are on the Po – but if once they pass it on their march to Naples – all Italy will rise behind them [...]. If you want to publish the Prophecy of Dante – you will never have a better time'.[29] But if, as Cheeke argues, 'Dante's' anticipation of future vindication embodies Byron's 'fantasy of success for his poem with an Italian audience' – and he did write to Hobhouse on 17 October 1820 that the Carbonari rebellion in Naples had 'acted as an Advertisement' for the poem[30] – the defensive preface betrays an anxiety about ventriloquising the national poet in his own verse form in order to encourage his countrymen to accomplish a political objective that, at the time, Byron wished for them more than they wished for themselves.[31]

On 24 February 1821, Austrian troops having in fact crossed the Po and marched south through the papal lands towards Naples, Byron received intelligence that the Neapolitan rebellion had collapsed, its leaders betrayed and the populace unmoved: 'thus the Italians are always lost for lack of unity among themselves'.[32] By 1 May, whatever hope he may have entertained that he might become poetically or militarily a 'mortal saviour' of Italy was definitively dashed, as his journal entry confirms, and in July Teresa Guiccioli's brother and father, who had initiated Byron into the Ravenna Carbonari, were condemned to Dante's own fate of exile from their native territory (although in their case *to* Florence).[33] The sense of urgency with which Byron had encouraged the publication of *The Prophecy of Dante* in the autumn of 1820 was lost by the time the poem was actually published on 21 April 1821 in the same volume as *Marino Faliero*, rather than, as Byron had urged in January of that year, with his translation of Pulci.[34] But he remained proud of the translation, which he boasted was 'the very best thing I ever wrote', and was exasperated by Murray's prevarications concerning the work's publication, on account of Pulci's supposed indecency and irreligion.³⁵ Composed between late October 1819 and late February 1820, it was eventually published, accompanied by the Italian text, not by Murray but by John Hunt in the fourth and final issue of *The Liberal* in April 1823.

In contrast to *The Lament of Tasso* and *The Prophecy of Dante*, in which the English poet effectively grants himself at least as prominent a role as those of the Italian poets he ventriloquises, the *Morgante Maggiore* is, as Byron's editor E. H. Coleridge described it, 'the offering of a disciple to a master'.³⁶ If in the two dramatic monologues Byron sought to present his claim to Italianness by justifying Dante and Tasso posthumously against their contemporary Italian antagonists, in the *Morgante* he sought, as Vassallo argues, indirectly to justify the style of *Don Juan*, the first two cantos of which had been criticised by reviewers as impious, by presenting as directly as his translating skills permitted Pulci's 'half-serious rhyme' (*DJ*, IV, 6).³⁷ Referring in his advertisement for the poem, perhaps written in response to Murray's anxieties about the translation, to the recent Pulcian adaptations of J. H. Merivale (*Orlando in Roncesvalles*, published in 1814) and Frere (*Whistlecraft*, published in 1817), Byron designated the Italian poet 'the founder of a new style of poetry lately sprung up in England'.³⁸ But unlike both Frere, who preserved Pulci's humour but carefully avoided his engagement with religious topics, and Merivale, who did more nearly the opposite, Byron conveyed as a totality Pulci's combination of levity and seriousness, a combination that Ugo Foscolo, in an article published in English in 1819, attributed to the desire to 'adhere to the forms and subjects of the popular story-tellers' while simultaneously rendering such materials 'interesting and sublime'.³⁹

In the poem's advertisement Byron addresses Pulci's irreverence explicitly in terms that were consistent with, even if not influenced by, Foscolo's argument. That the poet ridiculed monastic life does not demonstrate him to be irreligious, for neither the poet nor the poem would have fared well had the humour at the expense of religious figures been interpreted in Pulci's time or subsequently as derision of the Catholic religion itself.⁴⁰ The poem's juxtaposition of the sacred and the secular, of solemnity and jocularity, was its solution to the difficulty referred to in the Horatian epigraph to Canto I of *Don Juan*, namely of finding a way to speak suitably of common things

('Difficile est proprie communia dicere'), which in fifteenth-century Italy obviously included religion. Aligning the Italian poet with Fielding and Scott in the treatment of religious figures, describing him almost as if he were an English poet, Byron implies that Pulci had anticipated a serio-comic style that British writers since the mid eighteenth century were beginning to make their own. The implications of this defence of the *Morgante* for the reception of *Don Juan* remain unstated, however, for Byron is at pains in his advertisement, as indeed in the translation itself, to subordinate himself to Pulci. While the first paragraph of the advertisement suggests that the Italian poet may be closer to British writers than is evident from his tone, the second paragraph modestly claims that his translator may be further from a mastery of Italian than is evident from the translation: Byron 'was induced to make the experiment partly by his love for, and partial intercourse with, the Italian language, of which it is so easy to acquire a slight knowledge, and with which it is so nearly impossible for a foreigner to become accurately conversant'.[41] But just as Byron seems to reassert the national and linguistic boundaries that his first paragraph called into question, he introduces a subtle ambiguity in his final sentence:

> The translator wished also to present in an English dress a part at least of a poem never yet rendered into a northern language; at the same time that it has been the original of some of the most celebrated productions on this side of the Alps, as well as of those recent experiments in poetry in England, which have already been mentioned.[42]

Leaving unmentioned his own ongoing experiment in poetry, published on the northern side of the Alps – the fourth canto of which, published in 1821, acknowledged Pulci as 'the sire of the half-serious rhyme' (*DJ*, IV, 6) and a model – Byron locates himself on the southern side, thus allowing *Don Juan* to be understood as one of those 'most celebrated productions' of a literary heritage extending back to Pulci through Tasso and Ariosto. The division between Englishman and Italian is blurred, though not wholly effaced, as Byron simultaneously affirms his foreignness with respect to the Italian language and his sense of belonging to Italy, to 'this side of the Alps'. It was not by representing an Italian poet to Italians but by mediating an Italian poem to the English that Byron was able to construct a truly cosmopolitan poetic identity for himself in Italy.

Notes

1. F. Haskell, 'Preface', in A. Wilton and I. Bignamini (eds.), *The Grand Tour: The Lure of Italy in the Eighteenth Century* (London: Tate, 1996), pp. 10–12.
2. See, for example, his letter of 15 May 1764 to H. D. Berendis, in J. J. Winckelmann, *Briefe*, 4 vols, ed. W. Rehm (Berlin: de Gruyter, 1952–7), vol. III, pp. 39–40: 'The Duke of York, who was here for 12 days, is the greatest princely brute I know and does no credit to his rank or nation.'
3. See C. P. Brand, *Italy and the English Romantics: The Italianate Fashion in Early Nineteenth-Century England* (Cambridge: Cambridge University Press, 1957), pp. 32–45, 49–50.
4. The auction catalogue is reprinted in *CMP*, pp. 230–45.
5. See G. Mazzini, 'Byron e Goethe', in *Scritti editi ed inediti*, 106 vols (Imola: Galeate, 1915), vol. XXI, pp. 187–241 (pp. 199–207, 218, 222–7, 238).
6. See C. Bode, *Selbst-Begründungen: Diskursive Konstruktion von Identität in der Britischen Romantik* (Trier: WVT, 2008), p. 117.
7. Journal entry for 28–30 November 1813, in *BLJ*, vol. III, p. 225.
8. See *CPW*, vol. II, p. 234.
9. See P. Vassallo, *Byron: The Italian Literary Influence* (Basingstoke: Macmillan, 1984), who remarks that Byron likely encountered the sonnet in J. C. L. Simonde de Sismondi's *De la littérature du Midi de l'Europe* (p. 201), one of the works sold in the 1816 auction (see *CMP*, p. 241).
10. A. Jameson, *The Loves of the Poets* (London: Henry Colburn, 1829), I, p. 326. I owe this reference to McGann's commentary, in *CPW*, vol. IV, p. 479.
11. See *CPW*, vol. IV, p. 479; J. Black, *The Life of Torquato Tasso; with an Historical and Critical Account of His Writings* (London: John Murray, 1810), vol. II, pp. 406–12; *CMP*, p. 236. The poems were also reprinted in Pierantonio Serassi's *Vita di Torquato Tasso*, 2nd edn (Bergamo: Stamperia Locatelli, 1795), vol. II, pp. 41 n. 2 and 41–2 n. 3, a work on which John Cam Hobhouse drew in his *Historical Illustrations of the Fourth Canto of Childe Harold* (London: John Murray, 1818), and they would be discussed in 'The Lyric Poetry of Tasso', published anonymously in *The New Monthly Magazine and Literary Journal*, 5 (1822), 373–80.
12. 'O magnanimo figlio', 27–8, and 'O figlie di Renata', 33–5 and 37, in T. Tasso, *Opere di Torquato Tasso*, ed. B. T. Sozzi, 3rd edn (Turin: UTET, 1974), vol. II, pp. 797, 793–4. All translations of Italian into English in this chapter are mine.

13 *CPW*, vol. IV, p. 116.
14 J. J. McGann, 'Hero with a thousand faces: the rhetoric of Byronism', *Studies in Romanticism*, 31:3 (1992), 295–313 (p. 297). In abjuring suicide, 'Tasso' also has a smack of Hamlet, another figure wrongly perceived as mad: 'I would not die / And sanction with self-slaughter the dull lie / Which snared me here' (213–15) – see *Hamlet* (I, ii, 132).
15 See J. Luzzi, *Romantic Europe and the Ghost of Italy* (New Haven, Conn.: Yale University Press, 2008), Chapter 2.
16 Letter to Byron of 14 September 1821, in P. B. Shelley, *The Letters of Percy Bysshe Shelley*, ed. F. L. Jones (Oxford: Clarendon Press, 1964), vol. II, p. 347.
17 C. Pomarè, *Byron and the Discourses of History* (Farnham: Ashgate, 2013), pp. 138, 149. This parallel with the *Commedia* was pointed out by B. Taylor in 'Byron's use of Dante in *The Prophecy of Dante*', *Keats-Shelley Journal*, 28 (1979), 102–19 (pp. 107–8).
18 *BLJ*, vol. VII, p. 158.
19 *CPW*, vol. IV, pp. 214–15.
20 T. Medwin, *Medwin's Conversations of Lord Byron*, ed. E. J. Lovell, Jr (Princeton, NJ: Princeton University Press, 1966), p. 159.
21 Medwin, *Medwin's Conversations*, p. 158.
22 C. Franklin, 'Cosmopolitanism and Catholic culture: Byron, Italian poetry, and *The Liberal*', in L. Bandiera and D. Saglia (eds.), *British Romanticism and Italian Literature: Translating, Reviewing, Rewriting* (Amsterdam: Rodopi, 2005), pp. 255–68 (p. 255).
23 One can easily imagine that Byron had Southey in mind when he composed the condemnation of poetical flatterers in Canto III, and doubtless he did, but Thomas Moore records an omitted tercet – 'The prostitution of his Muse and wife, / [...] Shall shalt his bread and gives him means of life' – about a living Italian poet, certainly Vincenzo Monti, whom Byron had met and considered the 'Judas of Parnassus' because of his political temporising (T. Moore, *Life, Letters, and Journals of Lord Byron* [London: John Murray, 1838], p. 438). See also Byron's letter to Teresa Guiccioli of 7 August 1820, in *BLJ*, vol. VII, p. 151.
24 See *CPW*, vol. IV, p. 214; and Vassallo, *Byron*, pp. 35–6. Byron was sent a copy of Bossi's pseudonymously published *Versi*, including 'Al Lord Byron, celebre poeta inglese', in June 1817.
25 Dante, *Rime* no. 47 ('Tre donne intorno al cor'), 76, in D. Alighieri, *Opere minori*, ed. D. de Robertis (Milan: Ricciardi, 1979–84), vol. I, pp. 454–9 (see also Byron's note on Dante, in *CPW*, vol. IV, p. 141); *Epistole* no. 12, in Dante, *Opere minori*, vol. II, p. 596. The letter beginning 'Popule me, quid feci tibi?' (itself a quotation from Micah 6:3) is

recorded only in Bruni's biography of the poet, which Byron cites in his notes to the *Prophecy*. See *Le Vite di Dante, e del Petrarca* (Florence: All'insegna della stella, 1672), p. 47, and *CPW*, vol. IV, p. 504.

26 V. Alfieri, *Vita*, ed. G. Cattaneo (Milan: Garzanti, 2000), p. 224. The poem's connections with Perticari and Alfieri are examined by Vassallo, *Byron*, pp. 30–8.

27 See C. Duggan, *The Force of Destiny: A History of Italy since 1796* (London: Allen Lane, 2007), pp. 74–5. Byron's assumption, confided to his journal on 20 February 1821, that the pope's anathema against the Carbonari (shown to him by Alborghetti before its publication) would encourage 'a general and immediate rise of the whole nation' proved unfounded (*BLJ*, vol. VIII, pp. 48–9).

28 Stephen Cheeke, *Byron and Place: History, Translation, Nostalgia* (Basingstoke: Palgrave, 2003), p. 136.

29 *BLJ*, vol. VII, p. 172.

30 *BLJ*, vol. VII, p. 205.

31 Duggan observes that the revolutions in Naples, Piedmont, and Lombardy in 1820–1 failed in part because their well-born leaders, mostly officers or intellectuals, had failed to secure the support of the local populations (see *The Force of Destiny*, pp. 83–5).

32 Journal entry for 24 February 1821, in *BLJ*, vol. VIII, p. 49.

33 Journal entry for 1 May 1821, in *BLJ*, vol. VIII, p. 106.

34 Letter to John Murray of 19 January 1821, in *BLJ*, vol. VIII, p. 65.

35 Letter to John Murray of 12 September 1821, in *BLJ*, vol. VIII, p. 206. See also Byron's letters to Murray of 23 April 1820 and 1 March 1821, in *BLJ*, vol. VII, p. 83, and vol. VIII, p. 86.

36 E. H. Coleridge, 'Introduction' to the *Morgante*, in Lord Byron, *The Works of Lord Byron*, 13 vols, ed. E. H. Coleridge and R. E. Prothero (London: John Murray, 1898–1904), vol. IV, p. 280 (quoted by McGann, in *CPW*, vol. IV, p. 509).

37 Vassallo, *Byron*, pp. 151–3.

38 *CPW*, vol. IV, p. 247.

39 U. Foscolo, 'Narrative and romantic poems of the Italians', in U. Foscolo, *Opere*, ed. F. Gavazzeni (Milan: Ricciardi, 1974–81), vol. II, pp. 1567–1726 (p. 1646).

40 See *CPW*, vol. IV, p. 247.

41 *CPW*, vol. IV, p. 248.

42 *CPW*, vol. IV, p. 248.

2

Byron's ethnographic eye: the poet among the Italians

Gioia Angeletti

'It is from *experience*, not from *Books*, we ought to judge of mankind. There is nothing like inspection, and trusting to our own senses.'[1] This aphorism appears in a letter that Byron wrote to his mother as early as 1808, but the empiricist principle that informs it persisted as one of the central epistemological tenets of his whole career as a writer. Indeed, five years later, in 1813, in a letter to Annabella Milbanke, Byron expounded on the same concept, stating that the 'great object of life is Sensation – to feel that we exist – even though in pain'.[2] From 1816 onwards, this urge to sense and experience life affected his eight-year Italian sojourn, at the end of which 'his thirst for travel', to quote stanza 28 of *Childe Harold's Pilgrimage* I, was 'assuaged' by 'toil' and by a gradual moral and political disenchantment with Italy that redirected his wanderlust towards other destinations.

'Participant-observation' is 'the classic formula for ethnographic work', writes James Clifford, adding that because of its interaction with oral culture and real life – documents in-the-making – this work often 'leaves little room for texts' – in other words, for authoritative and incontrovertible 'textualization'.[3] In Byron's case, the ethnographic observation of the human and cultural geography of Italy is given textual form in his idiosyncratic letters and journals, where he does not merely represent Italianness but also interprets and reinvents it, often to confute conventional figurations of Italy. As with most ethnographers, Byron seeks both to grasp the exotic and foreign and to communicate them to his interlocutors. However, unsurprisingly enough, instead of a scientific method of ethnographic observation, recording and transmission, he adopts a method of his own. This is based on up-close, first-hand experience (what, for an ethnographer, would be fieldwork) and an 'emic' perspective, which shows his distance from other British travellers in Italy but, at the same time, cannot be taken as proof of his full integration into Italian culture.[4] As I have argued elsewhere, Byron's figurations or reconfigurations of Italy are palimpsests combining, often in complex and ambiguous ways, life experience and imagination, fact and fiction, *locus* and *topos*.[5] As a result, however sensorial and direct, his ethnography of Italy is eccentric because of its distinctive blend of objective and subjective elements. Though critics generally agree that Byron's letters and journals constitute an 'informal' autobiography, this aspect cannot be separated from their documentary value in relation to the contemporary social, ideological and political contexts of Britain and the Continent.[6]

This chapter focuses on the peculiar mode of Byron's reception and construction of Italianness in a selection of letters to British correspondents, which promote an appreciation of the contingent rather than the idealised Italy that captivated the imagination of most contemporary foreign tourists and visitors. On the one hand, the insistence on the contingent demonstrates how, by being 'immersed in "local colour"', the poet enjoyed an insider's perspective on Italian otherness that enabled him to capture its spirit more authentically than most contemporary visitors to the country, who tended to concentrate on its mythical aura.[7] On the other hand, this same insistence allows us to trace the ways in which Byron's insider knowledge was also the source of an increasing disenchantment with Italy and, consequently, one key reason for his gradual distancing of himself from the cultural, social and ethical values he previously associated with it.

Byron's poetics of domestication

As is well known, Byron's 'pilgrimage' to Italy was not inspired by the usual motivations of eighteenth-century Grand Tours, although his peregrinations around Europe confirm his interest in travelling and the essential meaning it gives to human life: 'A man must travel, and turmoil, or there is no existence', he wrote to Thomas Moore.[8] On leaving England in 1816, he looked for a temporary escape – which then became permanent – from the vexation caused by his disastrous marriage to and separation from Lady Byron. His letters and journals prove that in Italy he tended to wear his Italian mask by adopting local customs and traditions, as well as avoiding as much as possible the mass of English tourists crowding Italy's main cities. He appreciated Ravenna because, as he wrote to Lady Byron, 'it is out of the way of travellers & armies – and thus they have retained more of their originality. – They make love a good deal, – and assassinate a little.'[9]

In his letters, Byron often prided himself on his insider's perspective on Italy. Writing to Lady Byron from Ravenna in 1819, he benevolently mocked his acquaintance, and later partner in the project of the periodical *The Liberal*, Leigh Hunt for giving a false picture of the city in his *Story of Rimini*: 'he has made a sad mistake – about "old Ravenna's *clear-shewn towers* and *bay*" the city Lies so low that you must be close upon it before it is "shewn" at all – and the Sea had retired four miles at least, long before Francesca was born'.[10] Though admitting that Shakespeare and Otway 'had a million of advantages over' him, he confessed to John Murray that he has at least one over them, 'that – of having been at Venice – and entered into the local Spirit of it'.[11] In another missive to Murray, written a couple of weeks earlier, he wrote: 'I have *lived* among the Italians – not *Florenced* and *Romed* – and Galleried – and Conversationed it for a few months – and then home again – but been of their families [...] and correspondence in a part of Italy least known to foreigners [...] and you may be sure of what I say to you.'[12]

Nevertheless, seeing and knowing Italians and Italy from the inside did not mean feeling always fully acclimatised to their world. Byron's immersion in their customs and manners did not necessarily involve an accomplished acculturation into, or adaptation of, their lifestyle. Indeed, as Maria Schoina observes, he 'conceives of identity as an active process that involves inclusion and exclusion, identification and detachment, that is, a process in which the building of identity is at the same time an evasion of it'.[13]

These dynamics are clearly visible in the letter Byron wrote to Murray from Ravenna on 21 February 1820, in which he stresses the authenticity of his on-the-spot experience of Italy, while affirming his distance from England. Here he insistently deploys second-person pronouns and possessives to address Murray and the English ('ye of the North'), whom he thinks are unable to understand the southern mores and attitudes reflecting the spirit of liberty that inspired his expatriation in the first place. At the same time, however, Byron explains to Murray why he cannot produce the book on Italian manners that his publisher would like him to write:

> I have lived in their houses and in the heart of their families – sometimes merely as 'amico di casa' ['friend of the family'] and sometimes as 'Amico di cuore' ['friend of the heart'] of the Dama – and in neither case do I feel authorized in making a book of them. – – Their moral is not your moral – their life is not your life – you would not understand it.[14]

Byron emphasises the gap between Italy and Britain by repeatedly opposing 'you' (Murray and the English) to 'them' (the Italians), but where does his 'I' stand? The answer possibly lies in his observation that the Italians are 'capable of impressions and passions which are at once sudden and durable (what you find in no other nation) and who actually have no society (what we would call so) as you may see by their Comedies'.[15] In his bracketed phrase, Byron's singular use of an inclusive 'we' refers to a notion of society as a civic and political entity that he shares with Murray but of which he sees no equivalent, nor any alternative, in Italy. Significantly, writing to Isaac D'Israeli, the son of an Italian Jew from Cento, over two years later, he spoke of 'the laws of this lawless country', referring to Italy's lack of a central government and sense of national unity, two aspects of Italian life that triggered his gradual disenchantment with Italy and, at the same time, his *rapprochement* with his home country.[16] However paradoxical it may seem, especially in the last years of his Italian exile, Byron showed signs of a reconciliation with England, perhaps in an attempt to rehabilitate himself in the eyes of contemporary English readers.

That Byron's 'I' here is – as well as in the earlier letter to Murray – more English than Italian is confirmed by the revelation of his merely partial intimacy with Italian habits, traditions and *modus vivendi*, and his not feeling 'authorized' to publish a book about them. In Drummond Bone's words, Byron in Italy was 'cut-off from [his] cultural base, and yet unassimilated into a new environment'.[17] Rather than speak as if he were one of 'them', in his 1820 letter to Murray, Byron acts as a cultural mediator between the Italians and his British correspondent, a mediator who speaks about Italy from a privileged insider's perspective but one who also acknowledges the difference between himself and this cultural other.

However, in September of the same year, he returned to the idea of writing a book about Italy in order to give the English 'the loud lie', since they 'in general know little of the Italians' and most English travellers did not write truthful accounts of the country.[18] In August he wrote to Moore:

> I suspect I know a thing or two of Italy – more than Lady Morgan has picked up in her posting. What do Englishmen know of Italians beyond their museums and saloons [...]? Now, I have lived in the heart of their houses, in parts of Italy freshest and least influenced by strangers, – have seen and become [...] a portion of their hopes, and fears, and passions, and am almost inoculated into a family.[19]

Though the idea of 'inoculation' ambiguously suggests both deep insertion into and strangeness in a host environment, Byron insists that his compatriots see him neither as a tourist nor as a *flâneur* observing Italian people from a foreigner's perspective. Instead, he reiterates his empiricist epistemology based on direct sensorial experience ('have seen') and direct personal commitment ('become [...] a portion').

Byron's complex poetics of domestication – implying inclusiveness within the other, which, however, does not supersede estrangement – leads to his reception of the foreign culture as quotidian, while what was once native is often identified as strange, alienated or alienating. It is to this apparent loss of Englishness that the author of an 1822 article in *Blackwood's Magazine* referred when he noted that 'Byron has often forgotten, and often misremembered, his native country.'[20] Yet it is with the acquisition of Italianness that the letters and journals Byron wrote in Italy are primarily concerned, and if we read these texts as ethnographic writings we can see that their anthropological and cultural discourse displays a penchant for subjective participation and interpretive analysis, which traditional ethnographers tend to dismiss in favour of objective distance and disinterested observation.[21] In her review of James Fenimore Cooper's *The Bravo: A Venetian Story*, which appeared in the *Westminster Review* in 1832, Mary Shelley referred to the peculiarities of Byron's appropriated Italianness, and specifically his 'Venetianness', by noting that he 'was one of the few strangers who was admitted, or would choose to be admitted, behind the scenes of that singular stage [Venetian society]'.[22] Venice, of course, was for Byron a hyperbolical synecdoche of

Italy, and Mary Shelley's notion of his 'initiation' into Venetian life can be extended to his experience of Italy at large, from his relationship with Italian women from the most disparate social classes to his absorption and usage of the Italian language and Venetian dialect and his reception and, to a certain extent, eulogising of Italian customs, traditions and behaviour in opposition to their English equivalents. In particular, his learning of 'that soft bastard Latin' (to quote Byron's description of Italian in stanza 44 of *Beppo*) and of the Venetian dialect is part of his process of transculturation and integration into Italian society through the direct knowledge and appropriation of local customs. His remark to Murray that Venetian is for him 'something like the Somersetshire version of English' also shows an ethnographic and anthropological interest in linguistic otherness that is bound up with the direct experience and pragmatic knowledge of both the language and its regional and local variations.[23] Italian is *parole* rather than *langue* for Byron, serving communicative purposes rather than the aims of philological study.[24]

In other words, Byron's empirical engagement with Italy is part of a poetics of mobility and ironic *Weltanschauung*, whereby universally abstract truth is discarded in favour of epistemological enquiry based on factuality, improvised experience and a fragmented apprehension of reality. It is in this light that we can interpret the ethnographic interest in the anecdotal and the focus on apparently insignificant details that continually surface in Byron's letters from Italy.

Ethnographic investigations: fact versus fiction

Had he been alive when they were first published in 1836, Byron would undoubtedly have detested John Murray's *Handbooks for Travellers* for turning him into an icon to be exploited by the Victorian tourist industry.[25] However, influenced by these guidebooks, Victorians tended to identify Byron as the cosmopolitan European traveller par excellence, with 'the same "star quality" that distinguishes the *divi* of Hollywood and the recording industry'.[26]

In his study of European tourism and literature, James Buzard stresses the difference between the 'traveller' and the 'tourist', defining the former as someone who has a direct and private experience of scenes, places and people, while attributing to the tourist a consumerist attitude and a tendency to follow pre-established 'beaten tracks'.[27]

In Italy Byron did not entirely conform to either type, not only because of his outspoken disparagement of mass tourism but also because his experience of Italy was 'mediated' by his reading of representations of the country in the works of Shakespeare, Otway, Schiller, Radcliffe and Madame de Staël, among others. Henry Digby Beste's definition of 'resident' in his 1828 travelogue *Italy as It Is* may offer a better paradigm to identify Byron's position in Italy: 'a NARRATIVE of a residence in a foreign country will differ from a tour: the tourist may see and observe; the resident will reflect and compare'.[28] As we have seen, Byron's idiosyncratic 'narrative' is certainly much more than a series of observations of Italian otherness collated together, and, on the whole, the objects and nature of his annotations and reflections differ greatly from those of either a 'traveller' or a 'tourist'.

In his correspondence, Byron often dwells on anecdotal incidents and personal chronicles rather than on the cultural objects and geographical landmarks that would attract what Buzard identifies as the traveller or tourist. Like an ethnographer collecting first-hand materials, he focuses on what may appear as anthropological and ethnographic *marginalia* or *minutiae*, while also, on some occasions, endorsing a bottom-up approach to the local culture that favours the voice of the people over the official records and testimonies of historians and scholars.

In November 1816, Byron wrote to Moore and Augusta Leigh about his visit to Verona. He could not avoid mentioning the city's main tourist attractions – the amphitheatre and Juliet's tomb – but in both letters his interest lies not so much in these monuments per se as in the ways in which their historical meaning has become an integral part of the everyday life of Verona's inhabitants, to such an extent that the fiction associated with them turns into fact. In particular, Byron refers to 'the truth of Juliet's story', the 'authentic' rather than symbolic meaning of the tomb, so that even his own stealing of 'four small pieces of it', apparently souvenirs for his daughter and nieces, seems almost to hint at a desire to preserve a material specimen of the 'reality' of Juliet and Romeo's story, which is as important to the people and the local history of Verona as it is for its literary significance and reverberations.[29] Thus he wrote to Moore:

> I have been over Verona. The amphitheatre is wonderful [...]. Of the truth of Juliet's story, they seem tenacious to a degree, insisting on the fact – giving a date (1303), and showing a tomb. It is a plain, open,

and partly decayed sarcophagus, with withered leaves in it, in a wild and desolate conventual garden, once a cemetery, now ruined to the very graves. The situation struck me as very appropriate to the legend, being blighted as their love.[30]

Besides the undeniable legendary aura surrounding the two lovers, Byron's interest in this specific ruin – more than in 'all the antiquities – more even than the Amphitheatre' – lay in the more general cultural significance that it had for the inhabitants of Verona, in their insistence on the historical source of the legend, which for Byron was an additional ethnographic detail about the country.[31] Moreover, his attitude here foreshadows what he experienced in Venice in April 1817 and reported to Murray, confessing that he was more struck by the staircase where Doge Faliero was first crowned and then decapitated than the Rialto (which he visited 'for the sake of Shylock'): the former, in other words, seems to represent for Byron a *lieu de mémoire*, geographically and historically situated, rather than a *topos* whose import essentially depends on its purely literary associations, as is the case with the Rialto.[32]

Byron's cultural investigation of Italy is often triggered by details concerning individual stories and local anecdotes rather than by the official records of Italian history and historiography. For instance, this emerges during his well-known visit to the Ambrosian library in Milan in November 1816, where his attention was drawn not so much to 'sundry valuable MSS., classical, philosophical, and pious' as to the 'correspondence (the prettiest love-letters in the world) of Lucretia Borgia with Cardinal Bembo [...] and a lock of her hair, and some Spanish verses of hers'. Deliberately, Byron leaves the historical facts about one of the most controversial female figures of Renaissance Italy, and the Borgia family, in the background in order to concentrate on Lucrezia's personal story: 'to the scandal of the librarian', he writes to Moore, 'I stick to the Pope's daughter, and wish myself a cardinal.'[33] Once again, like an ethnographer collecting samples for his studies, Byron cannot resist preserving some relics (like the pieces of granite from Juliet's tomb), so he takes a single hair from a lock of Lucrezia's, and, since it was impossible to get copies of the letters, learns some of them by heart.

In the same ethnographic vein, showing Byron gleaning knowledge of Italian life from individual narratives and first-hand anecdotal details, the poet's account of his short stay in Bologna on 6 and 7

June 1819 to Murray passes over his 'picture-gazing' in the national gallery and focuses instead on his meeting with a janitor in the Certosa cemetery: 'an original of Custode who reminded [him] of the grave-digger in Hamlet'.[34] Byron describes the Custode as if he were a comedic actor, quoting or reporting his speeches about the buried (anonymous commoners such as a friar, or a Princess Barberini, whose tombstone is decorated with a bust by Bernini), and finally commenting on the more modest gravestones with only a few words inscribed on them, such as *'implora pace'* ('implores peace'). Byron aestheticises the caretaker by means of a familiar literary comparison in order to 'anglicise' him and make him closer to his addressee's cultural frame of reference. At the same time, though, he offers an anthropological testimony to what he sees as the Italians' theatrical and performative attitudes even in the most ordinary situations.

However genuine his curiosity about exotic burial traditions might have been, even in this case Byron could not avoid his compulsive self-referentiality: 'I hope, whoever may survive me and shall see me put in the foreigners' burying-Ground at the Lido [...] will see those two words and no more put over me.'[35] Since the poet's ethnographic eye never fixes on one single item unwaveringly, the pattern of his transcription of what he sees and hears is, on the whole, always the same: a constant repositioning of the focus from the outside to the inside, the foreign to the familiar, ethnography to autobiography. Though primarily focused on what is externally and objectively present, Byron's empirical attitude is inextricable from his irresistible impulse to see himself mirrored in the experience of the Italian other and thus to appropriate Italian customs, language and lifestyles in order to meet the demands of his narcissistic self. Nevertheless, what we read in this and other similar letters is an interest, first and foremost, in what is externally and objectively present, and in the wider ethnographic implications of what Byron sees in front of him.

As with the other episodes mentioned above, Byron's encounter with the caretaker is an example of how his letters and journals textualise first-hand experience. It is from fragments of personal 'histories' such as these, from pieces of subjective narrative and local sources of information, rather than from 'official' narrative histories, that Byron builds an Italian mosaic based on idiosyncratic, ethnographic discoveries.[36] And, of course, experiential knowledge involves, by definition, epistemological uncertainty, since it is based on necessarily circumstantial and limited data that may furnish the materials for inductive reasoning and general theories only at a second stage. Byron tends to stop at the initial phase of this ethnographic process, eschewing, as his *Weltanschauung* demands, absolute conceptualisations and epistemic systems. Aptly, in order to underline Byron's empirical approach, Ruskin commented that he 'spoke only of what he had seen, and known', thus raising a crucial ethnographic question concerning the relationship between knowledge and truth, partiality and neutrality.[37]

In a letter to Murray, Byron provided a philosophical explanation of the way in which his mind received the otherness of Italy – how his memory, in other words, stored multiple external inputs or stimuli – albeit in the awareness that his sensorial apprehension of Italy would always be limited and fragmentary, leaving him in a constant state of dissatisfaction, as well as making his Italian figurations seem incomplete. In particular, the letter focuses on his encounter with Rome, which, like Venice, may be interpreted as a Byronic synecdoche for the whole of Italy:

> I am delighted with Rome [...]. As a *whole – ancient & modern –* it beats Greece – Constantinople – everything – at least that I have ever seen. – But I can't describe because my first impressions are always strong and confused – & my Memory *selects* & reduces them to order – like distance in the landscape – & blends them better – although they may be less distinct – there must be a sense or two more than we have as mortals – which I suppose the Devil has – (or t'other) for where there is much to be grasped we are always at a loss – and yet we feel we ought to have a higher and more extended comprehension.[38]

Claiming that in Rome (and Italy at large) 'there is much to be grasped', Byron admits that his senses are overwhelmed by Italy and suggests that, as much as he tries to live according to an Italian 'way of life', appropriating its habits, rituals and routines, the *whole* of Italy will always elude his full understanding and his desire for a comprehensive experience and knowledge of the country.[39] In *Don Juan*, Byron returns to the idea of knowledge acquisition and confronting otherness through multisensory perceptual experience, referring to the 'use of our own eyes / With one of two small senses added' and to a 'sort of adoration of the real' that is 'but a heightening of the "beau ideal"' (II, 212). In *Beppo* he similarly promotes the 'real' over the 'ideal', referring to the sensuality of Venetian women and talking about 'Love in full life and length, not love ideal, / No, nor ideal beauty, that fine name, / But something better still, so very real' (*Beppo*, 13). Yet Byron remains aware that a knowledge of Italy primarily based on sensorial experience makes 'a higher and more extended comprehension' of the country in its entirety impossible. Thus, in his more personal writings, Byron attempts to convey that 'much' which can 'be grasped', that is, the multifarious materials and apparently inexhaustible vitality of Italy. Little could he suspect, at the time of writing this letter to Murray, that the hypersensual and vibrant reality of Italy (that 'labyrinth of external objects and [...] consequent reflections') would eventually stop providing him with reasons for permanently living there.[40]

'Love in full life and length', or when the 'real' overwhelms the 'ideal'

Before it became a source of disenchantment, directly experienced, present-day Italy, rather than its historical and mythical projections, appealed to Byron's ethnographic eye and pervaded his letters and journals. As is well known, Goethe admired his ability to give 'an air of reality' to anything he represented, conveying the quotidian matter-of-factness and the carnivalesque nature of the world by means of a seemingly improvised style, either in verse or prose.[41] Similarly, in *Praeterita*, Ruskin referred to the poet's ability to capture the 'living truth' of all the places he visited, to 'reanimate the real people whose feet had worn the marble I trod on'.[42] Like the 'love in full life and length' that he portrays in *Beppo* (12), most of the Italian phenomena he chronicled, described, or, in some cases, performed in his Italian letters do not belong to an ideal or transcendental Italianness. Instead, they are evocative of the existential irony and scepticism informing his aesthetics of mobility: 'How I do delight in observing life as it really is!' he tellingly wrote in his journal of 1813–14.[43]

So alluring was the contingent and transient 'living truth' of Italy, so overpowering its everyday existence that, on some occasions, Byron admitted that they even subdued his poetic '*estro*' (inspiration). In 1817, for example, he wrote to Murray:

> I have not done a stitch of poetry since I left Switzerland – & have not at present the '*estro*' upon me [...]. – If I write – I think of trying prose

[...] perhaps one day or other – I may attempt some work of fancy in prose – descriptive of Italian manners & of human passions – but at present I am preoccupied.[44]

In fact, sometimes Byron seems to be so occupied, rather than 'preoccupied', with present circumstances that his letter writing reads not so much like ethnographic reporting as a live recording of personal experiences, especially when they concern his sex life, the libertinism of which shocked even his friend Shelley.[45] Byron's yielding to the call of 'reality' and epicureanism, as well as his immersion in Italianness, are evident (and acted out) in a letter to Moore, where he expresses the *joie de vivre* derived from one of his numerous sexual experiences in Venice:

> At Venice we are in Lent, and I have not lately moved out of doors, – my feverishness requiring quiet, and – by way of being more quiet – here is the Signora Marianna just come in and seated at my elbow. Have you seen ***'s book of poesy? And, if you have seen it, are you not delighted with it? And have you – I really cannot go on. There is a pair of great black eyes looking over my shoulder, like the angel leaning over St. Matthew's, in the old frontispieces to the Evangelists, – so that I must turn and answer them instead of you.[46]

The poet's theatricality as a letter writer is well known. His letters to Murray are performative to the extent that Byron expected them to be circulated among their acquaintances. In this case, though, he is writing to his friend Moore, and therefore the informal style and *carpe diem* attitude of the letter are perhaps more than a mere pose to shock his interlocutor. Here, while Byron is certainly performing his immersion in Italian life, he also underlines his need for physical proximity, presence and even personal involvement in the process of understanding external reality. This is not simply a sexual issue and extends to his relationship to many other aspects of Italian culture and society.

When, for instance, in May 1817 he attended the execution of three robbers in Rome, he wrote a strikingly detailed and graphic account of the scene to Murray, stating that he 'was close – but was determined to see – as one should see every thing once – with attention'.[47] In the manner of an ethnographer, Byron used this and similar episodes as illustrative examples of 'field studies' or 'case reports' reflecting broader cultural, political or ideological aspects of Italy that he would then illustrate in other letters. So when he informed Murray about the murder of the commander of the papal troops in Ravenna just outside his house, he concluded, 'The whole town is in confusion. – You may judge better of things here by this detail than by anything which I could add on the Subject.'[48] Of course, Byron's cooperation with the Carbonari conspirators provided him with an insider's perspective on the contemporary political situation that made his testimony particularly interesting to the recipients of his letters.

The spectacularisation of reality produced by the Italian system of justice and punishment, whereby a real-life execution is transformed into a Gothic melodrama, appealed to Byron's own theatricality in both his life and works. Byron never overlooked the aesthetic impact that his representations of Italian culture and society could have on his audience. Hence the graphic and visual details he provides, which are always meant to convey and express a credible, because directly apprehended, reality. And yet, from this perspective as an insider, Byron did not simply go beyond romanticised idealisations of Italy but also developed an increasing disenchantment with its customs and inhabitants. Even in 1821, talking about the Italians, he famously confessed to Moore that, though 'there are some high spirits among them still', operas and 'macaroni are their forte, and "motley their only wear"'.[49] As his disenchantment grew through a combination of boredom and general weariness, Byron's ethnographic eye started looking at Italy from a newly ironic perspective, which led him to recognise his own strangeness in the midst of Italian alterity, that is to admit that perhaps his heart was not 'all meridian', and that he was a 'Citizen of the World […] able to find a country elsewhere', or even, as he wrote to Count Alfred D'Orsay in April 1823, a man 'of no Country'.[50] In July of the same year, he wrote to Goethe, saying, 'I am returning to Greece to see if I can be of any little use there.'[51] His urge was now to escape Italy and look for other kinds of excitement, and perhaps self-fulfilment, elsewhere.

Notes

1 Letter of 2 November 1808, in *BLJ*, vol. I, p. 173, Byron's italics.
2 Letter of 6 September 1813, in *BLJ*, vol. III, p. 109.

3   J. Clifford, 'Introduction: partial truths', in J. Clifford and G. Marcus (eds.), *Writing Culture: The Poetics and Politics of Ethnography* (Berkeley, Calif.: University of California Press, 1986), pp. 1–26 (p. 1); and J. Clifford, 'On ethnographic allegory', in J. Clifford and G. Marcus (eds.), *Writing Culture: The Poetics and Politics of Ethnography* (Berkeley, Calif.: University of California Press, 1986), pp. 98–121 (p. 118).

4   See T. N. Headland, K. Pike and M. Harris (eds.), *Emics and Etics: The Insider/Outsider Debate* (Newbury Park: Sage, 1990). Whereas an emic approach involves an analysis of a specific culture by resorting to the conceptual schemes and categories of that culture, an etic approach tends to apply theories and concepts from the scientific observers' external perspective.

5   See G. Angeletti, *Lord Byron and Discourses of Otherness: Scotland, Italy, and Femininity* (Edinburgh: Humming Earth, 2012), pp. 105–34.

6   R. Lansdown (ed.), *Byron's Letters and Journals: A New Selection* (Oxford: Oxford University Press, 2015), p. xi.

7   See R. Cardinal, 'Romantic travel', in R. Porter (ed.), *Rewriting the Self: Histories from the Renaissance to the Present* (London and New York: Routledge, 1997), pp. 135–55 (p. 137).

8   Letter of 31 August 1820, in *BLJ*, vol. VII, p. 170.

9   Letter of 20 July 1819, in *BLJ*, vol. VI, p. 181.

10 Letter of 20 July 1819, in *BLJ*, vol. VI, p. 181.

11 Letter of 8 October 1820, in *BLJ*, vol. VII, p. 194.

12 Letter of 23 September 1820, in *BLJ*, vol. VII, p. 180, Byron's italics.

13 M. Schoina, *Romantic 'Anglo-Italians': Configurations of Identity in Byron, the Shelleys, and the Pisan Circle* (Farnham: Ashgate, 2009), p. 91.

14 *BLJ*, vol. VII, pp. 43, 42.

15 *BLJ*, vol. VII, p. 43

16 Letter of 10 June 1822, in *BLJ*, vol. IX, p. 171.

17 Drummond Bone, 'Tourists and lovers: *Beppo* and *Amours de Voyage*', *The Byron Journal*, 28 (2000), 13–28 (p. 14).

18 Letter to John Murray of 28 September 1820, in *BLJ*, vol. VII, p. 184.

19 Letter of 31 August 1820, in *BLJ*, vol. VII, pp. 170–1.

20 Quoted in M. Parker, *Literary Magazines and British Romanticism* (Cambridge: Cambridge University Press, 2000), p. 122. However, such alleged obliviousness is refuted by all those letters, more and more frequent from 1820 onwards, in which Byron continuously mentions facts and details concerning British internal affairs, thus invalidating what he declares to Murray as early as 25 November 1816: 'I never see a newspaper & know nothing of England – except in a letter now & then from my Sister' (*BLJ*, vol. V, p. 134).

21 For an overview of the methods and approaches in anthropological research applicable to Byron's perception and figurations of Italy, see H. R. Bernard, *Research Methods in Anthropology: Qualitative and Quantitative Approaches* (Plymouth: AltaMira, 2011).
22 Quoted in Schoina, *Romantic 'Anglo-Italians'*, p. 103.
23 Letter of 4 December 1816, in *BLJ*, vol. V, p. 138. On Byron's learning the Venetian dialect, see also 'Detached thoughts', number 18: 'Lewis said to me – "why do you talk *Venetian* [...] to the Venetians? & not the usual Italian?" I answered – partly from habit – – & partly to be understood – if possible' (*BLJ*, vol. IX, p. 19).
24 See D. Saglia, *Lord Byron e le maschere della scrittura* (Roma: Carocci, 2009), pp. 138–42.
25 On Byron's general hostility towards tourist guidebooks, see K. Crook, 'Truth and sense on Italy: Byron's Guidebook', in L. M. Crisafulli (ed.), *Immaginando l'Italia: itinerari letterari del Romanticismo inglese* (Bologna: CLUEB, 2002), pp. 155–65.
26 J. Buzard, *The Beaten Track: European Tourism, Literature, and the Ways to Culture, 1800–1918* (Oxford: Clarendon Press, 1993), p. 122.
27 See Buzard, *The Beaten Track*, and J. Buzard, 'The uses of Romanticism: Byron and the Victorian Continental tour', *Victorian Studies*, 35:1 (1991), 29–49. On Byron as a Victorian icon of travel, see also G. Angeletti, 'From "the heightening of the beau ideal" to "palpable things": Byron, Clough and the poetry of experience', *La Questione Romantica*, 5:1–2 (2016), 97–114. On the commodification of Byron by later English travellers to Venice and by the Venetians themselves, see D. Laven, 'Sex, self-fashioning, and spelling: (auto)biographical distortion, prostitution, and Byron's Venetian residence', *Literaria Pragensia*, 23:46 (2013), 38–52.
28 H. D. Beste, *Italy as It Is; or Narratives of an English Family's Residence for Three Years in That Country* (London: Henry Colburn, 1828), p. i. Byron also employed 'resident' to refer to himself and distance himself from the 'traveller' in a letter to Murray dated 16 April 1820 about Italy's unstable political situation (*BLJ*, vol. VII, p. 77).
29 Letter to Augusta Leigh of 6 November 1816, in *BLJ*, vol. V, p. 127.
30 PS dated 7 November 1816 to letter of 6 November 1816, in *BLJ*, vol. V, p. 126.
31 Letter of 6 November 1816 to Augusta Leigh, in *BLJ*, vol. V, p. 127.
32 See P. Nora, 'Between memory and history: les lieux de mémoire', *Representations*, 26 (1989), 7–24. Byron's privileging of fact emerges clearly in one of his famous confessions to Murray: 'I hate things *all fiction* [...] there should always be some foundation of fact for the most airy fabric, and pure invention is but the talent of a liar' (Letter of 2 April 1817, in *BLJ*, vol. V, p. 203).

33 Letter of 6 November 1816, in *BLJ*, vol. V, p. 123.
34 Letter of 7 June 1819, in *BLJ*, vol. VI, p. 148.
35 Letter of 7 June 1819, in *BLJ*, vol. VI, p. 149.
36 Other examples concern his Venetian lovers, or references to apparently insignificant scandals, that show the impetuosity and inconsistency of Italians. Paradigmatic in this sense is Byron's recounting of an episode that occurred at the Fenice Theatre in Venice involving a Signor Cambon who was 'separated from his wife for mutual felicity' and 'had become the Cavaliero servente of another lady not separated – & the separated Lady had provided herself with a substitute for Signor Cambon. – But Signor Cambon upon seeing his moiety went into choler – and then into the box – reprobating his wife – and bestemmiando nobilmente [cursing nobly] her Cavaliero [...] much swearing & scuffling ensued – & both parties rolled skirmishing out into the passage'(Letter to John Cam Hobhouse of 19 December 1816, in *BLJ*, vol. V, p. 143).
37 J. Ruskin, *The Works of John Ruskin*, ed. E. T. Cook and A. Wedderburn, 39 vols (New York: Longmans, Green & Co. 1903–12), vol. XXXV, p. 149.
38 Letter of 9 May 1817, in *BLJ*, vol. V, pp. 221–2.
39 Letter to Moore of 24 December 1816, in *BLJ*, vol. V, p. 146.
40 Dedication, *Childe Harold's Pilgrimage*, IV, in *CPW*, vol. II, p. 122.
41 Quoted in R. S. Woof, *Byron: A Dangerous Romantic?* (Grasmere: Wordsworth Museum, 2003), p. 63.
42 J. Ruskin, *Praeterita: The Autobiography of John Ruskin (1885–89)* (Oxford: Oxford University Press, 1983), p. 140.
43 Journal entry for 17–18 December 1813, in *BLJ*, vol. III, p. 240. Byron's friend Lady Blessington referred to 'the extreme mobilité of his nature, which yields to present impressions' in Lady Blessington, *A Journal of the Conversations of Lord Byron with the Countess of Blessington* (London: Richard Bentley & Son, 1893), p. 95. For a general discussion of Byron's mobility, see Angeletti, *Lord Byron and Discourses of Otherness*, pp. 1–14.
44 Letter of 2 January 1817, in *BLJ*, vol. V, p. 157.
45 Curiously enough, Byron himself was sometimes astounded at Italian mores and morals – 'the most singular ever met with' – and at the 'singular' perversion of Italian women 'not only of action, but of reasoning' (letter to Moore of 25 March 1817, in *BLJ*, vol. V, p. 189).
46 Letter of 10 March 1817, in *BLJ*, vol. V, p. 186. On these experiences and, more generally, on the representation and role of Italian women in Byron's writings, see G. Angeletti, 'From place to topos: Byron's Italy as exotic discourse; women and places of the mind', in L. M. Crisafulli (ed.), *Immaginando l'Italia: itinerari letterari del Romanticismo inglese* (Bologna: CLUEB, 2002), pp. 183–202.

47 Letter of 30 May 1817, in *BLJ*, vol. V, p. 230.
48 Letter of 9 December 1820, in *BLJ*, vol. VII, pp. 247–8.
49 Letter of 28 April 1821, in *BLJ*, vol. VIII, p. 105.
50 See 'To the Po. June 2nd 1819': 'My heart is all meridian, were it not / I had not suffered now, nor should I be – / Despite of tortures ne'er to be forgot – / The Slave again, Oh Love! at least of thee' (45–8). Letter to John Taaffe, Jr, of 12 December 1821, in *BLJ*, vol. IX, p. 78; letter of 2 April 1823, in *BLJ*, vol. X, p. 156.
51 Letter of 22 July 1823, in *BLJ*, vol. X, p. 213.

3

From Lord Nelvil to Dugald Dalgetty: Byron's Scottish identity in Italy

Jonathan Gross

Byron found himself poised between three climates during the Carbonari uprisings of 1820: the climate of Italy, the climate of Scotland and the literary climate of Madame de Staël and Walter Scott. 'Politics somewhat tempestuous', he wrote in February 1821, 'and cloudier daily [...]. The weather is still muggy [...] – mist, mizzle, the air replete with Scotticisms [...]. Politics still mysterious.'[1] Though living in Italy, Byron analysed the Carbonari through allusions to Scotland and Scottish weather. There was an artistry to Byron's exile based on his careful reading of the novels of Scott and de Staël, of *Rob Roy* no less than *Corinne*. Through these readings, he never fully left one country when residing in another.[2] The process was dialectical, as Jane Stabler suggests.[3] Byron could transplant himself from the land of mist and fog, but the gloomy climate of Scotland, absorbed until the age of ten, dictated his actions in sunny Italy during a time of revolution, providing an 'air replete with Scotticisms' that he seemed, miraculously, to discover in Italy once he got there.

In de Staël's novel of 1807, *Corinne, ou l'Italia*, to proceed in chronological order, the Scottish Lord Nelvil (Oswald) is gloomy and melancholic without quite knowing why.[4] Oswald travels to Italy to cure his weak lungs, but his malady is psychological. Melancholy, as Byron and de Staël well knew, was the condition of sedentary writers. Food, exercise and diet were its cure, Richard Burton proclaimed in *Anatomy of Melancholy*, but so was sunlight.[5] Kay Redfield Jamison briefly discusses the relevance of sunlight to Byron's moods in Italy in her interesting book, *Touched with Fire*.[6] Without the help of a trained psychiatrist, Byron would have recognised in Oswald's 'deep sorrow' his own response to the Scottish climate:

> Oswald, Lord Nelvil, peer of Scotland, set out from Edinburgh to go to Italy during the winter of 1794 to 1795. He had a distinguished handsome face, was highly intelligent, bore a great name, and had independent means. A deep sorrow had, however, affected his health, and his doctors, fearing that his lungs had been damaged, had advised him to go south. (6)

Oswald experiences unexplained guilt over the death of his father, who haunts him (5). Italy becomes a place where Oswald's father cannot reach him, representing, like Byron's Italy, a privileged, male 'Romantic geography', to use Michael Wiley's term.[7] As a result, Oswald finds something sinful about travelling as far as Italy:

> Sometimes, too, he would reproach himself with deserting the places where his father had lived [in Scotland] – 'who knows whether the shades of the dead can follow those they love everywhere?' he would say to himself. 'Perhaps they are allowed to wander only near the places where their ashes are laid to rest; perhaps at this moment my father too is missing me but he lacks the strength to recall me from such a great distance!' (6)

Though Oswald leaves Scotland, a place associated with the supernatural, he still thinks about its ghosts. Oswald's melancholy inwardness connects him to Corinne, whose capacity for feeling and rebellion so entrance him.

De Staël published *Corinne* five years before Byron published *Childe Harold's Pilgrimage* I and II. The novel's psychological assessment of the Scottish character in exile had a profound influence on the poet.[8] De Staël describes Oswald's exile as follows:

> It is more painful to leave one's native land when one has to cross the sea to go away from it. [...] It is as if an abyss is opening up behind you and the return journey might never be possible. Moreover, the sight of the sea always makes a profound impression; it is the reflection of the infinite, to which our thoughts are continually attracted and in which they continually get lost. Oswald, leaning on the helm, his eyes fixed on the waves, was outwardly calm, for his pride combined with his shyness hardly ever let him show what he felt, even to his friends, but inwardly he was agitated by painful feelings.

(6–7)

The invocation of the 'abyss [...] opening up behind you', the impossibility of a 'return journey', the 'sight of the sea mak[ing] a profound impression', and the 'reflection of the infinite' are the most important insights we have into Oswald's feelings, and they are those of Byron in *Childe Harold's Pilgrimage* III as well, on his departure from his native land.

In *Corinne*, the hero struggles against Protestant reflection, guilt and conscience, before he embraces the warmth and pleasure of Catholic Italy, symbolised by Corinne's spontaneous lectures on art and beauty at the Capitol. '"Why give myself unremittingly to reflection?" [Oswald] would say to himself. "There is so much pleasure in an active life"', he muses (7). Yet, for Oswald, activity is defined as leaving Scotland to find adventures in Italy; once in Italy, Oswald has nothing to do, unlike Byron, who involved himself in Italy's revolutionary struggles. Oswald's lack of self-concern leads him into heroic action nevertheless – protecting the people of Ancona from a fire, protecting Jews from burning (despite, not because of, their religion) and saving lunatics from a fire. These actions are also products of his enlightened mind, which emphasises tolerance, benevolence and heroism, as well as perspicacious judgement. Oswald acts, but he does so with a Protestant conscience directed by his own inwardness. As a hybrid Italian with an English father, Corinne represents spontaneity, improvisation and joy, not the self-regulation, melancholy and duty that Oswald carries with him from the north, though de Staël forestalls the reductiveness of her title – which suggests the novel is only about its heroine and Italy – by providing characters with hybrid identities and by providing a Germanic fairytale aspect to her novel.[9] De Staël was prominent among the authors Byron read in Italy, and crucial to his self-fashioned identity abroad.

Byron commented on *Corinne* to explain his own melancholy to himself. 'My dearest Teresa – I have read this book in your garden', Byron famously wrote in the frontispiece of *Corinne* in Ravenna, before lamenting that they had ever fallen in love. 'You will not understand these English words', Byron explains, 'and *others* will not understand them – which is the reason I have not scribbled them in Italian.'[10] Byron writes in English in order *not* to be understood. Instead, he wishes to be recognised as resembling Oswald, if Teresa chooses to read de Staël's novel. Byron in Ravenna, like Oswald, must struggle between feeling deeply and expressing such feelings in a 'Staëlean' manner, which he associated with self-display. Was his marginalia written for Teresa or for his English-speaking audience and posterity? Either way, the half-Scottish Byron writes in an Italian translation of a Franco-Swiss writer's French book, the author having been condemned by the Corsican Napoleon to a ten-year exile, during which she is tutored by the Schlegel brothers and writes on German literature. As he does so, he identifies himself with her fictional Scotsman as he too finds himself in exile in Italy.

During his years in Italy, Byron also drew inspiration from *A Legend of Montrose* when he became involved with the Italian Carbonari. Writing from Ravenna, Byron asked for the novels of Walter Scott no fewer than ten times, and at moments that corresponded with the political crises in Italy and Byron's involvement with the Carbonari.[11] 'To me', he wrote to Scott in 1822, 'these novels have so much of "Auld lang syne" (I was bred a canny Scot till ten years old) that I never move without them – and when I removed from Raven[n]a to Pisa the other day – and sent on my library before – they were the only books that I kept by me – although I already have them by heart.'[12] Increasingly, Byron came to view Scott's novels as a guide for action in the fight for Italian freedom. After reading Scott's positive review of Canto III of *Childe Harold's Pilgrimage*,[13] Byron dedicated *Cain: A Mystery* to the 'Ariosto of the North',[14] thereby making Scott an honorary Italian and cementing the Scottish-Italian connection that this chapter seeks to foreground. Murray was confused by Byron's Ariosto allusion, but, as John Clubbe notes:

> [in] four words – 'Ariosto of the North' – [Byron] distilled his view of Scott: master of comedy; superb story-teller who blended in easy harmony narrative, description, and digression; and ironic epic poet who understood history and could body forth its essence in memorable characters and in narratives that, ostensibly fictional, captured historical truth.[15]

Byron quoted from Scott more often than any other writer except Shakespeare, and alluded to no fewer than fifteen of his works.[16]

Scott's hero in *A Legend of Montrose*, Dugald Dalgetty, resembles Byron. Raised in Aberdeen ('the learning whilk I had acquired at the Mareschal-College of Aberdeen'), Dalgetty's Scottish body is put to foreign service: 'my gentle bluid and designation of Drumthwacket, together with a pair of stalwart arms, and legs conform, to the German wars, there to push my way as a cavalier of fortune'.[17] Byron, who boasted repeatedly of his swimming prowess to Henry Drury, also became a 'cavalier of fortune', as he humorously noted in the brilliantly self-conscious poem, 'When a Man Hath No Freedom to Fight for at Home'.[18] He offered himself to the Italian and Greek revolutionary movements, training at the broadsword, keeping some of the very few horses in Venice at the Lido and engaging in pistol practice during his time abroad. 'My lord, my legs and arms stood me in more stead than either my gentle kin or my book-lear', Dalgetty notes, 'and I found myself trailing a pike as a private gentleman under old Sir Ludovick Leslie, where I learned the rules of service so tightly, that I will not forget them in a hurry' (215). Encouraged by Scott's novels, Byron used words such as 'whilk', 'pike' and other, often specifically Scottish, terms to define his political activity in Italy. But the model of Scott's Scottish fighters inspired him in other ways too. In *Rob Roy*, another Scott novel Byron ordered while in Italy, we see a portrait of the Duke of Argyll (Argyle in Scott's text): 'His whole peculiarities flashed on me at once', the narrator writes, 'the deep strong voice; the inflexible, stern, yet considerate cast of features; the Scottish brogue, with its corresponding dialect and imagery.' Campbell has 'sinewy' and 'strong' arms, traced to 'the old Picts who ravaged Northumberland [...] a sort of half-goblin, half-human being, distinguished, like this man, for courage, cunning, ferocity, the length of their arms, and the squareness of their shoulders'.[19] Here Scott delineates a body that Byron would 'grow into', much like Arnold in *The Deformed Transformed*, exchanging a lean, warlike body for the fat one he had acquired earlier in Italy despite his repeated efforts at exercise through broadsword training and horseback riding. Byron never travelled south of Rome to witness the Neapolitan uprisings at first hand.[20] The war-ready body that he adopted in Italy was a form he took from literary fictions. And, just as his swimming from Sestos to Abydos was inspired by the Roman poet Ovid, so Byron always had Walter Scott's literary fiction of the Scottish mercenary body close at hand to delineate a path forward.

If there was a 'Jew's Body', adumbrated in literature, so too was there a literary Scottish body, all the more attractive to Byron when he was, as it were, a fish out of water: a Scotsman in the Mediterranean.[21]

A Jew's body prevented him from obtaining Austrian citizenship, reputedly because of the weakness of his feet. Yet Jews fought bravely in Austrian and German wars, and Byron could compare himself to Shylock.[22] Byron donned particular identities and nationalities when it suited him, wearing them like so many garments in a costume drama. Armed with Scott's novels, Byron imagined that he could lend his strong body to military causes like Dugald Dalgetty.

On 24 April 1820 and on 4 May 1822, in letters to Scott, Byron described how he lived up to Scottish ideals of physical bravery and heroism. The first of these letters describes his annoyance at the pope's treatment of his troops. Byron's letter uses Scottish diction as a code to translate his Italian experiences. He begins with allusions to *Macbeth* ('skirr') and concludes with *A Legend of Montrose* ('sconce'):

> A very heavy rain & wind having come on – I did not get on horseback to go out & 'skirr the country' but I shall mount tomorrow & take a canter among the peasantry – who are a savage resolute race – always riding with guns in their hands. – I wonder they don't suspect the Serenaders – for they play on the guitar all night here as in Spain – to their Mistresses. – Talking of politics – as Caleb Quotem says – pray look at the *Conclusion* of my Ode on *Waterloo*, written in the year 1815[23] – & comparing it with the Duke de Berri's catastrophe in 1820, – tell me if I have not as good a right to the character of '*Vates*' in both senses of the word as Fitzgerald & Coleridge –
>
> 'Crimson tears will follow yet.'
>
> and have not they? – I can't pretend to foresee what will happen among you Englishers at this distance – but I vaticinate a *row* in Italy – & in which case I don't know that I won't have a finger in it. – I dislike the Austrians and think the Italians infamously oppressed, & if they begin – why I will recommend 'the erection of a Sconce upon Drumsnab' like Dugald Dalgetty.[24]

Byron imagines himself as an aristocratic overlord, of Scottish descent, surveying his troops.[25] He contrasts his masculine, Scottish behaviour, 'skirr[ing] the countryside', with 'the [Italian] Serenaders – for they play on the guitar all night here as in Spain – to their Mistresses'. As soon as he lets his masculine guard down, however, he remembers his true vocation as poet, and hawks 'Ode on Waterloo' (published as 'Ode from the French') to Scott like Caleb Quotem, a character in George Colman's *The Review, or the Wags of Windsor* (but borrowed from Henry Lee's play *Throw Physic to the Dogs*) who identifies himself as 'parish clerk and sexton here, My name is *Caleb Quotem*; I'm painter, glazier, auctioneer'.[26] Three identities 'chase each other' here: Scottish fighter, English poet and jack-of-all-trades.

Byron, then, cannot maintain the posture of Scottish soldier for long, even in this single letter. He has not, after all, gone out to 'skirr' the country but plans to do so tomorrow. The fact that he is connected to no standing army only adds piquancy to his allusions. But if Byron's identity in Italy is a constructed one, his favoured model is that of a Scottish mercenary. So powerful is this allusion that Byron concludes his letter by returning to it. He plans to erect 'a Sconce upon Drumsnab', which is tantamount to taking necessary precautions against military attack, 'like Dugald Dalgetty'. In Scott's novel, Dalgetty is a mercenary employed by Charles I during the earl of Montrose's campaign of 1644–5. Dalgetty's devotion to warfare, as opposed to the amatory involvements that form the heart of the novel (involving Allan M'Aulay, his friend the Earl of Menteith and Annot Lyle), offered Byron a way of imagining himself as a masculine actor rather than a Caleb Quotem jack-of-all-trades. During his years in Italy, Byron increasingly denigrated himself not only as a scribbler but as the fan-carrier of a woman – a *cavalier servente* rather than a cavalier[27] – a vocation he did not intend to pursue until the end of his life, ultimately leaving Italy for Greece in search of something rather more heroic.

As he read the novels of Walter Scott in Venice, Ravenna and elsewhere, Byron used Scott's fiction as a chance to emplot an escape from Italy through a hyper-masculinised version of himself, available through Scott's fictions. Much as he admired Italian art, and the poetry of Tasso, Ariosto and Pulci – not to mention the plays of Alfieri – Byron felt a simultaneous need to behave in a manner that would impress his British readers, particularly his Scottish publisher, John Murray, who was the recipient of many of his letters from Italy, which were also read by William Gifford, John Cam Hobhouse, Thomas Moore, Isaac 'D'Isreali' and others.[28] Having fought for various armies during the Thirty Years' War, on no particular side, Dalgetty becomes a martial version of the more effeminate Don Juan, who nevertheless sees military action in the Siege of Ismail. If Byron's Italian heroes were mostly impotent failures – mad, imprisoned, embattled or executed – Byron would outshine them, and do so as a someone who was half-Scottish by birth.[29] He would not be like the aged cuckold Faliero, nor the mad Tasso, nor the tortured Foscari, nor even the prophetic Dante. At a time of warfare, Scott's novels provided a way out of a psychological and political impasse, even if they were fictions, offering a vocation seemingly more noble even than that of the impotent prophet, vates or Cassandra.

Like Oswald, in Italy Byron is confronted with a choice between the life of contemplation and the life of action, finding neither to be wholly satisfactory. His 'Ode from the French' had already expressed regret at not having participated in a war with or against Napoleon:

> The Chief has fallen, but not by you,
> Vanquishers of Waterloo!
> When the soldier citizen
> Sway'd not o'er his fellow men –
> Save in deeds that led them on
> Where Glory smiled on Freedom's son –
> Who, of all the despots banned,
> With that youthful chief competed?
> Who could boast o'er France defeated,
> Till lone Tyranny commanded?
> Till, goaded by ambition's sting,
> The Hero sunk into the King?
> Then he fell: – So perish all,
> Who would men by man enthral!
> (22–35)

As a poet, Byron warns tyrants that 'Crimson tears will follow yet' (104). At the same time, he wishes to avoid the bystander role of Murat, King of Naples, who sold himself 'to death and shame / For a meanly royal name; / Such as he of Naples wears, / Who thy blood-bought title bears' (40–3). In Italy as in Spain, Napoleon helped to make mercenaries kings and kings mercenaries. Better to be a soldier, however, than king of Naples: 'There be sure was Murat charging! / There he ne'er shall charge again!' (69–70). Using the Scottish genre of flyting, Byron upbraids Britain and Napoleon, Wellington and Murat, for failing to live up to the heroic models of George Washington and Cincinnatus. But it was to the Scottish mercenaries of Scott's fiction that Byron looked for a model for his own 'heroic' actions in Italy.

Byron's second letter to Scott is signed with Napoleon's initials, NB (for Noel Byron). Where Napoleon earned his martial laurels, however, Byron merely asserts them. Yet, even as he poses as the 'grand Napoleon of the realms of rhyme' (*DJ*, XI, 55), he satirises himself by listing Napoleon's defeats. He envies John Cam Hobhouse's active involvement in politics and so describes to Scott his own political 'anxiety, rather than trouble, about an awkward affair here, which you may perhaps have heard of':

> Some other English, and Scots, and myself, had a brawl with a dragoon […]. He called out the guard at the gates to arrest us (we being unarmed); upon which I and another (an Italian) rode through the said guard; but they succeeded in detaining others of the party. I rode to my house, and sent my secretary to give an account of the attempted and illegal arrest to the authorities […]. Half way back […] I met my man, vapouring away, and threatening to draw upon me (who had a cane in my hand, and no other arms). I, still believing him an officer, demanded his name and address, and gave him my hand and glove thereupon. A servant of mine thrust in between us (totally without orders), but let him go on my command. He then rode off at full speed; but about forty paces further was stabbed, and very dangerously (so as to be in peril), by some *callum bog* [quoting *Waverly*, chapter 58] or other of my people (for I have some rough-handed fellows about me), I need hardly say without my direction or approval. The said dragoon had been sabring our unarmed countrymen, however, at the gate, after they were in arrest, and held by the guards, and wounded one, Captain Hay, very severely. However, he got his paiks [quoting *Rob Roy*, chapter 29] – having acted like an assassin, and being greeted like one. Who wounded him, though it was done before thousands of people, they have never been able to ascertain, or prove, nor even the weapon; some said a pistol, an air-gun, a stiletto, a sword, a lance, a pitch-fork, and what not. […] I enclose you copies of the depositions of those with us, and Dr. Craufurd, a canny Scot (*not* an acquaintance), who saw the latter part of the affair. They are in Italian.[30]

Byron uses English diction ('an awkward affair'; 'behaved very handsomely') to mask Scottish ferociousness, while identifying himself with neither the English nor the Scottish: 'Some other English, and Scots, and myself', he writes. '*Callum bog*' refers to polite Highland manners (as employed by Scott in *Waverley*[31]), but Byron uses the term ironically to expose the Scottish member of his encourage who stabbed the sergeant major in Italy: 'some *callum bog* or other of my people', he writes. Though living in Italy, Byron refers to the Scottish as 'my people', but then qualifies this Scottish self-identification by judging his 'people' as uncouth and disavowing their rash actions: 'I have some rough-handed fellows about me [who act], I need hardly say without my direction or approval.' Byron's positioning of himself in relation to Scottishness, Englishness and Italianness is ambiguous.

Indeed, national identities and the roles they play in these events are themselves blurred in Byron's account of the 'affair'. A canny Scot, Dr Craufurd, witnesses events, but Byron notes that no one can identify the weapons used, nor who used them. Was the injury achieved with a pistol, an air-gun, a stiletto, a sword, a lance or a pitchfork? Such weapons have potential national associations: a stiletto is stereotypically Italian, 'sword' and 'lance' are likely to be English, 'pitch-forks' might well evoke hordes of ferocious Scottish Highlanders. If Byron has such associations in mind here then he is implicitly comparing Scottish, English and Italian forms of warfare. But regardless of whether he consciously has this kind of comparison in mind or not, he does use Scottish vernacular, 'paiks', which means to give a person their just deserts, to imply his approval of Scottish aggression in this case. His use of the word 'paiks' identifies him with Scotland in another way too. William Dunbar first used 'paiks' in a literary context in 1513, and Byron's use of it here is another example of the distinctly Scottish flyting that T. S. Eliot attributed to Byron's best verse.[32] Even when deliberately obscuring his own sympathies, it seems that Byron cannot help hinting that they lie with the Scots.

Byron could, of course, identify himself with a broader Britishness. On 9 June 1820, he wrote to Thomas Moore, a London-based Irishman, mixing *Marino Faliero* with his own revolutionary enthusiasms. In writing this letter, Byron shows himself enacting a role for himself through his hero Faliero, an aristocratic hero who rebels against his own social class. Faliero was Byron's way of theatrically representing the Italian Carbonari uprising, but the play also alludes to the trial of Queen Caroline – and recalls Byron's intervention in Teresa's marriage to Alessandro ('passions of my own'), where Byron the writer appears as a fusion of Faliero and Steno: 'Steno' connotes 'stenography' or writing (or flyting, or, again, the Byronic verbal abuse associated with the graffiti scrawled on the ducal throne, which precipitates the action in the play). Faliero also represents Byron's aristocratic allegiances, which are signalled again by the theatricalised uniforms described below:

> I have incurred a quarrel with the Pope's carabiniers, or gens d'armerie, who have petitioned the Cardinal against my liveries, as resembling too nearly their own lousy uniform. They particularly object to the epaulettes, which all the world with us have on upon gala days. My liveries are of the colours conforming to my arms and have been the family hue since the year 1066.
>
> I have sent a trenchant reply, as you may suppose; and have given to understand that, if any soldados of that respectable corps insult my servants, I will do likewise by their gallant commanders; and I have directed my ragamuffins, six in number, who are tolerably savage, to defend themselves, in case of aggression; and, on holidays and gaudy days, I shall arm the whole set, including myself in case of accidents or treachery. I used to play pretty well at the broad-sword, once upon a time, at Angelo's; but I should like the pistol, our national buccaneer weapon, better, though I am out of practice at present. However, I can 'wink and hold out mine iron'. It makes me think (the whole thing does) of Romeo and Juliet.[33]

Byron strikes a bathetic pose, mocking his own military posturing, which translates a bad temper into a national cause. He does this by using phrases such as 'used to play pretty well at the broad-sword'. He displays a rather English self-deprecation here, and identifies himself as an English lord of Norman descent: 'My liveries are of the colours conforming to my arms and have been the family hue since the year 1066.' However, he also claims a shared identity with his Irish addressee: 'I should like the pistol, our national buccaneer weapon, better', imagining himself as a heroic Brit in Italy, waging war on his country's colonial rivals. Nevertheless, the 'longer he stayed away from England, the bitterer grew his feelings toward his native land – and the fonder became his recollections of Scotland', as Clubbe notes. 'In *Don Juan*, he repudiates English cant and turns instead to his Scottish inheritance, which he saw as uncorrupted by the all-pervading national vice.'[34]

Byron is not so absolute in his letter to Moore, citing three Shakespearian dramas to add context to his recent actions, punning on 'play' ('I used to play pretty well at the broad-sword'): here both a child's game and an English understatement for chivalric action. He is aware he appears absurd (they 'particularly object to the epaulettes'), but revels in it and suggests that his ferocity will turn what appears Italian burlesque and *commedia dell'arte* into something heroic. He makes use of a curiously contrapuntal narrative, using a Spanish word – 'soldados' – to separate himself from a strictly English, Scottish or even Italian identity. At the same time, he sees his actions as very English: Byron employs 'ragamuffins' as if he were Falstaff in *Henry IV* (V, iii, 36), and, like Corporal Nym in *Henry V*, can 'wink and hold out his iron' (II, i, 51). But, equally, even as Byron's tone suggests he sees something farcical in his involvement in Italian politics, his fierce determination to fight on reminds us of his underlying identification with, and desire to emulate, Scott's heroic mercenaries.

Byron's Scottish publisher introduced Byron to Scott, who helped him consolidate his Scottish identity, acting as a father figure from the fatherland. However, Byron's Scottish identity became most pronounced in Italy, where he explained Italian customs about the body, marriage and sex to an astounded British audience. 'I "scotched not killed" the Scotchman in my blood, / And love the land of "mountain and of flood"', Byron wrote in Canto X of *Don Juan* (19), begun in Pisa and completed in Genoa. According to Clubbe, the '"perfervidum ingenium Scotorun" ["ardent Scottish temper"] of the later Byron, which he thought he inherited from his mother, manifests itself especially in his growing sensitivity to the Scottish quality of "heart" and in his continuing willingness to give of himself emotionally for people and causes'.[35] But this Scottishness manifested itself in other ways as well, not least through particular personal connections.[36] Taken by surprise in Pisa, Byron only has a 'cane' in his hand, a gentleman's accoutrement and a potential weapon but also a sign of his deformity, which he shared with Scott, perhaps one reason why both writers were hyper-masculine but chose sedentary professions, which in his case Byron continually disowned. Then there is 'the Arimaspian Murray',[37] the Arimaspians being a one-eyed tribe from the north of Scythia who warred with griffins over the gold they guarded – Murray was blinded in one eye from a wound received as a schoolboy.[38]

However, while all disabled in some way, Byron, Scott and Murray were nevertheless physically robust, overcoming their afflictions, and thereby displaying a trait that Scott explored in *A Legend of Montrose* by connecting Scottish forms of warfare, which Byron promised to employ in Italy, to Alexander the Great and the Macedonian phalanx. As Byron chose between pistols, air-guns, stilettos, swords, lances and pitchforks during his years in Italy, he would have had Scott's history of warfare firmly in mind since he ordered Scott's novel from Murray. And military heroism lies at the heart of Byron's sense of Scottishness while in Italy.

'Lowlanders were as constantly engaged in war as the mountaineers, and were incomparably better disciplined and armed', Scott writes, while the

> favourite Scottish order of battle somewhat resembled the Macedonian phalanx. Their infantry formed a compact body, armed with long spears, impenetrable even to the men-at-arms of the age, though well mounted and arrayed in complete proof. [...]
>
> This habit of fight was in a great measure changed by the introduction of muskets into the Scottish Lowland service, which not being as yet combined with the bayonet, was a formidable weapon at a distance, but gave no assurance against the enemy who rushed on to close quarters. The pike, indeed, was not wholly disused in the Scottish army; but it was no longer the favourite weapon [...]. Such was the natural consequence of standing armies, which had almost everywhere, and particularly in the long German wars, superseded what may be called the natural discipline of the feudal militia.[39]

When Byron went to Greece and raised a band of Suliotes, he was continuing the military tradition that Scott describes, one Scott traced to Alexander. That Byron relied on klefts, rather than European-trained armies, only reinforces this commitment to the style of warfare portrayed in *A Legend of Montrose* and *Rob Roy*. Byron's seemingly absurd claim that his broadsword exercises would prepare him to fight disciplined Turkish troops becomes more credible when one realises, Homeric helmets in pink boxes aside, that Byron took seriously his aristocratic responsibility to defend liberty by the sword as well as the pen, through his poetic vocation to inspire the imaginations of the Italians (and then the Greeks) to return to the heroism of their ancestors. As a mercenary, Byron was, albeit with humour, fulfilling the destiny of the Scottish mercenary warrior, one whose body, as much as his mind, was so memorably described in Scott's novels.

Perhaps Byron and Scott protested too much about Scottish heroism because of their shared deformity. Scott did not address his own deformity in his work until *The Black Dwarf*. When Augusta Leigh read this work in December 1816, she assumed Byron was the author; Byron denied his authorship three times, but once he had read *Tales of My Landlord*, of which it formed a part, Byron understood why she was so 'positive' in her 'erroneous persuasion'.[40] Publication of Byron's *The Deformed Transformed* followed, with its hero exchanging his deformed body for that of the warrior Achilles, but Byron's letters from Italy, directly inspired by Scott's two novels as well as de Staël's Scottish hero in *Corinne*, show his vexed relationship to bodies. The fighting body of Scotland was always at war with the sensual, pleasure-loving body of Venice and Ravenna, one barely preserved from effeminacy by pistol practice and broadsword exercises.

Yet this only gives another biographical spin to the fact that Byron's love of Italy and involvement in its politics were powerfully inflected by his identification with Scotland, and that he never felt himself more Scottish than when residing in Ravenna, Venice, Genoa and Pisa. After all, it was in Italy that Byron affirmed that his '"heart warms to the Tartan" or to any thing of Scotland which reminds me of Aberdeen and other parts',[41] longed for 'Auld Lang Syne' and insisted that he was 'half a Scot by birth, and bred / A whole one' (*DJ*, X, 17). Byron's marginalia in Teresa Guiccioli's copy of de Staël's *Corinne*, where he feels he will become an impotent spectator like Oswald, and his countervailing use of metaphors drawn from Scott's *A Legend of Montrose*, show that Byron's sense of Scottish masculinity everywhere informs his actions in Italy and his judgement of those Neapolitan uprisings he not only witnessed and chronicled but participated in and helped to inspire.

Notes

1 Journal entries for 10 and 16 January 1821, in *BLJ*, vol. VIII, pp. 21, 28.
2 See M. Schoina, *Romantic Anglo-Italians: Configurations of Identity in Byron, Shelley, and the Pisan Circle* (Farnham: Ashgate, 2009); R. Beaton, *Byron's War: Romantic Rebellion, Greek Revolution* (Cambridge: Cambridge University Press, 2014); K. R. Jamison, *Touched with Fire: Manic-Depressive Illness and the Artistic Temperament* (New York: Free Press, 1996), pp. 149–90.
3 See J. Stabler, *The Artistry of Exile* (Oxford: Oxford University Press, 2013), pp. 15–18.
4 Quoted here in translation from Madame de Staël, *Corinne, or Italy*, trans. S. Raphael (Oxford: Oxford University Press, 2009). Page numbers follow quotations in the main text.

5 R. Burton, *Anatomy of Melancholy* (Chicago, Ill.: Ex-Classics Project, 2010), p. 36.
6 Jamison, *Touched with Fire*, pp. 149–59.
7 Wiley explores 'what constitutes physical, mental, moral, and spiritual self hood' in M. Wiley, *Romantic Migrations: Local, National, and Transnational Dispositions* (New York: Palgrave, 2008), p. 147; and M. Wiley, *Romantic Geography: Wordsworth and Anglo-European Spaces* (Basingstoke: Palgrave, 1998).
8 For a full discussion of de Staël's influence on Byron, see J. Wilkes, *Lord Byron and Madame de Staël: Born for Opposition* (Aldershot: Ashgate, 1999).
9 J. Isbell, 'Introduction', in de Staël, *Corinne, or Italy*, p. viii.
10 Letter to Teresa Guiccioli of 23 August, 1819, in *BLJ*, vol. VI, p. 215.
11 See J. Murray, *Letters of John Murray*, ed. A. Nicholson (Liverpool: Liverpool University Press, 2007): *Rokeby* (p. 9); *Lay of the Last Minstrel* (p. 60 n.); *Lady of the Lake* (p. 52 n.); *Bridal of Triermain* (p. 118); *Waverley* (pp. 118, 120 n.); *Guy Mannering; the Antiquary* (p. 169 n.); *Tales of My Landlord* (pp. 181, 197); *Old Mortality, The Heart of Midlothian, A Legend of Montrose* (p. 262 n.); *The Bride of Lammermoor* and *Ivanhoe* (p. 298); *The Abbot, Kenilworth, The Fortunes of Nigel* and *Halidon Hill* (p. 466 n.).
12 Letter of 12 January 1822, in *BLJ*, vol. VI, pp. 486–7. See also J. Clubbe, 'Byron and Scott', *Texas Studies in Literature and Language*, 15:1 (1973), 67–91 (p. 77).
13 *Quarterly Review*, 16 (October 1816), 172–208.
14 Byron calls Scott the 'Ariosto of the North' in his letters to John Murray of 7 August and 17 September 1817, in *BLJ*, vol. V, pp. 255, 266.
15 Clubbe, 'Byron and Scott', p. 68.
16 Clubbe, 'Byron and Scott', p. 77.
17 W. Scott, *A Legend of the Wars of Montrose*, ed. J. H. Alexander (Edinburgh: Edinburgh University Press, 1995), pp. 7, 16.
18 Letters of 3 May 1810 and 17 June 1810, in *BLJ*, vol. I, pp. 237, 246.
19 W. Scott, *Rob Roy*, ed. D. Hewitt (Edinburgh: Edinburgh University Press, 2008), p. 143.
20 See A. Schmidt, *Byron and the Rhetoric of Italian Nationalism* (Basingstoke: Palgrave Macmillan, 2010), p. 41.
21 See S. Gilman, *The Jew's Body* (London and New York: Routledge, 1991).
22 See, for example, Byron's letters from Venice to Hobhouse (27 May 1818), Douglas Kinnaird (27 May 1818) and John Murray (6 April 1819), in *BLJ*, vol. VI, pp. 41, 106.
23 Byron here refers to his 'Ode from the French', published anonymously in the *Morning Chronicle* on 15 March 1816.

24 *BLJ*, vol. VII, pp. 84–5.
25 Byron had used the verb 'skirr' once before in *The Siege of Corinth* (692), and 'skirr'd' in *Cain* (III, i, 64) and *The Two Foscari* (III, i, 293). Byron draws on *Macbeth*: 'send out moe Horses / Skirr the countrie round' (V, ii, 37).
26 G. Colman, *The Review, or The Wags of Windsor* (New York: D. Longworth, 1804), pp. 17, 19.
27 For further discussion of Byron's role as a *cavalier servente*, see Diego Saglia's chapter later in this volume.
28 See T. Guiccioli, *Lord Byron's Life in Italy*, trans. M. Rees, ed. P. Cochran (Newark, Del.: University of Delaware Press, 2005); A. Nicholson's preface to *The Letters of John Murray*, p. xxi. Murray's father was John McMurray, 1737–93, of Edinburgh.
29 For a discussion of Byron's heroes that also links their failures to Scotland, via Byron's Calvinistic upbringing in Aberdeen, see A. Rawes, 'Byron's Romantic Calvinism', *The Byron Journal*, 40:2 (2012), 129–42.
30 *BLJ*, vol. IX, pp. 153–4.
31 'The Highland politeness of Callum Bog – there are few nations, by the way, who can boast of so much natural politeness as the Highlanders – the Highland civility of his attendant had not permitted him to disturb the reveries of our hero' (W. Scott, *Waverley*, in *The Complete Works of Walter Scott, with a Biography and His Last Additions and Illustrations* [New York: Conner & Cooke, 1833], vol. II, p. 71).
32 See T. S. Eliot, 'Byron', in *On Poetry and Poets* (New York: Noonday Press, 1943), pp. 223–39 (p. 223).
33 *BLJ*, vol. VII, pp. 117–18.
34 Clubbe, 'Byron and Scott', p. 70.
35 Clubbe, 'Byron and Scott', p. 70.
36 For a wider discussion of the importance of Scots in a number of Byron's social networks, in Italy and elsewhere, see M. Pittock, 'Byron's networks and Scottish Romanticism', *The Byron Journal*, 37:1 (2009), 5–14.
37 Letter to Douglas Kinnaird of 13 September 1812, in *BLJ*, vol. VIII, p. 208.
38 See Nicholson, Preface to *The Letters of John Murray*, p. xix.
39 Scott, *A Legend of the Wars of Montrose*, p. 153.
40 See Nicholson's note, *The Letters of John Murray*, p. 199, and *BLJ*, vol. V, pp. 171, 175, 191, 220.
41 Clubbe, 'Byron and Scott', p. 70, quoting Byron's letter to Scott of 12 January 1822, where Byron is also quoting Chapter 35 of *The Heart of Midlothian* (*BLJ*, vol. IX, p. 87).

4

The garden of the world: Byron and the geography of Italy

Mauro Pala

Geography as mindscape

In *La Nouvelle Héloïse*, the protagonist Saint-Preux contemplates the Swiss landscape to the point of identifying himself with it, inaugurating a characteristic tendency that runs throughout European Romanticism: the seeking out of correspondences, partial or absolute, temporary or eternal, between observer and place. Earlier commentators on travel, of course, laid the ground for Rousseau. In his reading of the Grand Tour, for example, Addison maintains that the traveller's eye is both introspective and expands towards the infinite.[1] But the Romantic tradition that followed Rousseau went much further. Byron's poetry certainly far exceeds the idea of introspection as conceived of by Addison, to arrive at a wholly original synthesis of first-person experience, figurative estrangement and the revisitation of history by means of an intimate, impressionistic, imaginative revisioning of Italy.

The present-day convergence between geography and critical theory in studies of the representation of landscape stresses the observer's total involvement in his/her experience of place. This transformation of geography into a discipline interested in the psychological and social aspects of landscape has been achieved by scholars such as Bertrand Westphal, Michael Jakob, Michael Dear and Douglas Richardson, among others.[2] Their innovative topographical methods are well suited to the polymorphism and polysemy of Byron's Italian landscapes: seen through the lens of geocriticism, Byron's Italy displays all the characteristics of what Gaston Bachelard calls 'topoanalysis', the psychological study of environments.[3] Here it is the observer's relation to the places they observe, and not simply those places, that is repeatedly reconsidered, reimagined and reconfigured.

Though Byron's poetry depicts the geography of Italy through a poetics built on an engagement with a real and historical environment, the poet himself often tends to overshadow this environment, exploiting its imaginative, spiritual and personal possibilities alongside its historical ones. As a result, the reader is confronted with Byron's perspective on a landscape as much as with that landscape per se. The observer, in the act of observing, takes centre stage to the point, for example, of completely overwhelming the fiction that gives *Childe Harold's Pilgrimage* its name:

> With regard to the conduct of the last canto, there will be found less of the pilgrim than in any of the preceding, and that little slightly, if at all, separated from the author speaking in his own person. The fact is, that I had become weary of drawing a line which every one seemed determined not to perceive.[4]

A fictional means of engaging with place, Childe Harold is largely dispensed with in *Childe Harold* IV, in favour of 'the author speaking in his own person' as he directly encounters a range of landscapes, cityscapes and landmarks. Consequently, as W. J. T. Mitchell puts it, Byron's 'picturing, imagining, perceiving, likening and imitating' of place are not the background to a narrative of self but rather the constitutive elements of that narrative.[5] The direct experience of place becomes the basis of a whole poetic praxis, rather than an added embellishment. For Byron, as for other Romantic expatriates, Italy becomes a catalyst for new aesthetic ideas, modes and forms through which 'the interplay of new physical contexts with intellectual and imaginative inheritances' creates a radically new 'artistry of exile'.[6] The representations of specific Italian topographies in *Childe Harold* IV, which have, as Stephen Cheeke points out,[7] been too hurriedly dismissed as second-hand, are the fundamental elements of the poetics of the canto, then – a work that Byron himself defines as 'a composition which in some degree connects me with the spot where it was produced, and the objects it would fain describe'.[8] At the centre of the canto's Italian poetics is the Byronic self.

Nevertheless, the canto's representations of Italy are part of 'a creative process and an actual sequence of physical and material connection'.[9] As such, Byron's representations of Italian places look both inwards and outwards. While they dramatise 'the author speaking in his own person', they also show how Italian ruins in particular testify to the decadence of a nation now subjugated, indeed almost obliterated, by foreigners. They also highlight the cynicism and materialism of modernity more generally, as they expose the way in which moral ideals, particularly classical and especially Roman ideals, have been debased to trite clichés. But for Byron, the geography of Italy also offers a potential new beginning: 'Watering the heart whose early flowers have died, / And with a fresher growth replenishing the void' (*CHP*, IV, 5). As Byron's re-engagement with places familiar to the reader of his own time deconstructs the rhetoric already associated with those places, it transforms this very rhetoric into a personalised account of 'the flux of everything which is most immediate' – within but also in front of the poem's speaker.[10] This is particularly true of Byron's engagement with Italian ruins in *Childe Harold* IV.

Italy: a 'graced' ruin

As early as the eighteenth century, the dictates of British fashion, according to prevalent opinion among the Whigs, favoured Italy over France. Not limited to the sphere of aesthetics, Italian influences were also evident in the historiography of the period, which was inclined to award primacy to the figures of illustrious men as moral models in politics and to advance a notion of history in which, following Giambattista Vico's cyclical reading of historical change, periods of splendour and decadence alternate through the centuries.[11] For Byron and his contemporaries, the ruins of Italy offered unrivalled opportunities for singling out and depicting such cycles and transitions. For Byron, moreover, the variety of Italy's ruined landscapes also facilitated the frequent digressions through which, denying the totalising harmony normally attributed to Italy, he draws attention to the country's complex and problematic relationship with modernity owing to its continuing immersion in its classical past.[12]

The ruins of Italy in *Childe Harold* IV thus confirm the 'wayward' trajectory that characterised the Byronic 'Grand Tour', which, unlike earlier classical itineraries, reveals Byron to be not merely looking for models from the past but also 'struggling with his own years, with the age he lives in, with history and the unknown that convention ignores even when reality demands their notice'.[13] To these ends, Byron develops a topographical and figurative language that transforms his verse into an instrument for rereading history as well as a tool for introspection. The dislocation and disorientation which Byron experienced in his early years in Italy are initially synthesised in *Childe Harold* IV into a narrativised Italian panorama, then into a poetic investigation of Italy in which observation goes beyond geography per se to explore the past and the present, self and otherness.

As a result, Italy in Byron's work already appears as a complex and heterogeneous reality, a peculiar cultural geography. But his poetry from Italy also displays a 'spatial awareness' that 'acquires critical intensity as the outcast maps the distance between himself and home'.[14] This double perspective (of 'being here' and 'not being there'[15]) grounds a poetics of conscious self-reinvention: for his audience at home, on the one hand, and in the face of his immediate experience of Italy, on the other. Byron's double glance at Italy and England results in a self-consciously multiple and performative use of the former. In his depictions of the country, 'self-making and text-making' are 'parallel acts; indeed [...] precisely the same act viewed from differing perspectives', an act that focuses 'intensely and with precision' on the creation of both a Byronic Italy and an Italian Byron rooted in genuine and personal experience.[16] Ruins, decay, 'palaces [...] crumbling to the shore' (*CHP*, IV, stanza 3) play a central role in each of these creations from the outset of the canto:

> I stood in Venice, on the Bridge of Sighs;
> A palace and a prison on each hand:
> I saw from out the wave her structures rise
> As from the stroke of the enchanter's wand
> A thousand years their cloudy wings expand
> Around me, and a dying Glory smiles
> O'er the far times, when many a subject land
> Look'd to the winged Lion's marble piles,
> Where Venice sate in state, thron'd on her hundred isles!
>
> (1)

From the start, Byron highlights his own presence right there on the spot and emphasises the centrality of his perspective. Venice becomes an idealised instrument for self-realisation and a stage for self-assertion. The city becomes a deserted and ethereal place where history, seen as a concatenation of events, seems to have ended, even though, emerging as 'from the stroke of the enchanter's wand', the city embraces the poet with the wings of the Lion of Saint Mark and 'A thousand years their cloudy wings expand / Around me'.[17] Venice, a city 'declined to dust', little more than 'empty halls' (15) and crumbling palaces (3), appears to elude all questions of a political or historical nature that might refer to the present. In this moment, the city is the effect it has on the viewer, as its embrace competes with the sense of constraint associated with prisons and expands through the movement of the city's structures rising from below. Here, Venice is the rapid succession of the different frames of mind it conjures up in the viewer.

A fluidity of thoughts and feelings, and the effects of these, thus seem to be the main impact of the Venetian cityscape on the observer. This fluidity makes Venice 'the greenest island of [Byron's] imagination' but also enables the poet to include in his writing 'a new kind of tolerance for kinds of doubleness' when confronting Venice:[18]

> She looks a sea Cybele, fresh from ocean,
> Rising with her tiara of proud towers
> At airy distance, with majestic motion,
> A ruler of the waters and their powers:
> And such she was; – her daughters had their dowers
> From spoils of nations, and the exhaustless East
> Pour'd in her lap all gems in sparkling showers.
> In purple was she robed, and of her feast
> Monarchs partook, and deem'd their dignity increas'd.
>
> (2)

If the Venetian cityscape is a matter of feeling, it is also a matter of 'kinds of doubleness' because Venice is here read not only as an encapsulation of dreams and desires but also a product of history that constantly evokes not only its own past but the pasts of other places too. We see this in the association between Venice and the goddess Cybele, the mother goddess, transformed from a chthonic divinity into a sea goddess, her myth travelling from East to West, through ancient Greece and Rome, before finally arriving in Venice. The towered tiara on Cybele's head represents a power that extended over potentially unlimited time and space, as 'exhaustless' as the East itself. Venice in this stanza thus summarises two main historical components of Byronic Italy. On the one hand, it embodies a sense of decadence and decay connected with the course of European history; on the other, it signifies the geographical and historical meeting of

East and West. As Saree Makdisi notes, Venice offers 'a multidimensional "border" into the space and time of the Orient, a space-time that has its own distinct pattern of temporal ruptures and losses, but, on its own terms, is a discrete spatial-temporal sphere, different from that of the West'.[19] As a result, in Byron's Venice, the space-time of the Orient 'exists alongside that of the Occident, in opposition to it, rather than as a rupture contained by – or within – an otherwise homogeneous Western *Jetztzeit*'.[20] If Byron's 'dying' Venice is a stage for the performance of the Byronic self, it is also a confrontation with multiple histories – past and present, East and West.

Venice is also presented as a highly literary cityscape, as Byron eschews mimetic description in the stanzas that follow in favour of 'a kind of code' which, 'once registered as a diversion (or a possible diversion), points the reader toward other [...] contexts of reading' the city.[21] Byron affirms that his strong relationship with Venice dates back to his childhood – 'I lov'd her from my boyhood – she to me / Was a fairy city of the heart' – an essentially literary fantasy generated by Byron's reading of 'Otway, Radcliffe, Schiller, Shakespeare's art', which 'stamp'd her image in me' (*CHP*, IV, 18). However, the felt experience of Venice's historical fate overrides this literary Venice once Byron is confronted with its present-day reality, where the glory of Venice is dying, and the city, which was 'a ruler of the waters' (2), now 'Sinks, like a sea-weed, into whence she rose' (13). Venice is 'lost and won / Her thirteen years of freedom done' (13). And the city is dearer to Byron in her current state of historical ruin than either the 'fairy city' of literature or the 'ruler of the waters and their powers' (2) of past centuries: 'Perchance even dearer in her day of woe / Than when she was a boast, a marvel, and a show' (18). Georg Simmel's interpretation of ruins helps us to understand Byron's thinking here:

> The ruin of a building [...] means that where the work of art is dying, other forces and forms, those of nature, have grown; and that out of what of art still lives in the ruin and what of nature already lives in it, there has emerged a new whole, a characteristic unit [...] a unity which is no longer grounded in human purposiveness but in that depth where human purposiveness and the working of non-conscious natural forces grow from their common root [...] the ruin often strikes us as so often tragic [...] because destruction here is not something

coming senselessly from the outside but rather the realization of a tendency inherent in the deepest layer of the existence of the destroyed [...] in the case of the ruin, with its extreme intensification and fulfilment of the present form of the past, such profound and comprehensive energies of our soul are brought into play that there is no longer any sharp division between perception and thought.[22]

Ruins in the Byronic landscape are an instrument of nature in precisely Simmel's sense of this, and, as such, mark the limits of human action. The ruin reveals a timelessness that Byron identifies with nature by means of an association which might at first seem paradoxical in a country so rich in history as Italy. However, Simmel also points us to another aspect of ruins – their manifestation of 'a tendency inherent in the deepest layer of the existence of the destroyed' and their 'extreme intensification and fulfilment of the present form of the past' – which enables us to see how Byron's aesthetic of ruin is a fundamentally historical, as well as an experiential, one. A ruined Venice is 'even dearer in her day of woe / Than when she was a boast, a marvel, and a show' because, rather than manifesting a single history, or even a single moment in history, the city now manifests the 'deepest layer' of – and the 'fulfilment' of – history itself.

Nevertheless, Byron's insistence on ruins also calls to mind Edward Gibbon's philosophy of history and prose. Just like the poet, the historian superimposes the narration of *Decline and Fall* onto significant events from his own life.[23] Drawing on Patricia Meyer Spacks' analysis of autobiography, Charlotte Roberts highlights the role – the 'persona' – and the attitude that Gibbon assumes in his maturity with respect to the material he has analysed. This gives rise to what Roberts terms a 'marmoreal' style, where the adjective does not so much refer to the fragments of marble and stone that Gibbon describes in his work, as to his total identification with the object narrated against the background of eminently autobiographical writing.[24] While the poet envisages Roman history precisely like the historian – and the majority of the Italian patriots of that time – that is as an integral part of Italian history, like Gibbon he also, as a 'ruin amidst ruins' (25), presents decline as both a historical state and an existential one.

Ruins are not only a distinctive feature of the Italian landscape, then, but also the essence of Byron's representation of that landscape, the element giving shape to the entire composition of *Childe Harold* IV, in which Italy is a garden of art whose remains are preferable to the fruit growing elsewhere. However, ruins do not always function in the same way as crumbling, sinking Venice. As Byron tells Italy later in the canto:

> Thou art the garden of the world, the home
> Of all Art yields, and Nature can decree;
> Even in thy desart, what is like to thee?
> Thy very weeds are beautiful, thy waste
> More rich than other climes' fertility;
> Thy wreck a glory, and thy ruin graced
> With an immaculate charm which can not be defaced.
>
> (26)

The garden of Italy recalls Eden. Even if in ruins (a 'wreck'), Italy overturns the biblical Fall by being enveloped by the fascination of art, sheltered from the setbacks of history and protected by a law (a *nomos*) which 'Nature' decrees and regulates. This occurs because a privileged relationship exists between 'Nature', which inspires 'Art', and Italy, a relationship previously felt in Venice: 'States fall, arts fade – but Nature doth not die, / Nor yet forget how Venice once was dear' (3). Italy '*is* the loveliest, and must ever be / The master-mould of Nature's heavenly hand', and its ruins make this special relationship manifest, as 'Nature' 'charms' and 'graces' those ruins with 'weeds' that are 'beautiful' (25). For Byron, Italy's ruins simultaneously fulfil history's inherent 'tendency' towards 'destruction' and function as the sites of nature's redemption of history.

Given Byron's dual focus both on himself in Italy and on Italy's influence on the self, it should come as no surprise that he seeks out a kind of personal redemption that mirrors the salvation found in the Italian landscape. Identifying himself with the ruins of Italy, both being ruined and desolated by 'life', he finds this redemption in the imaginative contemplation of those ruins.[25] Standing a 'ruin amidst ruins' and 'meditat[ing] amongst decay' (*CHP*, IV, 25), he finds that the 'beings of the mind' are 'Essentially immortal' and thus 'create / And multiply in us a brighter ray / And more beloved existence' (5). The poet's mind, now 'a fragment' of what it was, and identifying itself with ruin, acquires a 'being more intense' than corporeality.[26] A 'ruin', a 'fragment', a 'nothing', he finds himself 'gaining' as he 'gives' the life he 'images', positing a highly intimate relationship between himself and the ruins he depicts. Describing the act of writing, Byron famously says:

> 'Tis to create, and in creating live
> A being more intense, that we endow
> With form our fancy, gaining as we give
> The life we image, even as I do now.
> What am I? Nothing; but not so art thou,
> Soul of my thought! with whom I traverse earth,
> Invisible but gazing.
>
> (*CHP*, III, 6)[27]

'Imaging' the life of thought, poetry is so important that the self ceases to exist in its absence. The self is therefore the product of a dynamic relationship between the imagination and what stimulates it. For Byron, responding to and imaging Italian ruins is an engagement with history, a text-making and a self-making.

Expanded by the 'genius of the spot'

Byron puts Addison's theory of the traveller's eye into practice as he opens up the landscape of travel literature to both the interior and the exterior. On the one hand, his emphasis is on potentially boundless introspection.[28] In this sense, he reasserts the poet's centrality and the potential for self-making in encounters with the geography of Italy. Viewed from Byron's perspective, the topography of Italy, 'made of various, most of the time contrasting, features works as a context in which consciousness can recognize its opposite and thereby make it possible for the self to realize itself'.[29]

On the other hand, it confronts head-on the dialectic of past and present that gives that topography its historical meanings. Byron's depictions of Italy can also be ascribed to a Europe-wide aesthetic and ideological tendency which, from the end of the eighteenth to the early nineteenth century, transformed notions of the Italian peninsula from a museum into a mausoleum and, in 'linking [itself] to [the] storied Italian past, [...] tended either to ignore or dramatize the shortcomings of contemporary Italy, which emerged paradoxically in the Romantic age as the culturally impoverished antithesis of its own illustrious heritage'.[30] Byron repeatedly recalls the Italian past in order to criticise – but also as a potential means of redeeming – the alienation and materialism of modern times.

Thus, in Venice, 'Tasso's echoes are no more' (*CHP*, IV, 3) yet the city has produced a literary heritage that might repopulate 'the solitary shore' (4). Florence, while representing the glories of the Renaissance, which made Italy famous all over the world, has also long been guilty of not properly celebrating its most famous men of letters: 'Byron's encomium of Santa Croce and its fallen heroes dramatises the notable absence of those cultural avatars who lie outside of the cathedral's walls: the *tre corone* (three crowns), Dante, Petrarch, and Boccaccio.'[31] However, always open to 'doubleness', Byron conjures up Santa Croce in a way that makes it both cast a shadow over present-day Italy and, potentially, inspire it. Perhaps partly prompted by Ugo Foscolo's *Dei Sepolcri*,[32] the poetry has this church, which is also a sepulchre, contain in its 'holy precincts [...] / Ashes which make it holier, dust which is / Even itself an immortality' (*CHP*, IV, 54) – Michelangelo's, Alfieri's, Galileo's and Machiavelli's (56). The Italian past gifts the present both absence and plenitude, ingratitude and generosity, lack and 'immortality' (54). What at first glance looks like another example of the contemporary tendency to turn Italy into a mausoleum that chastises the modern peninsula with the remains of its past greatness is, in fact, a rather more complex textual inscription. With its 'double' legacy, Santa Croce is part of the topography of places that share strong conflicting symbolic connotations and thereby constitute Byronic Italy in *Childe Harold* IV – from Venice to Tasso's and Ariosto's burial places and the Coliseum. Even as Byron draws on a contemporary trend he also makes it his own and reinterprets it by deploying as well as subverting its increasingly clichéd rhetorical manoeuvres.

The double nature of these places simultaneously contributes to the construction of the Italian Byron. Byron's openness to the doubleness of places linking life and death (churches, sanctuaries, cemeteries and battlefields) evokes the notion of *trasgressio*, the exceeding of limits – the boundary or *limes* between self and other – which are here transcended via the *limen*, a porous membrane that connects, rather than divides, different surfaces or territories and enables movement and circulation across them.[33] For Frederick Garber, '*Childe Harold* is a poem of self as well as place. To carry that point further, it is a poem of places *for* the self as well as places *of* the self. The former are those where the self seeks location, the latter the locations within the self.'[34] Yet Byron blurs even these distinctions, self-consciously transforming himself, in his responsiveness to Italy, from Byron in Italy into an Italianised Byron. Doubleness is again key here: as Byron projects doubleness onto the geography of Italy, so he dramatises his own sensitivity to that doubleness. Thus, in the face of the contemporary insistence on modern Italy's irredeemable cultural and political impoverishment, Byron can transform himself into the champion of those patriotic Italian ideals enshrined in Santa Croce even while lamenting the fact that nothing remains of Italy's ancient glory:

> Though there were nothing save the past, and this,
> The particle of those sublimities
> Which have relaps'd to chaos: – here repose
> Angelo's, Alfieri's bones, and his,
> The starry Galileo, with his woes;
> Here Machiavelli's earth return'd to whence it rose.
>
> These are four minds, which, like the elements,
> Might furnish forth creation: – Italy!
> [...]
>   thy decay
> Is still impregnate with divinity,
> Which gilds it with revivifying ray;
> Such as the great of yore, Canova is to-day.
>
>   (*CHP*, IV, 54–5)

If the Italian past offers ideal models for the present, Italy's present contains more than degeneration and decline. As the contemporary Canova is 'such as the great of yore', it is evident that Italy still has great 'minds' that might regenerate it. And it is important that Byron should choose an artist as his *exemplum* here, and not, for instance, a political leader. The revitalising 'minds' he finds in Italy are those that are 'impregnate with divinity', that create something 'essentially immortal' and 'multiply in us a brighter ray / And more beloved existence'. Such minds transcend political oppression and division, as the section on the Venus de Medici makes plain:

> The ambrosial aspect, which, beheld, instils
> Part of its immortality; the veil
> Of heaven is half undrawn; within the pale
> We stand, and in that form and face behold
> What Mind can make, when Nature's self would fail:
> And to the fond idolaters of old
> Envy the innate flash which such a soul could mould.
>
>   (*CHP*, IV, 49)

In the act of looking at the Venus, we 'behold' the peaks the mind can reach. What we see exceeds both our expectations and the object itself. What we admire in the Venus is ultimately not the statue per se, but rather the effect of an 'innate flash' that finds its receptacle in the mind. Indeed, as Alan Rawes aptly remarks, 'the Venus is another "Being of the Mind" like Shylock, the Moor, and Pierre: it began as a thought, a flash innate to Mind [...]. The statue points to, and draws our attention to, something else and greater than itself.'[35] Again and again in Italy, Byron encounters evidence of 'something [...] greater' than, but nevertheless available in, the peninsula's present. And, as Byron sees more than Italy in Italy, so he himself is 'Expanded by the genius of the spot' (*CHP*, IV, 155) – Byron simultaneously becomes more than himself. Clearly, the 'spatial situatedness' hypothesised by Cheeke has greater relevance and value than the mere fact of being at a place.[36]

We can get a purchase on this aspect of Byron's Italian experience by exploring the poet's concept of 'the Mind' and what he says about Italy's influence on it. 'Time hath taught / My mind to meditate what then it learn'd' (76), Byron states, suggesting a process whereby time teaches the mind how to think. But this process is inaugurated by the lesson taught by the *genius loci*: 'Pass not unblest the Genius of the place!' (68). The genius of a place can exert a terrifyingly sublime power, which, in ways that recall Giovanni Battista Piranesi's views of Rome, becomes palpable in Byron's account of the Coliseum – 'The seal is set. – Now welcome, thou dread power! / Nameless, yet thus omnipotent' (138) – a power that allows for an overcoming of spatial and temporal limits as well as a projection of the self back into the past, where, unseen, it can observe all things: 'Thus we become a part of what has been, / And grow unto the spot, all-seeing but unseen' (138). As with the experience of the Venus de Medici, this is a moment beyond the rational understanding of the 'learned', the 'wise', the 'artist and his ape' – 'Let these describe the undescribable: / I would not their vile breath should crisp the stream / Wherein that image shall forever dwell' (53). It is also a moment of infinite thought, as the Coliseum becomes an 'exhaustless mine / Of contemplation' (128). The same experience is to be found in St Peter's:

> thy mind,
> Expanded by the genius of the spot,
> Has grown colossal

> [...]
> Thou seest not all; but piecemeal thou must break,
> To separate contemplation, the great whole;
> And as the ocean many bays will make,
> That ask the eye – so here condense thy soul
> To more immediate objects, and control
> Thy thoughts until thy mind hath got by heart
> Its eloquent proportions, and unroll
> In mighty graduations, part by part,
> The glory which at once upon thee did not dart,
>
> > Not by its fault – but thine: Our outward sense
> > Is but a gradual grasp.
> > > > (155–8)

Byron's Italy and the Italian Byron once again coincide here as Italy 'expands' Byron's 'mind'. Under the guidance of the mysterious *genius loci*, the viewer of such essential features of the Italian landscape as the Coliseum and the dome of St Peter's is taught 'what Mind can make'. The viewer can access 'the fountain of sublimity' (159), though only by learning self-discipline and perseverance, 'condens[ing]' the 'soul', 'control[ling]' 'thoughts' and proceeding by 'gradual grasp'. The result is that we, 'growing', 'thus dilate / Our spirits to the size' (158) of what we see but at first can 'seest not' (157). In the words of Michael Cooke, Byron's representation of Italy lends revelatory dimensions to the phenomena of the Grand Tour and the very experience of travel. The 'things' of travel are not to be acquired but mysteriously 'entered' and learnt in a way that fuses the innermost capacity with their uttermost powers. Uncertainty, surprise and disarray beset various moments during Byron's itinerary, but his emerging and dilating sense of time eventually enables him to synthesise these moments into a sense of 'human power, of life itself'.[37]

Elsewhere Byron chooses a Gothic register to relocate the sublime to the Roman 'marble wilderness' (79), as in his celebrated description of the Palatine:

> Cypress and ivy, weed and wallflower grown
> Matted and mass'd together, hillocks heap'd
> On what were chambers, arch crush'd, column strown
> In fragments, chok'd up vaults, and frescos steep'd
> In subterranean damps, where the owl peep'd,
> Deeming it midnight: – Temples, baths, or halls?

> Pronounce who can; for all that Learning reap'd
> From her research hath been, that these are walls –
> Behold the Imperial Mount! 'tis thus the mighty falls.
>
> (107)

If Italian sites such as the Coliseum and St Peter's are revelatory of something more than Italy – of 'human power, of life itself' – then sites such as the Palatine reveal only emptiness, absence and loss. Here Rome, embodied by Niobe, dispossessed, 'Childless and crownless, in her voiceless woe' (79), a negative mirror image of the Venetian Cybele, points forward to the final trajectory in *Childe Harold's Pilgrimage* – one that leads the poetic self away from the geography of Italy and towards the ocean. But the trajectory is not ultimately towards emptiness. Taught by Italy to see 'life itself' in the details of its landscapes and cityscapes, Byron turns to the ocean to see the 'image of Eternity' (183). Written against the backdrop of contemporary philosophical debates about nature and its relation to the human mind, Byron's poem will not rest in the kind of ideas offered by Friedrich Schelling, following in Georg Wilhelm Friedrich Hegel's footsteps and positing an interpenetration of subjective/human and rational/natural.[38] Rather, for Byron, the longed-for communion with Italian landscapes and landmarks pushes his poetry far beyond merely 'human power' and towards what Cooke calls the power 'of life itself'.

A 'topoanalytic' approach to *Childe Harold* IV can thus help us to situate Byron in relation to a wider 'foundational struggle over the meaning of place' in Romanticism, and to more precisely identity his contribution to that struggle.[39] In *Childe Harold's Pilgrimage*, the geographies of Italy are never deployed as a mere background. They are never simply settings, allegories or a means of distancing Byron from the British political scene. For all their standard tropes and well-known symbols, his depictions of Italian landscapes and cityscapes cannot be written off as poetic appropriations of an inert geocultural otherness. Rather, as complex, heterogeneous and personal negotiations with real places and their attendant histories, they realign self, other, imagination, the physical, the metaphysical, past and present in ways that not only make place an essential element of the consciousness observing it but also make that observing consciousness an essential element of place.

Notes

1. M. Jakob, *Paesaggio e letteratura* (Firenze: Olschki, 2005), p. 123.
2. See M. Dear, J. Ketchum, S. Luria and D. Richardson, 'Introducing the geohumanities', in M. Dear, J. Ketchum, S. Luria and D. Richardson (eds.), *Geohumanities: Art, History, Text at the Edge of Place* (Abingdon and New York: Routledge, 2011), pp. 3–4. See also Henri Lefebvre's remark that the 'history of space must account for both representational spaces and representations of space, but above all for their interrelationships and their links with social practice. The history of space thus has its place between anthropology and political economy'. H Lefebvre, *The Production of Space*, trans. D. Nicholson-Smith (Oxford: Blackwell, 1991), p. 116.
3. B. Westphal, 'Foreword', in R. Tally Jr (ed.), *Geocritical Explorations: Space, Place, and Mapping in Literary and Cultural Studies* (Basingstoke: Palgrave Macmillan, 2011), pp. ix–xv (p. ix).
4. Dedication, *CHP*, IV, in *CPW*, vol. II, p. 122.
5. W. J. T. Mitchell, *Iconology: Image, Text, Ideology* (Chicago, Ill.: University of Chicago Press, 1986), p. 1.
6. J. Stabler, *The Artistry of Exile: Romantic and Victorian Writers in Italy* (Oxford: Oxford University Press, 2013), p. 24.
7. 'I will suggest that in fact the notion of being there represents the most powerful and complex aspect of Byron's work, even as it is perhaps the most obvious and immediate element of Byron's enduring fame [...] indeed it is part of the point in offering the traveller fragments of Byron's poetry that such passages would not only reverberate more powerfully when read in the actual places they describe, but that reading them would somehow constitute a participation in or recreation of Byron's presence in the same place.' S. Cheeke, *Byron and Place: History, Translation, Nostalgia* (Basingstoke: Palgrave Macmillan, 2003), p. 6.
8. Dedication, *CHP*, IV, in *CPW*, vol. II, p. 121.
9. Cheeke, *Byron and Place*, p. 96.
10. J. S. Duncan and N. S. Duncan, 'Roland Barthes and the secret histories of landscape', in T. J. Barnes and J. S. Duncan (eds.), *Writing Worlds: Discourse, Text and Metaphor in the Representation of Landscape* (London, New York: Routledge, 2001), pp. 18–37 (p. 21); J. J. McGann, *The Romantic Ideology: A Critical Investigation* (Chicago, Ill.: The University of Chicago Press, 1985), p. 127.
11. A. A. Schmidt, *Byron and the Rhetoric of Italian Nationalism* (Basingstoke: Palgrave Macmillan, 2003), p. 13.
12. J. Stabler, *Byron, Poetics and History* (Cambridge: Cambridge University Press, 2009), p. 44.

13 P. M. G. Cooke, 'Byron, Pope and the Grand Tour', in A. Rutherford (ed.), *Byron: Augustan and Romantic* (London: Macmillan, 1990), pp. 165–80 (p. 170).
14 Stabler, *The Artistry of Exile*, p. 104.
15 On the concept of 'being there' and its complications, see Cheeke, *Byron and Place*, pp. 6–7.
16 F. Garber, *Self, Text and Romantic Irony: The Example of Byron* (Princeton, NJ: Princeton University Press, 1988), p. 7.
17 See T. Tanner, *Venice Desired* (Oxford: Blackwell, 1992), p. 20.
18 Tanner, *Venice Desired*, p. 24.
19 S. Makdisi, *Romantic Imperialism: Universal Empire and the Culture of Modernity* (Cambridge: Cambridge University Press, 1998), p. 124.
20 Makdisi, *Romantic Imperialism*.
21 J. J. McGann, 'Byron and "The Truth in Masquerade"', in R. Brinkley and K. Hanley (eds.), *Romantic Revisions* (Cambridge: Cambridge University Press, 1992), pp. 191–209 (p. 192).
22 Quoted in Tanner, *Venice Desired*, p. 28.
23 C. Roberts, *Edward Gibbon and the Shape of History* (Oxford: Oxford University Press, 2014), p. 150.
24 Roberts, *Edward Gibbon*, p. 153.
25 J. J. McGann, *Fiery Dust: Byron's Poetic Development* (Chicago, Ill.: University of Chicago Press, 1968), p. 128.
26 As Thomas McFarland notes, 'In his journal [Byron] recorded his liking for "my Fragment. It is no wonder that I wrote one – my mind is a fragment".' T. McFarland, *Romanticism and the Forms of Ruin: Wordsworth, Coleridge and Modalities of Fragmentation* (Princeton, NJ: Princeton University Press, 1988), p. 23.
27 See V. Newey, 'Authoring the self: *Childe Harold* III and IV', in B. Beatty and V. Newey (eds.), *Byron and the Limits of Fiction* (Liverpool: Liverpool University Press, 1988), pp. 148–90 (p. 148).
28 Jakob, *Paesaggio e letteratura*, p. 123.
29 Garber, *Self, Text and Romantic Irony*, p. 73.
30 J. Luzzi, *Romantic Europe and the Ghost of Italy* (New Haven, Conn.: Yale University Press, 2008), p. 54.
31 Luzzi, *Romantic Europe and the Ghost of Italy*, pp. 56–7.
32 'Although nothing Byron wrote influenced Foscolo, one poem by Foscolo – his most important – did, in two very different ways, influence Byron when he came to write two of *his* most important.' P. Cochran, *Byron and Italy* (Newcastle: Cambridge Scholars, 2012), p. 195.
33 See B. Westphal, *Geocriticism: Real and Fictional Spaces*, trans. R. T. Tally (Basingstoke: Palgrave Macmillan, 2011).
34 Garber, *Self, Text and Romantic Irony*, p. 44.

35 A. Rawes, *Byron's Poetic Experimentation:* Childe Harold, *the Tales and the Quest for Comedy* (Aldershot: Ashgate, 2000), pp. 124–5.
36 Cheeke, *Byron and Place*, p. 8.
37 Cooke, 'Byron, Pope, and the Grand Tour', p. 176.
38 See E. Behler, *Frühromantik* (Berlin: Walter de Gruyter, 1992).
39 Cheeke, *Byron and Place*, p. 9.

5

'Something I have seen or think it possible to see': Byron and Italian art in Ravenna

Jane Stabler

When Byron first arrived in Ravenna in June 1819, the feast of Corpus Christi blocked the route of his carriage. Ravenna was 'fervent in keeping up the traditions and customs of the past', Teresa Guiccioli noted, 'the streets through which the procession would pass were strewn with flowers [...] sumptuous tapestries and pictures adorned the houses [...] and vehicles were not allowed access'.[1] Byron, we might say, was stopped in his tracks in Ravenna by that religious festival with all its associated art and iconography. In this chapter, I want to look at the relationship between Byron's *Cain* and the church art of Ravenna as a way of reading Byron's response to Italian art beyond well-known classical and Renaissance paintings and sculptures. It is a speculative argument, but *Cain* is a 'speculative' drama that fosters a dialogue with the unknowable.[2] In the Renaissance tradition, man is the measure of all things. Man is not the measure of all things in Byzantine mosaics, and this profoundly different world view is a vital context for Byron's poetry and drama after 1819, even though his letters and journals contain far more about Ravenna's political situation than its medieval art and architecture.

No written record remains of what Byron thought of the Ravenna mosaics. This may be disappointing, but Byron also lived in Venice for four years without describing the interior of St Mark's. Perhaps he never went inside, but if he did, to what extent did or does his silent experience of that interior matter? It is a question for editors as much as for literary critics. To what extent are we justified in tracing the influence of things that we think a poet might have seen, or know that he did see, but that he never actually describes? How might Byron's critics and editors identify those things that were 'so much in [his] head' that he felt it redundant to stipulate when or how they entered his consciousness;[3] how are we to determine the levels of influence that one artefact (lexical, musical or visual) might exert over a verbal one, perhaps years later? To ask these questions is to open a debate about the nature of critical evidence as well as the working of aesthetic allusion; this chapter will address such matters by suggesting some of the ways in which the visual art of Ravenna might have shaped the creativity of Byron's *Cain*.

In bringing Byron's experience of Italian religious art to the fore, I wish first of all to modify Bruce Haley's view that Byron 'hated most religious pictures'.[4] Haley's verdict is based on Byron's off-hand account of the Manfrini Palace collection:

> You must recollect however – that I know nothing of painting – & that I detest it – unless it reminds me of something I have seen or think it possible to see – for which [reason] I spit upon & abhor all the saints & subjects of one half the impostures I see in the churches & palaces [...]. I never yet saw the picture – or the statue – which came within a league of my conception or expectation.[5]

Understandably, most critical attention has been focused on Byron's writing about his highly charged encounters with canonical works of Western art in collections such as the Manfrini Palace, the Uffizi and the Vatican galleries – *Childe Harold's Pilgrimage*'s meditations on the Venus de Medici, the Dying Gaul, the Laocoon and the Apollo Belvedere, and the praise of Giorgione and Canova in *Beppo*. Bruce Haley, James Heffernan, Maureen McCue, Jerome McGann and Jonathan Sachs all explore Byron's relationship with monumental art and ruins.[6] But their combined focus – rich and rewarding though it is – truncates Byron's experience of Italian art to the monolithic, the titanic and the heroic, overlooking the ways in which other less-celebrated aspects of Italian art might influence Byron's poetry beyond those famous passages of ekphrasis.[7]

When confronted with canonical artworks, Byron tends to adopt an attitude that is either iconoclastic (spitting upon the saints, for example) or competitively determined to outdo all previous homage. There is, however, a difference between the arresting ways in which Byron responds to the famous works of art that had to be seen by eighteenth- and nineteenth-century tourists, and the more subtle ways in which the Italian visual arts might inform and infuse his perception. I want to consider Byron's assimilation of Italian art as an encounter with the fabric of a living culture, not just as a one-off response to the highlights of a well-worn tourist trail. At a temporal distance from the immediate act of perception, Byron's memories of Italian art inevitably become more creative acts, arousing his fascination with not just what was seen but also with ways of seeing and knowing.

In Canto V of *Don Juan* (written in the autumn of 1820 when Byron had settled in Ravenna), Byron voices his guidebook *ennui* and versifies a high-cultural resistance to the exhausted trope of description:

> I won't describe; description is my forte,
>   But every fool describes in these bright days
> His wond'rous journey to some foreign court,
>   And spawns his quarto, and demands your praise –
> Death to his publisher, to him 'tis sport;
>   While Nature, tortured twenty thousand ways,
> Resigns herself with exemplary patience
> To guide-books, rhymes, tours, sketches, illustrations.
>   (*DJ*, V, 52)

Nevertheless, for the rest of Canto V, Byron does describe, albeit with a degree of ironic disdain. Leading his readers through the interior of a palace on the Bosphorus, the narrator of *Don Juan* loads his stanzas with detail and a sense of its superfluous excess – 'articles which nobody required' (*DJ*, V, 64).[8] The sultan's priceless works of art, which are wonderful to Juan and Johnson, but mundane to Baba, are awarded an evocative simile, and the carpet appears 'As if the milky way their feet was under / With all its stars' (*DJ*, V, 66). To render the immediacy of the aesthetic encounter, Byron intersperses description with the deictic, inviting the reader to visualise the scene by gesturing to 'A certain press or cupboard niched in yonder / In that remote recess, which you may see – / Or if you don't the fault is not in me' (*DJ*, V, 66). This moment of self-reflexive narration exemplifies a tension between Byron's proven facility with ekphrasis and his poetics of inference. I want to suggest that Byron's formal techniques for gesturing to what lies out of sight form a link between the narrative style of *Don Juan* and the blank verse of *Cain*, and that the bridge between the material and the immanent is a significant feature of Ravenna's vernacular art.

Byron's main textual signal of insinuation is the dash. In the manuscript fair copy of Canto V, there is a dash after 'the fault is not in me', which was converted first into a full stop (in pencil on the manuscript) and finally into a comma (in the first edition) by John Murray's editorial team. It is worth pausing over this mark and what it tells us about Byron's attitude to the relationship between the visible and the invisible.[9] Byron's dashes can stand in for commas, conjunctions or rests, but they can also invite the reader to interpolate something that is off the page – most famously, perhaps, the long dash in 'The lady Astarte, his —' in *Manfred* (III, iii, 47), which did appear in print whereas the dash after Manfred's "tis not so difficult to die.' did not.[10] Byron's heavier and longer manuscript dashes reach out to the unsayable, whether sacred or profane. They form part of a graphic repertoire of pause and syncope that touches, at one end of the generic spectrum, with comic theatre and bawdy humour, but at the other with the ineffable of deep emotion or even religious awe. The stroke of ink that extends into space often appears as a pathway into the unknown, which the reader might choose to follow or not (if, indeed, the reader who was the editor allowed the dash to go forward into type). When Byron invites the reader to use their imagination in co-producing either the precisely realised details of ekphrasis or the mysterious suggestion of the dash, he brings to a momentary crisis the relationship between the visible and invisible worlds. This relationship is a significant element in both Italian religious art and Romantic theory. It is also, as we shall see, at the heart of *Cain*.

Ravenna was Byron's home for most of 1820 and 1821. From there he wrote to Thomas Moore on 31 August 1820:

> What do Englishmen know of Italians beyond their museums and saloons […]? Now, I have lived in the heart of their houses, in parts of Italy freshest and least influenced by strangers, – have seen and become (*pars magna fui*) a portion of their hopes, and fears, and passions, and am almost inoculated into a family. This is to see men and things as they are.[11]

His proud Virgilian allusion to having played a great part, to being a 'portion', and to being an inoculated particle in a larger body tell us that his various involvements (amatory and martial) in Ravenna led Byron to reflect on the relationship between social parts and the whole. This, as I shall suggest, is also a key element of what we might see as a mosaic aesthetic, but in the early nineteenth century, Ravenna's intricately fabricated basilicas were generally underestimated: 'this corner of Italy is not sufficiently visited', as a later nineteenth-century guide declared, although he found it to be 'more Constantinople than Constantinople itself'.[12]

Italian art had been the acknowledged standard of aesthetic perfection for British artists since the formation of the Royal Academy, but it was a selective ideal of the high Renaissance of Michelangelo and Raphael, the climactic third period of Vasari's *Vite de' più eccellenti pittori, scultori, ed architettori*.[13] Mosaic composition is not mentioned in Sir Joshua Reynolds' *Discourses*; it had to be glossed in Warton's 1785 edition of Milton's works as 'a kind of painting in small pebbles'.[14] Mosaic's tangible strangeness for early eighteenth- and nineteenth-century British tourists is captured by Lady Mary Wortley Montagu, when she describes St Sophia in Constantinople and comments on the surprising visibility of the images of the saints. The mosaic work of the dome, however, she reported, 'decays very fast, and drops down. They presented me with a handful of it; its composition seems to me a sort of glass, or that paste with which they make counterfeit jewels.'[15] Rarely, eighteenth- or early nineteenth-century antiquarians find beauty in mosaic art, but more often it is seen as curious, stiff, primitive, great in its rudeness, just plain rude and exemplifying barbarity. Tobias Smollett sums up the prevailing disdain when he glances at the mosaics in St Peter's, Rome:

> The mosaic work, though brought to a wonderful degree of improvement, and admirably calculated for churches, the dampness of which is pernicious to the colours of the pallet, I will not yet compare to the productions of the pencil. The glassyness (if I may be allowed the expression) of the surface, throws, in my opinion, a false light on some parts of the picture; and when you approach it, the joinings of the pieces look like so many cracks on painted canvas.[16]

Among Byron's contemporaries, William Wordsworth's mention of the 'rude fidelity' of a mosaic typifies its habitual association with the primitive while Percy Shelley uses mosaic art as an image for what is inferior or second best in *A Defence of Poetry*.[17] Byron includes 'mosaic stone' in *The Siege of Corinth* (920), and one of his letters home records the 'beautiful Mosaic' at Aventicum in 1816.[18] He does not describe the much more extensive wall mosaics in Ravenna, but we know that he went to look at them.

In June 1819, 'Dante's tomb, the classical pine wood, [and] the relics of antiquity' provided Byron with 'a sufficient pretext' for visiting Teresa Guiccioli in Ravenna.[19] He referred impatiently to 'this farce of visiting antiquities', and Teresa claims that 'he rapidly exhausted the round of visits to the historic buildings of Ravenna'.[20] Teresa's memoir and Byron's letters tell us that he visited the Sepulchre of the Exarchs and the church of St Vitale. His saturation with images of martyrs (perhaps the foot procession of martyrs in St Apollinare Nuovo) might inform his exasperated comment to Teresa at the height of his infatuation: 'Love has its martyrs like religion.'[21] Silence need not, however, imply lasting hostility or rejection. Although Byron does not write about any of the churches in detail, Teresa reveals that he gave 'alms in plenty' to 'churches and poverty-stricken convents' and that he funded the restoration of the fittings and the organ of 'a large Ravenna church'.[22] Bernard Beatty (in this volume) and Gavin Hopps provide convincing accounts of Byron's inclination to be more receptive to forms of Catholicism once he settled in Italy, and the Eastern orthodoxy of Ravenna is a significant manifestation of this tangible form of Christianity.[23] Besides quotidian familiarity with his hometown, however, there is another reason why, in 1821, Byron might have been reminded of the mosaics on his doorstep.

On 6 August of that year, Percy Bysshe Shelley arrived in Ravenna.[24] If Byron's manuscript dating is accurate, Shelley arrived in the middle of the composition of *Cain*, and it seems likely that their intermittent debate about religion informs the composition of Cain – though perhaps not as much as Shelley wanted.[25] Byron aimed to startle English readers in his shift to neoclassical drama in *Marino Faliero*, *Sardanapalus* and *The Two Foscari* and then to the 'mystery' form of *Cain*. His unprecedented experiment with a medieval dramatic mode occurred as Byron found himself being bound into a traditional Italian family structure, buttressed by Teresa Guiccioli's patterns of religious observance and embedded in the omnipresent early Christian architecture of Ravenna. This visual context offered a distinctive way of handling a religious topic that had always intrigued him. Mosaics fall outside the generic competence of humanistic Western art. Ravenna's inscrutable two-dimensional mosaic forms provide a different sort of aesthetic experience from the soft curves of the Venus de Medici or Raphael's mistress or Titian's mistress.[26] As one can see from his views on the Manfrini collection in Venice, Byron's enthusiasm for art is usually predicated on its proximity with the human (often the female), just as his appreciation of the sublime in the 'Letter to John Murray Esqre' depends on there being some perceptible human activity in the foreground. The art of Ravenna does not accord with the idea that we find beautiful what is 'near' or what reminds us of us (as Cain loves Adah). It is a separate, more algebraic, aesthetic. On more than one level, British tourists in Ravenna find themselves staring at the unfamiliar and the incomprehensible.

Two days into his visit, Shelley visited the church of St Vitale, the Basilica of St Apollinare in Classe and the tombs of the Christian emperors. From his letter to Mary, it sounds as if Shelley went round 'in Albe's carriage' without Byron, but Byron, as we know, had completed the tourist circuit in Ravenna two years earlier and seems to have been keen to point other visitors in the direction of Ravenna's antiquities.[27] When J. Mawman arrived in Ravenna, just after Shelley's departure, Byron offered 'his Carriage & horses in case Mr. M. would like to make the round of the remarkable buildings'.[28] Even if Byron and Shelley did not talk about these 'remarkable buildings' in their after-dinner conversations, they evidently discussed Shelley's failure to get into one of them as Byron fired off an angry letter to the papal legate when Shelley was denied admission to Ravenna's Duomo.[29]

Shelley found the buildings 'very peculiar & striking' and 'remarkable', but this was mainly for their height: 'Heaven alone knows how they contrived to lift it', he says of one granite dome.[30] Shelley was unimpressed by the art of the Christian imperial family: 'The tombs are massy cases of marble adorned with rude & tasteless sculpture of lambs & other Christian emblems', he wrote back to Mary. 'It seems to have been one of the first effects of the Christian religion to destroy the power of producing beauty in art.' Echoing the verdict of many earlier travellers, Shelley refers to the starry decoration of the vaulted chamber over the tomb of Galla Placida as 'rude mosaic'.[31]

We cannot know, of course, exactly what condition the mosaics were in when Shelley saw them, but Henry James's account of Ravenna fifty years after Byron and Shelley were there gives us a glimpse of the mosaics themselves and the effect they had on a Western visitor.

I will draw on James's descriptions to reconstruct something of what Byron and Shelley encountered. By reading Jamesian ekphrasis alongside *Cain*, we can begin to trace a possible dialogue between Byron's drama and the mosaics. One of James's most revealing comments is about the way he finds all the images merging in his mind: 'I have no space for a list of the various shrines [...] and, to tell the truth, my memory of them has already become a very generalised and undiscriminating record.'[32] As we saw in Byron's memory (and forgetfulness) of the Manfrini Palace, every description of a work of art is already an interpretation.

Standing in for our representative nineteenth-century viewer, James experienced a tension between 'Regular pictures full of movement, gesture and perspective' (for example Guido's fresco in the Duomo) and 'emblems of primitive dogma [...] slabs [...] covered with carven hieroglyphics of an almost Egyptian abstruseness – lambs and stags and fishes and beasts of theological affinities even less apparent'. The ability of the mosaics to outlast time and the sheer scale of the creative labour also struck him, and he wrote of his 'deep amaze [...] that, while centuries had worn themselves away and empires risen and fallen, these little cubes of coloured glass had stuck in their allotted places and kept their freshness'.[33] Even for someone like Byron, who had seen St Sophia, the mosaics of Ravenna would have offered a vertiginous awareness of scale, which I would map on to 'the million millions / the myriad myriads' in *Cain* (I, i, 521–2) and 'the unborn myriads of unconscious atoms' seen by Lucifer (II, ii, 42). It is at least possible that the 'un-numbered and innumerable / Multitudes, millions, myriads' (I, i, 447–8) and the 'myriads of starry worlds' (II, ii, 360) that Cain describes are energised by a memory of all those tiny pieces.

Byzantine mosaics were designed to create the effect of light. An inscription from the episcopal palace in Ravenna gives the wall its own words to tell viewers what they were seeing. Translated into English, the mosaic's self-description runs as follows:

> Either light was born here, or captured here it reigns free; it is the law, from which the current glory of heaven excels. The roofs deprived [of light] have produced gleaming day [...]. See, the marble flourishes with bright rays, and all the stones struck in starry purple shine in value, the gifts of the founder, Peter. To him honor and merit are granted, thus to beautify small things, so that although confined in space, they surpass the large. Nothing is small to Christ.[34]

This is, of course, the opposite of what Lucifer teaches Cain. Mosaics focus attention on a harmonious relationship between parts and the whole, but instead of the orthodox understanding that man is a beloved part of something much bigger, Lucifer's aim is to sharpen Cain's suspicion that he is a radically disconnected particle floating in a universe that has been doomed to destruction by its heartless creator.

The nature of God and his attitude to the rest of his creation is one of the central issues of *Cain*. The image of Christ in St Vitale's church as recorded by James is a representation of Shelley's (but not necessarily Byron's) worst nightmare in this respect: 'The great Christ [...] is quite an elaborate picture, and yet he retains enough of the orthodox stiffness to make him impressive in the simpler, elder sense. He is clad in a purple robe, even as an emperor.'[35] There is a deliberate kinship in Ravenna's mosaics between representations of Christ and the Emperor Justinian, who wanted to be presented as the meeting point of political order and religious orthodoxy. Byron's Lucifer, like Shelley in *Prometheus Unbound*, sees divine power as omnipotent tyranny and Lucifer's depiction of God on his 'vast and solitary throne' (I, i, 148) might recall the Christ in St Vitale's church or in St Apollinare Nuovo. We do not, of course, see God in *Cain*. Byron's God is as inscrutable in *Cain* as he is in Genesis, which is why Byron could insist that his drama was at once 'orthodox' but also 'not quite canonical'.[36]

In *Cain*, we watch human characters struggling to realise natural and supernatural forms they do not understand. Cain wonders at the shapes of mammoths and sea monsters (II, ii, 132–42, 190–6), and both Cain and Adah try to describe the 'Haughty, and high, and beautiful' (II, ii, 54) angels and mighty phantoms they meet: 'as the silent sunny noon / All light they look upon us' (I, i, 509–10). The eerie inscrutability of these beings is matched by James's apprehension of the mosaic angels in St Apollinare Nuovo:

> Upon all these strange things, the strange figures in the great mosaic panorama look down [...]. What it is these long slim seraphs express I cannot quite say, but they have an odd, knowing, sidelong look out of the narrow ovals of their eyes which, though not without sweetness, would certainly make me murmur a defensive prayer or so were I to find myself alone in the church towards dusk.[37]

The mosaics on Ravenna's walls are not simply visual decoration; they are a means of communion, opening the material church building out to eternity. The religious function of the mosaic icon is as a channel between two worlds. James slightly misreads the mosaic's purpose as didactic illustration: 'It is an interest simple [...] almost to harshness, and leads one's attention along a straight and narrow way.' That 'harshness' is, as we have seen, what earlier tourists recognised; James writes of 'strange stiff primitive Christian forms' and notes that when in Rome one is distracted by the sensuous excess of paganism underlying Catholic art, but 'Ravenna [...] began with the Church, and all her monuments and relics are harmoniously rigid'.[38] In the expression of doctrinal and formal rigidity we can identify a kinship between the Ravenna mosaics and the poetics of *Cain*.

Shelley had already disapproved of the 'severe and unharmonising traits' of *Marino Faliero*, but Byron persisted in wanting to '[break] down the *poetry*' and for his plays to be 'rigidly historical', 'simple and severe', 'Doric and austere'.[39] In his volume of three plays, 'a tragedy', 'an historical tragedy' and a 'mystery', linguistic attenuation and fragmentation were part of the experiment: 'I have broken down the *poetry* as nearly as I could to common language', he says of *The Two Foscari*, and we might see the 'rugged' or 'jerky' rhythms of Cain (to use Truman Guy Steffan's adjectives) as a poetic form of mosaic.[40] The repeated interruptions of stichomythia or 'subdivisions of dialogue' about which reviewers complained (whereby a single line of verse is shared by more than one speaker) are almost a visual recreation of the glittering tessellated surface of mosaic, the cracked or fissured surface that Smollett so much disliked.[41]

Byron introduces Cain using the formulation 'in the following scenes', indicating the static form of 'Mystery play' tableau. The prayers that initiate the first act take us through the episodes of creation, and each provides a shift of scale from the awe-inspiring creation of light and dark to the much more troubling introduction of creatures at close quarters when Zillah's praise of God includes 'Oh God who loving, making, blessing all, / Yet didst permit the serpent to creep in' (I, i, 18–19). And this brings us to the realisation of original sin, which Byron handles brilliantly by letting us feel it as the weight of dramatic irony. We know what will happen to Cain, but it still seems to happen by accident, and yet it is impossible to avert.

When he 'tread[s] on air, and sink[s] not' (II, i, 1), Cain becomes one with the giant mosaic figures floating in space against their glittering backgrounds, but his overexposure to cosmic wonder makes him unfit to participate in mundane or familial religious ritual.

The touristic experience of Byron and Shelley in Ravenna might also be evinced in Byron's use of the dynamics of the guided tour to dramatise the way Cain's vision of the universe becomes Lucifer's creation and by Cain's resentment at being obliged to admire he knows not what. To turn Cain against the mysteries of the universe, Lucifer has only to behave like a bored chaperone: 'behold! Is it not glorious?', he says, languidly, asking Cain to 'point out' the site of Paradise (II, i, 97–8, 33–4). The second act is full of Lucifer's visual prompting: 'look back', 'Look there!' 'what yonder', 'Behold!', 'Behold these', 'Approach the things [...] and judge their beauty near' (II, i, 118, 120, 197; II, ii, 86, 249–50). And perhaps like Shelley's tour of Ravenna's antiquities, the glimpses of Eden and immortality just make Cain into a boring dinner companion: 'The overpowering mysteries of space [...] have made me / Unfit for mortal converse' (III, i, 179–84). Adah, meanwhile, is happy to leave the invisible where she did not find it. She looks in a different way from Cain and can accept without questioning the idea of hidden possibility. Adah appreciates the way 'unnumber'd stars / Spangle the wonderful mysterious vault / With things that look as if they would be suns' (I, i, 512–14), but she is wary of the lure of visual attraction and resists Lucifer's invitation to adore the symbols of the invisible.

Cain's desire to get outside dramatic irony should make him into a scientist, but he always falls back into a different sort of empiricism, sounding like an early nineteenth-century tourist in a gallery, determined to cram in all the best sights and compass or number or measure everything he is shown: 'I have looked out / In the vast desolate night in search of him' (I, i, 270–1) Cain says of death – 'let me [...] see them nearer' (II, i, 117) he says about the lights in the blue wilderness; 'let me look on it' (II, i, 145); 'show me' (II, ii, 366, 397); 'I see them but I know them not' (II, ii, 168); 'And to what end have I beheld these things / Which thou hast shown me?' (II, ii, 417).

In doctrinal terms, Byron's insistence in the play's preface that his subject 'has nothing to do with the New Testament', and that 'there is no allusion to a future state in any of the books of Moses, nor indeed in the Old Testament', does and does not partake of the spirit of the mosaics in Ravenna.[42] There is, indeed, a noticeable lack of direct representation of New Testament images in the church of St Vitale. The apse is dominated by Christ on the globe flanked by angels and St Vitale and Bishop Ecclesius; the mystic lamb against a starry sky presides over the vault of the presbytery, but the most obvious biblical images are scenes of Abraham's hospitality to the angels and the averted sacrifice of Isaac in the lunettes on the left-hand side of the altar, while on the right-hand side of the altar Abel is shown offering a sacrificial lamb. The mosaics depict Christ as simultaneously the sacrifice and the priest, prefigured in the Old Testament figures of Abel, Melchizedik and Isaac. Through typology, the scenes of Old Testament sacrifice prefigure the New Testament Eucharist – exactly as Lucifer does with his warning 'that Son will be a Sacrifice' (I, i, 166). Byzantine icons allow a worshipper to move between the dimensions of time and space and to enter the presence of the mystery depicted; the overlapping of temporal schemes in the mosaic panels might represent a visual intertext for the vistas of time through which Lucifer leads the dazzled Cain.

In the hospitality of Abraham icon in St Vitale's church, the three seated figures are portrayed almost identically, with no real distinguishing features. Their visual similarity aids understanding of the process of typology. The scenes of sacrifice set on the walls above the altar are versions of the liturgical drama of sacrifice in the Eucharist, a drama repeated over the altar of St Apollinare in Classe. The relationship between the visible and the invisible must be completed by the viewer – as intimated by Adah: 'How know we that some such atonement one day / May not redeem our race?' (III, i, 85–6). The hand that appears over the sacrifice of Isaac (and above many of the other Old Testament scenes) is the hand of God, symbolising God's acceptance of sacrifice and his intervention in human history. In Byron's imagination, the hand that looms the largest is a human hand stained with blood – 'Incarnadine' (III, i, 398–9) – allowing us to recognise Cain as the prototype for all the murders and imagined murders of history, including that of Macbeth. The image of the 'multitudinous seas incarnadine' (*Macbeth*, II, ii, 59) cannot quite come into focus as Byron tells us that Cain has never seen the ocean so Cain's metaphor is that the water of the four rivers of Eden could not cleanse him (III, i, 522). The four rivers of Eden are depicted under the Christ in St Vitale's apse.

One irony of Byron's drama is that Cain's hatred of violence and his awe at the beauty of the cosmos might so easily have become a religious instinct; his lack of comprehension might have been an acceptable form of worship. Alienation from modern life, muddle or confusion can sometimes be part of an icon's impact, David Brown reminds us. It is a mistake, Brown suggests, to have too simplified a theory of meaning, to suppose that symbols only work if they are fully comprehended.[43] Cain's confrontation with the mysteries of time and space, especially his 'Oh, thou beautiful / And unimaginable ether!' (II, i, 98–117) speech, almost tilts into being a hymn of praise. In the manuscript, extensive dashing traces Cain's delirious, incredulous wonder, 'Intoxicated with eternity? – –', and stammering before the vast enigma of creation: 'How beautiful – ye are! How beautiful – / Your works – or accidents – or whatsoever / They be! –'. In the duration of the dashes Cain sways between visions of unaccountable design and something begotten not made; the most speculative passages of the play in Act II are actually the parts that come closest to orthodox joy and reverence.

The process of showing or beholding or peering or gazing is at the heart of the relationship between visual image and written text, and helps to explain why *Cain* was written in Ravenna. The questions of how one can look steadily at the mysteries of the universe are philosophical, formal and ethical. While watching the execution of three men in Rome 1817, Byron found his hand shaking so much that he could scarcely hold the opera glass. In Ravenna he had to witness retributive justice on a different scale. The suffering of the families who were uprooted in the wake of the failed uprising moved Byron profoundly: 'It has been a miserable sight to see the general desolation of families', he wrote, 'it is a kind of thing which cannot be described without equal pain as in beholding it'.[44] 'I gazed', Byron writes as the narrator of *Don Juan*, over the shooting of the military commandant at his door in Ravenna, '(as oft I have gazed the same) [...] But it was all a mystery' (*DJ*, V, 38–9). How to behold it is the key question. How does one look steadily at individual or general desolation? What is the role of the artist in such matters?

One answer is the kind of art devoted to the small scale – this is the 'tender' Dante that the Romantics respond to, the episode of Paolo and Francesca (which Byron adapted while in Ravenna), the affective ekphrasis of the *Inferno* where the poet swoons to see so much agony as the cost of one moment of human passion. Beauty that one has to be close to is one sort of art; it is the sensual world of Adah and the little Enoch, the art of human features and 'sweetness': 'his little cheeks, / In their pure incarnation, vying with / The rose leaves strewn beneath them' (III, i, 10–12). Byron's writing in *Cain* shows that his response to the visual arts divides between the Manfrini Palace treasures, 'a face to go mad for', and another realm that is without body, parts or passions.

A close reading of one dramatic exchange about invisible influence will help to draw together the possible parallels between mosaic art and Byron's medieval mystery play. In Act II, scene 1, as Cain grapples with different scales of vision, he finds the worlds he has seen to be less bright than 'the fire-flies and the fire-worms' which 'Sprinkle the dusky groves and the green banks / In the dim twilight' (II, i, 123–5). Lucifer works to exacerbate Cain's new sense of littleness:

> Thou has seen both worms and worlds,
> Each bright and sparkling, – what dost think of them?
>
> Cain. That they are beautiful in their own sphere,
>   And that the night, which makes both beautiful
>   The little shining fire-fly in its flight,
>   And the immortal star in its great course,
>   Must both be guided.
>   (II, i, 126–32)

This is, as Steffan calls it, 'one of Byron's faulty sentences'.[45] The trouble is that we do not know whether it is a bit of carelessness or a deliberate disruption of syntax. In the manuscript, the dashes that fall after 'sphere', 'flight', 'course' and 'guided' suggest Cain's probing of the darkness and Lucifer's knowing silence. Lucifer has just invited Cain to look back at the earth. In the manuscript, the dialogue of Cain and Lucifer includes one line broken by Cain's double dash and concluded by Lucifer's mirroring of this symbol: 'I cannot see it. – – / Yet it sparkles still. – –'. The dashes are extra-metrical: even though they look as if they stand in for missing words, the two speech units add up to ten syllables. Cain and Lucifer are locked into a line that is whole and broken at the same time. The dashes work to convey Cain's baffled confrontation with invisible presence and Lucifer's ability to flood the void with meaning. Byron then opens a grammatical aporia with the line, 'And that the night which makes both beautiful', a fragment of meaning which remains incomplete. It is a gap in sense that gestures to something else Cain cannot see. But it lets through a significant thought. The night, Byron says elsewhere, is 'a religious concern'.[46] Cain sort of does but sort of does not recognise God in dark matter. Act II gazes at the 'multiplying masses of increased / And still-increasing lights' (II, i, 100–1) but also at the darkness that surrounds them and engulfs them. Mosaics create light, but in so doing, they also make darkness visible.

Two months after Shelley left Ravenna, Byron moved to Pisa. There he showed his drama to the Shelley circle, and Percy realised ruefully that he had not managed to shake Byron's tendency to recur to the 'delusions of Christianity'.[47] Mary Shelley heard it slightly differently: 'To me it sounds like a revelation [...]. One has perhaps stood on the extreme verge of such ideas and from the midst of the darkness which has surrounded us the voice of the Poet now is heard telling a wondrous tale.'[48] The echo of the prophet Isaiah is fitting. Steffan assumes that the art of *Cain* is flawed, but I think it is more likely to be part of a deliberate, utterly uncompromising rigidity: the God of Byron's mystery play does not look like Jupiter or a Tory or an Austrian or the Emperor Justinian. He has to be much worse than that. 'I form the light, and create darkness: I make peace, and create evil: I the Lord do all these things', says the God of Isaiah (45:7). Byron's drama, like the mosaic icons of Ravenna, is a moment of contact with the unknowable, the unseeable and the unsayable. In its starkness, the form of *Cain* departs from all Byron's previously stated aesthetic preferences, but not from what he could see around him in Ravenna's religious art.

Acknowledgements

I am grateful to the Leverhulme Trust for the Research Fellowship that enabled this research and to the Harry Ransom Center at the University of Texas at Austin for allowing me to consult and quote from Byron's draft manuscript of *Cain*.

Notes

1 T. Guiccioli, *Lord Byron's Life in Italy*, trans. M. Rees, ed. P. Cochran (Newark, Del.: University of Delaware Press, 2005), p. 142.

2   See Byron's letter to Thomas Moore of 8 March 1822, *BLJ*, vol. IX, p. 123.
3   Letter to John Murray of 12 October 1817, in *BLJ*, vol. V, p. 268.
4   B. Haley, *Living Forms: Romantics and the Monumental Figure* (Albany, NY: State University of New York, 2003), p. 170.
5   Letter to John Murray of 14 April 1817, in *BLJ*, vol. V, p. 213.
6   See J. A. W. Heffernan, *Museum of Words: The Poetics of Ekphrasis from Homer to Ashbery* (Chicago, Ill.: University of Chicago Press, 1996), p. 133; M. McCue, *British Romanticism and the Reception of Italian Old Master Art, 1793–1840* (Farnham: Ashgate, 2014), p. 116; J. J. McGann, *The Beauty of Inflections: Literary Investigations in Historical Method and Theory* (Oxford: Oxford University Press, 1985), p. 325; J. Sachs, *Romantic Antiquity: Rome in the British Imagination, 1789–1832* (Oxford: Oxford University Press, 2010); C. Chard, *Pleasure and Guilt on the Grand Tour: Travel Writing and Imaginative Geography, 1600–1830* (Manchester: Manchester University Press, 1999); S. Cheeke, *Writing for Art: The Aesthetics of Ekphrasis* (Manchester: Manchester University Press, 2008); C. Kenyon Jones, '"Of painting I know nothing": Byron's response to some European art', *Newstead Abbey Review* (2016), 32–46.
7   However, see Richard C. Sha's diagnosis of a profound ambivalence to monuments in *Childe Harold's Pilgrimage* in *Visual and Verbal Sketch in British Romanticism* (Philadelphia, Pa.: University of Pennsylvania Press, 1998), p. 188, and Janice Hewlett Koelb's questioning of modern criticism's very limited definition of ekphrasis in *The Poetics of Description* (Basingstoke: Palgrave Macmillan, 2006).
8   Cheeke notes the relationship between ekphrasis and digression in *Writing for Art*, p. 19.
9   For a recent exploration of the rhetorical force of dashes in stanzas 96 and 97 of *Childe Harold* III, see S. J. Wolfson, '"This is *my* lightning"; or sparks in the air', *SEL*, 55 (autumn 2015), 751–86. Wolfson reads the speed of the manuscript dashes as 'a lightning on the page that seems too impatient for any other punctuation' (p. 765). Murray's team opted for commas. Byron delegated the meaning of manuscript dashes to his editors (whether in the house of John Murray or John Hunt), who had the task of interpreting whether the mark was being used as an edgy lighting conductor or as a contemplative musical rest.
10 The dash in stanza 66 of *Don Juan* V replicates Laurence Sterne's art of *verbum sat* – see *The Life and Opinions of Tristram Shandy*, ed. Graham Petrie (London: Penguin, 1986), p. 427.
11 *BLJ*, vol. VII, pp. 170–1.
12 M. Valery, *Historical, Literary, and Artistical Travels in Italy* (Paris: Baudry's European Library, 1842), pp. 415–16.

13　See J. Hale, *England and the Italian Renaissance* (London: Fontana, 1996), pp. 55–78, for Vasari's role in the formation of English taste.
14　John Milton, *Paradise Regain'd… to which is added Samson Agonistes; and Poems Upon Several Occasions* (London: Strachan and Rivington, 1785), p. 373.
15　Lady M. Wortley Montagu, *Letters Written During Her Travels in Europe, Asia, and Africa to Persons of Distinction, Men of Letters &c. in Different Parts of Europe* (London: Thomas Martin, 1790), p. 135.
16　T. Smollett, *Travels through France and Italy*, 2 vols (Dublin: Robert Johnston, 1766), vol. II, p. 115.
17　William Wordsworth, 'On Re-visiting Dunolly Castle' (l. 5), in *Wordsworth: Poetical Works*, ed. T. Hutchinson and E. de Selincourt (Oxford: Oxford University Press, 1985); P. B. Shelley, *Percy Bysshe Shelley: The Major Works*, ed. Z. Leader and M. O'Neill (Oxford: Oxford University Press, 2003), p. 697.
18　Letter to John Cam Hobhouse of 26 May 1816, in *BLJ*, vol. V, p. 78.
19　Guiccioli, *Lord Byron's Life in Italy*, p. 142.
20　Letter to Teresa Guiccioli of 11 June 1819, in *BLJ*, vol. VI, p. 154; Guiccioli, *Lord Byron's Life in Italy*, pp. 144, 146, 152.
21　Letter of 14 June 1819, in *BLJ*, vol. VI, p. 156.
22　Guiccioli, *Lord Byron's Life in Italy*, p. 248.
23　Gavin Hopps, 'Gaiety and grace: Byron and the tone of Catholicism', *The Byron Journal*, 40:1 (2013), 1–14.
24　See P. B. Shelley, *The Letters of Percy Bysshe Shelley*, 2 vols, ed. F. L. Jones (Oxford: Clarendon Press, 1964), vol. II, p. 330.
25　See C. E. Robinson, *Shelley and Byron: The Snake and the Eagle Wreathed in Fight* (Baltimore, Md.: Johns Hopkins University Press, 1976), pp. 195–201.
26　See Byron's letter to John Murray of 26 April 1817, in *BLJ*, vol. V, pp. 217–19.
27　Letter of 8 August 1821, in Shelley, *Letters of Percy Bysshe Shelley*, vol. II, p. 321.
28　Letter to J. Mawman of 31 August 1821, in *BLJ*, vol. VIII, p. 195.
29　Letter to Count Giuseppe Alborghetti of 15 August 1821, in *BLJ*, vol. VIII, p. 180.
30　Letter to Mary Shelley of 8 August 1821, in Shelley, *Letters of Percy Bysshe Shelley*, vol. II, p. 321.
31　Letter to Mary Shelley of 8 August 1821, in Shelley, *Letters of Percy Bysshe Shelley*, vol. II, p. 322.
32　H. James, *Italian Hours*, ed. John Auchard (Harmondsworth: Penguin, 1995), p. 299.
33　James, *Italian Hours*, p. 299.

34 D. M. Deliyannis, *Ravenna in Late Antiquity* (Cambridge: Cambridge University Press, 2010), p. 192.
35 James, *Italian Hours*, p. 298.
36 Letter to Douglas Kinnaird of 4 November 1821 (in *BLJ*, vol. IX, p. 56) and letter to Thomas Moore of 19 September 1821 (in *BLJ*, vol. VIII, p. 216).
37 James, *Italian Hours*, pp. 297–8.
38 James, *Italian Hours*, p. 297.
39 Letter to Horace Smith of 14 September 1821, in Shelley, *The Letters of Percy Bysshe Shelley*, vol. II, p. 349; letters to John Murray of 14 July and 16 February 1821, letter to Douglas Kinnaird of 27 September 1821, in *BLJ*, vol. VIII, pp. 152, 78 and 223.
40 Letter to Douglas Kinnaird of 27 September 1821, in *BLJ*, vol. VIII p. 152; T. G. Steffan, *Lord Byron's Cain* (Austin, Tex.: University of Texas Press, 1968), pp. 92, 108. For a more recent discussion of 'Byron's labour to disfigure his poetry for dramatic effect', see M. Callaghan, 'The struggle with language in Byron's *Cain*', *The Byron Journal*, 38:2 (2010), 125–34 (p. 125).
41 See, for example, the *British Review*, 19 (December 1822), p. 78. For *Cain*'s reception, see Steffan, *Lord Byron's Cain*, and R. Mortenson, *Byron's Waterloo: The Reception of Cain, A Mystery* (Seattle, Wash.: Iron Press, 2015).
42 *CPW*, vol. VI, p. 229.
43 D. Brown, *God and Enchantment of Place: Reclaiming Human Experience* (Oxford: Oxford University Press, 2004), pp. 49, 20.
44 Letter to Thomas Moore of 2 August 1821, letter to John Murray of 14 July 1821, in *BLJ*, vol. VIII, pp. 165, 152.
45 Steffan, *Lord Byron's Cain*, p. 197.
46 'Detached thoughts', No. 100, in *BLJ*, vol. IX, p. 46.
47 Letter to Horace Smith of 11 April 1822, in Shelley, *The Letters of Percy Bysshe Shelley*, vol. II, p. 412.
48 Letter to Maria Gisborne of '?20–21 December [1821]', in M. Shelley, *The Letters of Mary Wollstonecraft Shelley*, ed. B. Bennett (Baltimore, Md.: Johns Hopkins University Press, 1991), vol. I, p. 212.

6

'Something sensible to grasp at': Byron and Italian Catholicism

Bernard Beatty

Byron, aged ten, moved from Presbyterian Aberdeen to Newstead Abbey in 1798. The abbey was despoiled at the Reformation but still bore witness to 'the old faith and the old feelings' (*DJ*, XV, 46) that had shaped it. It was, presumably, Byron's first direct exposure to any kind of Catholicism. Some twenty-five years later and in Italy, he is still writing about it and presenting it as a secular house that still preserves something of its sacral, specifically Catholic, character. He is clearly sympathetic to this, but the first references in his poetry to Catholicism tell a different tale.

The most significant of these is in the lines on Mafra in *Childe Harold's Pilgrimage* I. There,

> mass and revel were alternate seen;
> Lordlings and frères – ill sorted fry I ween!
> But here the Babylonian whore hath built
> A dome where flaunts she in such glorious sheen,
> That men forget the blood which she hath spilt
> And bow the knee to Pomp that loves to varnish guilt.
>
> (29)

This is Byron's first exposure to Catholicism in practice, and he responds like John Knox. The Catholic Church is Scarlet Woman and Babylon. It, or She, is murderous, rich, showy and illicitly powerful. There is a shocking alliance between religion and pleasure ('mass and revel') and between church and state ('Lordlings and freres'). Guilt, varnished or not, is Catholicism's home territory. But then it is also Byron's.

No one commented adversely on these lines when they were published since what they say had been agreed commonplaces since the

Gunpowder Plot. The major Romantic writers were mostly scornful of Catholicism (Coleridge, Scott and Mary Shelley are, to some extent, exceptions) though they might use some of its terminology when it suited them. Wordsworth, for instance, unlike Byron and Coleridge, was vehemently opposed to Catholic Emancipation and appalled by the idea that his daughter would want to marry a practising Catholic.[1] Shelley's preface to *The Cenci* berated the gap, as he saw it, between morality and the practice of religious belief in Italy. Byron's distant relation, Lord George Gordon, had led violent anti-Catholic riots in London only thirty years before Byron's lines were written.

Byron presents himself as a similarly appalled outsider here, but in the tales written immediately after the first cantos of *Childe Harold's Pilgrimage*, he can be both sympathetic outsider and even insider to Catholic experience. In *The Giaour*, for instance, the main character joins a Franciscan abbey (this is Byron's undeliberate mistake since male Franciscans do not have abbeys) and makes a long confession to a friar who 'shrived him on his dying day' (1332). The confession is more Rousseauistic than Catholic since the Giaour, like Byronic heroes in general, is guilty but not penitent. He wishes to display rather than change himself. On the other hand, in *Parisina* (published in 1816 but written earlier), Byron's first Italian poem, Hugo confesses like a good Catholic, and the narrator appears to share his conviction:

> As his last confession pouring
> To the monk, his doom deploring
> In penitential holiness,
> He bends to hear his accents bless
> With absolution such as may
> Wipe our mortal stains away.
> (413–18)

This is the first time that Byron, or, here, his narrator, has adopted a Catholic voice, and, as it happens, it is also an Italian one. This is a pattern that will be repeated. As Byron acknowledges in his preface, Gibbon was the source of his story, but Gibbon, briefly a Catholic convert and then anti-Christian ('Sapping a solemn creed with solemn sneer' says Byron in stanza 107 of *Childe Harold* III), gives no suggestion as to Hugo's Catholic end. Though set in Italy, the tale lacks, as Peter Cochran notes, the local colourings that characterise his Eastern tales.² Byron had not been to Italy yet and, anyway, wants a stark and schematic effect. Part of this schema is clearly to contrast Hugo's externally witnessed repentance and peace with Azo's wholly repressed guilt and anguish. This is the main aesthetic reason for Hugo's confession, but it is interesting how precisely Byron understands the sequence of confession, which depends upon expressed penitence, then the priest's absolution which, in turn, wipes away 'mortal stains'. The vocabulary ('mortal' here denotes the category of mortal as opposed to venial sins) is technical and accurate. It is in marked contrast with the luridly Gothic presentations of confession in Radcliffe's *The Italian*, which lie behind *The Giaour*. Radcliffe, too, has a penchant for Franciscan abbeys.

The same precision startles the reader of *The Siege of Corinth*, set in the Venetian territory of Corinth. Like *The Giaour*, the poem moves between contrasted Muslim and Catholic worlds. The besieged Venetians cluster in a church where Mass has earlier been said. Byron forces us to register this vividly:

> On its table still behold
> The cup of consecrated gold;
> Massy and deep, a glittering prize,
> Brightly it sparkles to plunderers' eyes –
> That morn it held the holy wine,
> Converted by Christ to His blood so divine,
> Which His worshippers drank at the break of day
> To shrive their souls ere they joined in the fray,
> Still a few drops within it lay.
>
> (953–61)

Once again, there is an aesthetic and thematic reason for this detail. As I have argued elsewhere, the poem, like *Hamlet*, establishes careful contrasts between different ways of being dead or alive after death, and this is one of them.³ In the most important of the details (the remains of Christ's blood still in the chalice), it is not accurate, for any Mass involves careful ablutions, yet the overtly tangible detail clearly intrigues the poet in itself but does so only in so far as, once again, the narrator takes an insider Catholic position on the sacrament. This is not Protestant wine as symbol but wine actually changed ('Converted by Christ') into blood. In Catholic theology, taking communion does not absolve mortal sins, which contradict it, but it does forgive lesser sins.[4] So Byron is right about 'shriving their souls' too. On its publication in 1816, this was perhaps the most precise and sympathetic account of transubstantiation in English since Crashaw and Dryden (both converts to Catholicism). We will return to these drops of blood in the conclusion of this chapter.

Byron's other Italian poems – *The Lament of Tasso*, *Beppo*, *The Prophecy of Dante* and his translation of part of *Morgante Maggiore* – were all written in Italy. Byron had visited Ferrara, wrote *Beppo* in Beppo's Venice and *The Prophecy of Dante* in Dante's Ravenna, so allusions to place are more vivid, especially in *Beppo*, which depends upon them. Catholicism is now *in situ*.

In comparison with his other Italian texts, in *Beppo* Byron is more outsider than insider. This may seem odd since the poem depends upon Byron's ostentatious foregrounding of his insiderly knowledge of Italian ways. But that is the point. Byron is writing as a very Italianised Englishman writing for an English audience so, though he will flaunt his enthusiasm for Venetian habits of life rather than English ones, he will do so, albeit in *ottava rima*, in a very English voice that naturally utilises standard Protestant ways of ridiculing Catholicism. Thus, Catholic 'repentance' coincides with a determination to sin (stanza 1); Catholic clergy have too much power and are mainly concerned with getting money by saying Masses for the dead to relieve the pains of Purgatory (stanza 2 and, similarly, 98); Catholicism is a religion of excessive austerity and of excessive licence (stanzas 7–9). These are the only direct references to Catholicism.

Yet the placing of the poem's action in relation to the liturgical year is real enough and new. If we read Byron's letters before 1816, his references to Christmas are perfunctory and to Easter non-existent. He lives in secular time. But once in Italy this changes. He notices when it is Holy Week, he notices the punctuation and shaping of the year by religious festivals, he notices the bells for Vespers and the Angelus that punctuate the day. He does so because he is increasingly an insider, and every Italian does so. As Shelley notes with horror, Catholicism in Italy 'is interwoven with the whole fabric of life'.[5] *Beppo* inaugurates a pattern of attention to this fact.

Byron's poetry had always been concerned with sin and guilt, but, when placed in Italy, as we have seen in *Parisina*, sin is forgivable either sacramentally or by an open tolerance of waywardness, especially of sexual waywardness. Thus, when he says in stanza 24 of *Beppo* that 'in Christian countries' it is easier, indeed expected, that married women will have lovers, he mainly means Catholic countries such as Italy. And so the end of the poem, where, in effect, Beppo forgives Laura and the count for having been lovers and settles happily into a modus vivendi with them, seems to be a Catholic ending as well as a comic one. Indeed, the two go together. Byron can, for the first time, sustain long comic poems in Catholic Italy.

This is quite possibly the first time that this note, which depends upon a delicate interplay between forgiveness and transgression rather than a Protestant insistence on their conjoined separation in the very midst of salvation (Luther's famous 'simul peccator et iustus'[6]), had been fully sounded in English poetry since Chaucer who, like Byron here, lived in a Catholic world. 'Luther's greatest merit', said Nietzsche approvingly, 'was to have had the courage of his sensuality'. Nietzsche associates Luther here with his claim that there 'is no inherent contradiction between chastity and pleasure', but Luther's enthusiasm for marriage was quite separate from his earlier attempt at monastic asceticism, which he later rejected and Nietzsche, son of a Lutheran pastor, disliked Catholic asceticism.[7] In Chaucer's Catholic world and that of *Beppo*, there is distinction, interplay and reciprocity between forgiveness and transgression, just as Byron associates the monks of Newstead Abbey with both licence and austerity. Laura's Venice still embodies this.[8] Byron was as at home on monastic San Lazzaro as he was in the carnival.

The remaining Italian poems wholly abandon the outsiderly non-Catholic narrator. They are either dramatic monologues, for Byron played a decisive role in creating the genre, or translations from Italian. Either way, the speaking voice assumes Catholic belief, which, in turn, whether the mode is *opera buffa* or *seria*, presupposes specifically Catholic doctrines. These are the same doctrines in which Byron insisted that his illegitimate daughter, Allegra, was to be educated.

None of these poems is primarily a religious poem, but religion is not extrinsic to their concerns. Both Tasso and Dante (by which, for the moment, I will mean Byron's Tasso and Byron's Dante) regard their poems as religious in orientation and see themselves as inspired by God in their writings. In Dante's case, this means Byron's present poem, which he is voicing, as well as *La Divina Commedia*, for, in a striking passage that opens Canto II, he claims that the same inspiration that filled Israel's prophets is upon him (1–9). In an even more startling claim, he weeps over Florence as Christ did over Jerusalem and wishes, like Christ, to be a mother hen to its inhabitants (I, 60–4). Like the psalmist, he sees the cries for justice by suffering Italians 'rising o'er / The seraph voices' and reaching the Almighty (III, 18–19).

More specifically Catholic, both Tasso and Dante fuse religious vocabulary with erotic devotion to the feminine as some sort of deity. Tasso's Leonora is worshipped as a shrine on saintly ground. He is in awe of her as he is of God himself (129–35). Dante's Beatrice blesses him 'with her light' (I, 11–12), and she is his 'sole pure seraph' (I, 20). Dante may see himself as Isaiah redivivus, but he addresses God as Trinity with the same precision of reference that we have already encountered (I, 13–14). Catholic Italy has made Byron more precisely and variedly theological than his bedrock, thin but powerful, Calvinist-tinged, assumptions about election and damnation, which wholly excluded the feminine from devotional sensibility and doctrinal insight, have done. Byron's advertisement to his translation of the first canto of *Morgante Maggiore* confirms this, but in an interesting and important formulation he defends the coexistence of reverence and irreverence in Catholicism:

> It has never yet been decided entirely, whether Pulci's intention was or was not to deride the religion, which is one of his favourite topics. It appears to me, that such an intention would have been no less hazardous to the poet than to the priest, particularly in that age and country, and the permission to publish the poem, and its reception among the classics of Italy, prove that it neither was nor is so interpreted. That he intended to ridicule the monastic life, and suffered his imagination to play with the simple dulness of his converted giant, seems evident enough; but surely it were as unjust to accuse him of irreligion on this account, as to denounce Fielding for his Parson Adams [...] or Scott for his exquisite use of the Covenanters.[9]

Byron is as much concerned with what would be acceptable, even expected, 'in that age and country' (fifteenth-century Italy) as with the personality and views of Pulci himself. He was often to emphasise this point.

The conjunction of reverence and irreverence is not unique to Catholic Italy for Byron compares it to Fielding's England and Scott's version of seventeenth-century Scotland, but Byron's interest in it is increased because Pulci was a priest. The Covenanters themselves, after all, made a sharp distinction between reverence and irreverence – it is only barely religious Scott who can unite them centuries later. Protestant Fielding was deliberately writing in the manner of Catholic Cervantes. His Parson Adams is a saintly simpleton rather than a corrupt figure. Yet neither Fielding nor Scott could possibly write the curious mixture of precise theology and comically intimate invocation which we find in stanzas 1 and 2 of Byron's *Morgante*:

> In the beginning was the Word next God,
>   God was the Word, the Word no less than He:
> This was in the beginning, to my mode
>   Of thinking, and without him nought could be.
> Therefore, just Lord! from out thy high abode,
>   Benign and pious, bid an angel flee,
> One only, to be my companion, who
> Shall help my famous, worthy, old song through.
>
> And thou, oh Virgin! Daughter, mother, bride,
>   Of the same Lord, who gave to you each key
> Of heaven and hell, and everything beside,
>   The day thy Gabriel said, 'All hail' to thee,
> Since to thy servants pity ne'er denied,
>   With flowing rhymes, a pleasant style and free,
> Be to my verses then benignly kind
> And to the end illuminate my mind.

It is precisely this mixture of insider reverence and intimacy with Catholic doctrine and devotion and outsider cockiness that interested Byron. Teresa Guiccioli said that one of his main aims in writing was to 'demonstrate how much was permitted in a Catholic country, and in an age of living faith'.[10] Similarly, the divine world is both masculine and feminine for the invocation is to God and to Mary. Mary is particularly associated with helping Pulci's poetry to be supple and femininely attractive: 'con dolce rime e stil grato e soave' ('with sweet rhymes and a graceful and gentle style').[11]

Byron translated Pulci while he was writing Canto III of *Don Juan*, though he first encountered Pulci through Merivale's translation of the last four cantos in 1814. He clearly wished to associate his own translation with the writing of *Don Juan*. He described the first canto of *Don Juan* as being 'in the style of Beppo – and Pulci – forgive me for putting Pulci second it is a slip – "Ego et Rex meus"'.[12] The

Latin formula ('I and my king') is attributed to Cardinal Wolsey and implies false arrogance in putting himself before Pulci as responsible for the style of *Don Juan*. And we find Pulci's mingling of Catholic doctrine and feeling with a light-hearted move away from it in the 'Ave Maria' stanzas of *Don Juan* (III, 102–4), which were written, so far as we can tell, at almost the same time that he was translating him.

Writing about these stanzas, Gavin Hopps convincingly takes issue with Jerome McGann and Moyra Haslett, who both see the stanzas as mocking the Immaculate Conception, which they grotesquely misunderstand as the conception of Christ rather than of Mary herself. By a careful reading of these stanzas, Hopps demonstrates that Byron's allusion is both vaguer and more complex than this and, certainly, not simply 'irreverent'.[13] Yet McGann and Haslett both correctly presume that Byron thinks with some theological precision here and elsewhere. For we find a similar mix of theological insight and irreverence mingled with faith when Byron talks about believing in Mary's 'mystical virginity', 'the usual Origin of Evil' and 'the whole Trinity' (*DJ*, XI, 6) or being drawn to the idea of transubstantiation.[14] It seems likely that it is Byron's exposure to Italian Catholicism in past texts and present habits that explains this. Certainly, the move from sneering at churches in Portugal and Spain defiled by 'monkish incense' (*CHP*, I, 67) to his extraordinary praise of St Peter's as an 'eternal ark of worship undefiled' (*CHP*, IV, 154) is a huge shift. Whereas Byron now sees St Peter's as a new and better temple, Wordsworth was adamant that Catholicism could never be 'a temple of the true God'.[15] How else can we explain this shift in Byron? Neither Catholicism in other countries nor the Orthodox Church in Greece ever gain Byron's reverent attention. Yet St Peter's is 'Christ's mighty shrine above his martyr's tomb!' (*CHP*, IV, 153). And Byron hails Italy in the most un-Protestant of voices as

> Parent of our Religion! Whom the wide
> Nations have knelt too for the keys of heaven!
> Europe, repentant of her parricide,
> Shall yet redeem thee.
>
> (*CHP*, IV, 47)

It is striking that Byron here associates Italy's right to political liberty with the claims of Catholicism to be the oldest form of Christianity ('the best religion as it is assuredly the oldest of the various branches of Christianity'[16]) and to hold a proper spiritual power unique to it.

If we turn now more directly to the life rather than poems of Byron we might expect that his experience of Italian Catholicism would begin with his first acquaintance with Italy in 1816, but this is not the case. On 19 August 1810, Byron returned to Athens and lodged in the Franciscan Capuchin Convent. By this time he had already written those *Childe Harold* stanzas that are so critical of Portuguese and Spanish Catholicism. The monastery was then a common lodging place for European visitors. There was only one friar there, Father Paolo. It had been founded in 1658 for the Franks in the city, and it came to be run by Italians. Father Paolo administered to some forty Catholics in the city. All the boys in the convent had Italian names like Byron's favourite Niccolo Giraud, though his family was French. Byron notes that some were Greeks, and, jokingly, he calls them 'Schismatics', that is he sees them from a Catholic point of view.[17] Byron sets himself to learn Italian, not least because Italian was the lingua franca there, translating not only Horace into Italian but also some 'prayers out of the Mass ritual'.[18] What was Byron's attitude to Father Paolo? There is some little known information about this.

In 1825, a French doctor called Lauvergne was in Chios where he met Father Paolo, forced to leave Athens because of the Independence War. Lauvergne asked about his memories of Byron and then wrote them up. He says that 'the ministry and gentleness of Fr Paolo' had so conquered his lordship's affections that the latter, ordinarily enigmatic in all his social relations, gave way with him to all the peculiarities of his character'. Paolo himself is reported as saying that Byron came to him once in profound melancholy and 'asked to live in a friar's cell, to eat with us'. 'He clasped my hands as he called me Father.' There is then a very long account purporting to be Byron's remembered words about the causes of his melancholy – much the sort of confession that the Giaour makes. It is difficult to know how much credence to give to this – it happened fifteen years earlier, but clearly something happened. This is how it ended:

> Then he moved towards a corner of my room, and taking down a beautiful crucifix which I had brought from Rome, he put it in my hands. I offered it to Byron, saying to him: 'Here is the comforter of the misfortunate.' He took it with rapture and kissing it several times

he added with his eyes bathed in tears: 'My hands will not desecrate it for long, and my mother will soon be the guardian of your precious memento.'[19]

Byron's kissing the friar's crucifix is a reverse image of the dying Lara's rejection of the crucifix held out to him (*Lara*, II, 477–85) for which the suddenly pious narrator rebukes him (II, 486–8), but this is not Byron becoming a Catholic, though it helps to explain why Scott only a few years later thought that he might do so in a markedly ascetic form and that Byron 'seemed to allow I might be right'.[20] It is clear, however, that Byron associates Catholicism, here in Italian and monastic form, with undercurrents in his being, with guilt and forgiveness, and with the tangible as sign of the spiritual, for he grasps the friar's hands, takes and kisses the crucifix. The dying Manfred explicitly rejects the proffered Catholicism of the Abbot, but he, too, asks for the Abbot's hand and is holding it while he dies (*Manfred*, III, iv, 109).

There is another element here, though, which becomes the hallmark of Byron's later relationship with Italian Catholicism. According to the story, Byron wanted to live in a friar's cell, to immerse himself in a way of life. His later excursions to San Lazzaro were perhaps as much to associate himself with monastic life as with learning Armenian. Even without the story, the convent in Athens was Byron's normal address despite various lengthy excursions for some eight months. He lived, though in Greece, within the norms of Italian Catholic life. His flirtation with this continued whereas his flirtation with pederasty at the same time did not, until he left Italy in 1823 and was once again in Greece. The movement in and out of an insiderly relationship to Italian Catholicism begins here.

When Byron does eventually settle in real Italy as opposed to an Italian outpost, we find the same pattern of familiarity, but with a difference. Byron used frocked or unfrocked priests, Don Perelli and one Don Giovanni,[21] as go-betweens in the early stages of his affair with Teresa and employed one, Lega Zambelli, as his steward. He knew both cardinal legates in Ravenna and their secretary, Count Alborghetti, extremely well and even sent some medicine to the cardinal. ('If he takes it properly it will do him good.'[22]) Teresa's separation from her husband was authorised directly by Pope Pius VII, who, as a bishop, had officiated at the wedding of Teresa's grandparents.[23] Byron, slightly ironically, therefore called him 'the most just of all Popes', but he usually speaks of him with respect.[24] On the occasion of the Neapolitan uprising he is reported to have said:

> I respect the Pope very much: he has qualities that command esteem; I should have been displeased had he shown less concern; but I should like to see Catholics make common cause with the others in order to give Italy a political point of view different from that which it has now.[25]

Byron gave money to churches and monasteries for all sorts of reasons ('two crowns to the Prior of San Matteo for coming to bless the house [...] a crown for the Madonna of Montenero', etc.).[26] His habitual generosity came increasingly to resemble Catholic acts of charity to the poor (his Pisan accounts list gifts to 'a poor old lame woman', 'two Franciscan nuns' and 'ten poor men'), and he saw it as this: 'met an old man. Charity – purchased a shilling's worth of salvation'.[27] Byron's valet reminisced after Byron's death: 'I have seen my Lord repeatedly, on meeting or passing any religious ceremonies, [...] dismount his horse and fall on his knees, and remain in that posture till the procession had passed.'[28] The contrast with Goethe's, Coleridge's, Shelley's or the Brownings' relationship to Italian Catholicism is obvious. They look down on it or see through it. Byron does not. Here, for instance, is what he said, according to Teresa, to Pietro Gamba in 1821:

> Time and reflection have changed my mind on these subjects, and I consider Atheism as a folly. As for Catholicism, so little is it objectionable to me, that I wish my daughter to be brought up in that religion, and some day marry a Catholic. If Catholicism, after all, suggests difficulties of a nature which it is difficult for reason to get over, are these less great than those which Protestantism creates? Are not all the mysteries common to both creeds? Catholicism at least offers the consolation of Purgatory, of the Sacraments, of absolution and forgiveness; whereas Protestantism is barren of consolation for the soul.

Teresa comments that this 'profession of faith, expressed by such a man as Lord Byron, in a calm and dispassionate tone, produced a great impression upon the young count'.[29] It is not quite a profession of faith but shows a sympathetic understanding of it. That he had, as he claimed, changed his mind can be seen in the distance between his attraction to transubstantiation when in Italy with his earlier remark to Dallas on 21 January 1808: 'I have refused to take the Sacrament because I do not think that eating Bread or drinking wine from the hand of an earthly vicar, will make me an Inheritor of Heaven.'[30] His earlier self is doubly Protestant in his suspicion of earthly mediators and in his assumption that Eucharistic bread and wine are no more than bread and wine.

The difference between this Ravenna world and Byron's Athenian world is that the latter was a male one, but in Italy, though he has wide and relaxed relations with clerical figures of all ranks (while acquiring some elements of a specifically Italian anti-clericalism), women dominate his life as courtesans, mistresses, convenors of *Conversazioni* and, in Teresa Guiccioli's case, almost as his wife, through whom he became, for the first time in his life, part of a family.[31] Both Teresa and her grandparents often mothered his daughter, Allegra.[32] Through them he acquired a different perspective on Catholicism, but it was one in which, again, reverence and irreverence are mixed. For instance, he notes that his main Venetian mistress 'was very devout – and would cross herself if she heard the prayer-time strike – sometimes – when that ceremony did not appear to be much in unison with what she was then about'.[33] Presumably he means in the midst of lovemaking. At the same time, strong women become more and more important and vocal in his poetry. They are often lightly or strongly associated with religious belief. At the same time, too, and often associated with this, forgiveness and rebirth after some kind of death become as real a force as guilt in such poems as *Mazeppa*, *The Vision of Judgment*, *Don Juan* and *The Island*. I would call this, roughly, a Marian cluster in his verse. Precisely as such it seems to have enabled Byron to articulate much more clearly and distinctly, in *Cain* and *Heaven and Earth*, the tangle of Calvinist emphases on election and damnation that had hovered around his pre-Italian writings.

We can link these elements with two others, clearly connected in the curious way that things are unexpectedly connected in Byron. The first is given by my title – 'something sensible to grasp at'. The second will take us back through *The Siege of Corinth* to Byron's understanding of written language. Italian Catholicism is the matrix of both.

Byron's often quoted words, implicitly present throughout this essay, on 'tangible religion' occur when he expresses his surprise to Thomas Moore that *Cain* has created an uproar. He says that he himself thought it 'a speculative, and hardy, but still a harmless production' and then goes on to say this about Catholicism:

> I am really a great admirer of tangible religion; and am breeding one of my daughters a Catholic, that she may have her hands full [...]. What with incense, pictures, statues, altars, shrines, relics, and the real presence, confession, absolution, – there is something sensible to grasp at. Besides it leaves no possibility of doubt: for those who swallow their Deity, really and truly, in transubstantiation, can hardly find anything else otherwise than easy of digestion.
> I am afraid this may sound flippant, but I don't mean it to be so.[34]

We should note the contrast here between the adjectives for *Cain* ('speculative, and hardy'), both of which imply aloof separation from interacting life, and the interactive physical processes ('tangible', 'hands full', 'grasp at', 'swallow', 'digestion') that are the life and also the attraction of Catholicism. Both sides of this equation are reflected in the play. Cain murders Abel, in part, because he dislikes the tangible religion of sacrifice. He is at home in speculation and the sky and in dislike of an intangible God who elects and damns without, so to speak, any suggestion that he might make himself available, ludicrously and humbly, to be swallowed. Byron's increasing knowledge of Catholicism has enabled him to revisit his earlier quasi-Calvinist assumptions with greater articulacy. But it has also given him an increasing sense of Catholic possibility: Adah, in her defence of Seraphic Love's superiority to Luciferian knowledge (*Cain*, I, i, 420–2), is a proto-Catholic, feminine voice in this starker world.

This second, positive response to Italian Catholicism as 'tangible' is the opposite of that of most English travellers to Italy of the time. William Rae's reaction to sacramentalism, detailed in his 1835 *Records of a Route through France and Italy; with Sketches of Catholicism*, is one of sustained outrage. When he sees devout Catholics rushing towards some newly blessed holy water in Turin, for instance, he denounces 'the tendency of Catholicism to unspiritualise religion; to divest it as much as possible of its mentality if such a term be allowable by rendering all that is connected with it tangible, material, corporeal'.[35] Byron's use of 'grasp at' is particularly helpful in revealing his different attitude. It is linked with the apparently flippant usage that Allegra, as a Catholic, will have 'her hands full'. We can link it, too, with Father Paolo's memory that Byron took a crucifix and 'put it in my hands'. This is in marked, one might say deliberate, contrast with his words to Dallas when he was twenty about refusing 'the sacrament from the hand of an earthly vicar'. The earliest uses of 'grasp', often with 'at', refer to the blind trying to find their way in darkness.[36] Byron's use of 'grasp at' in this context is both that of an agnostic seeking and of a Doubting Thomas who finds belief through the reciprocities of touch. Catholicism offers this. Calvinism and all Byron's pre-Italian religious experience do not. We can also link it with the marked difference between the first intangible ghost in Canto XV of *Don Juan* and the second one whose identity is discovered when Juan's arm 'pressed upon a hard but glowing bust' (XVI, 122), which is set as an *exemplum* in an extended discourse in the final cantos about the relationship between faith, fiction and evidence. One joy in reading Byron is in gradually coming to recognise the extraordinary jumps and connections between the apparently disparate in his customary thought. This is innate in him, but Italy (Aurora and Fitz-Fulke, from opposite directions, disrupt an Anglo-Saxon world) authorises him as confident spokesman of his customary bias.

Byron emphasises the tangible, but it is clearly quite wrong to see this, as materialist critics such as McGann and Jerome Christensen have confidently done, as endorsing the material world's evidentiality against the illusory world of spirit. McGann, in particular, valiantly battled to enlist Byron against the other Romantics, as seen particularly through the eyes of American secular, transcendentalist critics (Abrams, Bloom, Hartman). He was right to do so but wrong in thinking that Byron's undermining of their spilt religion meant that he was an assured sapper of religion as such. Sometimes he is, more usually he is not. The whole point of Byron's paragraph is that the tangible is an assured sign of the spiritual. Byron, no theologian as such, instinctively intuits sacramental theology in a way that would not become recognised in Protestant England until the Oxford Movement. Newman was received into the Catholic Church by Dominic Barberi, an Italian Passionist, some twenty years after Byron's death, but he understood Catholicism in a particularly English way, much as Byron's specifically Italian Catholic experience enabled him to produce, as it were out of nowhere, his English Catholic heroine Aurora Raby. Byron borrows from Pulci's poem the common comic device of giving physical attributes to angels, so that the angels in *The Vision of Judgment* can sprain their wings and cough.[37] Elsewhere in his poetry he gives entirely convincing realisation to spirits, angels and demons. He is heir to Dante as well as

Pulci for he is on both sides of the fence or, more particularly, on the fence itself, 'the horizon's verge' (*DJ*, XV, 99), where spirit turns into matter and matter into spirit.

Byron's pivotal position is that of the human composite placed, as Byron's favourite poet put it, 'on this isthmus of a middle state'.[38] It is also, in a much commented upon passage, that of the writer as such:

> But words are things, and a small drop of ink,
>   Falling like dew, upon a thought, produces
> That which makes thousands, perhaps millions, think;
>   'Tis strange, the shortest letter which man uses
> Instead of speech, may form a lasting link
>   Of ages.
>
> (*DJ*, III, 88)

Here the material object, ink, turns into a thought for 'think' literally contains 'ink'. That is the main point. A writer thinks, the thought turns into ink, the reader turns it back into thought again but could not do so without the ink. But it is complicated by the way that it is the ink itself which falls 'like dew, upon a thought', which implies a causal fertile energy within the material ink. The poet is not simply a spiritual outsider using material ink as instrument since the ink itself, so to speak, is inside the 'think'. Byron discovers his thought already written in the act of writing with ink. This miracle repeats itself in reverse with every reader.

This marks a movement in Byron from orator to writer. He is always both, of course, but from the time of writing his first Italian-idiom poem we catch him observing his own physical act of writing, when his 'pen is at the bottom of a page' (*Beppo*, 99). Such references proliferate in *Don Juan*. But this 'small drop of ink' is also linked to the 'few drops' of Christ's blood which remain in the chalice in *The Siege of Corinth* – a miracle of a different kind but of a similar kind. Byron does not directly make the connection, but his intense perception that the boundaries between matter and spirit can be and are mysteriously crossed in both directions explains his instant understanding of transubstantiation, of the conjunction of the material and the intellectual in writing, and of the material and the spiritual in lovemaking which are the two poles, narrator and narrative, in *Don Juan*. These reach their fullest expression in the interplay between narrator, ghosts, repressed Adeline, fleshly Fitz-Fulke and attractive

Catholic virgin Aurora Raby in the last cantos of *Don Juan*. All this is set in England but written in Catholic Italy where, spiritually, Byron found something sensible to grasp at. I doubt they could have been written anywhere else.

Notes

1. For Wordsworth's attitude to Catholicism, see K. Jones, *A Passionate Sisterhood* (London: Virago, 1998), pp. 260–1.
2. See https://petercochran.files.wordpress.com/2009/03/parisina.pdf, p. 1.
3. B. Beatty, 'Determining unknown modes of being: a map of Byron's ghosts and spirits', in G. Hopps (ed.), *Byron's Ghosts: The Spectral, the Spiritual and the Supernatural* (Liverpool: Liverpool University Press, 2013), pp. 30–47 (p. 37).
4. The most recent and authoritative *Catechism of the Catholic Church* (1997) states that, as 'bodily nourishment restores lost strength, so the Eucharist strengthens our charity, which tends to be weakened in daily life; and this living charity wipes away venial sins' (www.vatican.va/archive/ENG0015/_INDEX.HTM#fonte, p. 1394).
5. Preface to *The Cenci*, in P. B. Shelley, *Shelley's Poetry and Prose*, ed. D. H. Reiman and S. B. Powers (New York: Norton, 1977), p. 241.
6. M. Luther, *Luther's Works*, 55 vols, ed. J. Pelikan and H. T. Lehmann (St Louis, Miss.: Concordia, 1955–85), vol. XXV, p. 260.
7. F. Nietzsche, *The Birth of Tragedy and The Genealogy of Morals*, trans. F. Goffering (New York: Doubleday, 1956), p. 232.
8. Byron is fascinated by the same conjunction of carnival licence and Lenten penance and fasting in Catholic Spain (see *CHP*, I, 78).
9. *CPW*, vol. IV, pp. 247–8.
10. T. Guiccioli, *Lord Byron's Life in Italy*, trans. M. Rees, ed. Peter Cochran (Newark, Del.: University of Delaware Press, 2005), p. 197.
11. L. Pulci, *Morgante Maggiore*, I, stanza 2, in L. Pulci, *Morgante e opere minori*, ed. Aulo Greco (Torino: UTET Libreria, 2004).
12. Letter to John Cam Hobhouse of 11 November 1818, in *BLJ*, vol. VI, p. 76.
13. See G. Hopps, 'Gaiety and grace: Byron and the tone of Catholicism', *The Byron Journal*, 41:1 (2013), 1–14.
14. See Byron's letter to Thomas Moore of 8 March 1822, in *BLJ*, vol. IX, p. 123.
15. Jones, *Passionate Sisterhood*, p. 261.

16 Letter to Richard Belgrave Hoppner of 3 April 1821, in *BLJ*, vol. VIII, p. 98.
17 Letter to John Cam Hobhouse of 23 August 1810, in *BLJ*, vol. II, p. 12.
18 Letter to John Cam Hobhouse of 23 August 1810, in *BLJ*, vol. II, p. 13.
19 H. Lauvergne, *Souvenirs de la Grèce, pendant la campagne de 1825* (Paris: Le Normand Fils, 1826), pp. 233–40. Lauvergne's 'Note on Lord Byron' is translated, quoted in full, and discussed by C. W. J. Eliot in his 'Lord Byron, Father Paul, and the artist William Page', *Hesperia*, 44:4 (1975), 409–25. See also Eliot's 'Gennadeion Notes, III: Athens in the time of Lord Byron', *Hesperia*, 37:2 (1968), 134–58. Rosalys Coope and Pete Smith's magnificently informative book on Newstead Abbey details a visit to Byron's study by F. C. Laird in 1811. Laird is fascinated by 'a very curious antique crucifix'. It could well be the one from Father Paolo's cell. It was extremely unusual, of course, for a non-Catholic to have a crucifix in a private room. Anglicans at that time, and Nonconformists at all times, disliked them, while Coope and Smith go on to tell us that 'old Joe Murray [Byron's servant] removed the crucifix and it does not feature in the 1815 [Sale] Catalogue.' R. Coope and P. Smith, *Newstead Abbey, a Nottinghamshire Country House: Its Owners and Architectural History, 1540–1931* (Nottingham: Thoroton Society of Nottinghamshire, 2014), p. 98 and n. 46.
20 J. G. Lockhart, *Memoirs of the Life of Sir Walter Scott*, 4 vols (Paris: Baudry's European Library, 1837), vol. II, p. 105.
21 See Byron's letter to Teresa Guiccioli of 28 September 1820, in *BLJ*, vol. VII, p. 185.
22 Letter to Teresa Guiccioli of 17 July 1820, in *BLJ*, vol. VII, p. 131.
23 Guiccioli, *Lord Byron's Life in Italy*, p. 224.
24 Letter to Teresa Guiccioli of 7 August 1820, in *BLJ*, vol. VII, p. 152.
25 Lord Byron, *His Very Self and Voice: Collected Conversations of Lord Byron*, ed. Ernest J. Lovell Jr (New York: Macmillan, 1954), p. 240.
26 D. L. Moore, *Lord Byron: Accounts Rendered* (London: John Murray, 1974), p. 266.
27 Moore, *Lord Byron*, p. 264; journal entry for 26 January 1821, in *BLJ*, vol. VIII, p. 35.
28 Byron, *His Very Self and Voice*, p. 210.
29 Byron, *His Very Self and Voice*, p. 246.
30 *BLJ*, vol. I, p. 148.
31 Teresa wrote ecstatically in French on one of Byron's letters that he had promised to be her husband. See L. Marchand, *Byron: A Portrait* (London: John Murray, 1971), p. 327.
32 Unlike Byron, Teresa's aged grandparents visited Allegra at Bagnacavallo (see Guiccioli, *Lord Byron's Life in Italy*, p. 252).

33 Letter to John Murray of 1 August 1819, in *BLJ*, vol. VI, p. 197.
34 Letter to Thomas Moore of 8 March 1822, in *BLJ*, vol. IX, p. 123.
35 W. Rae, *Records of a Route through France and Italy; with Sketches of Catholicism* (London: Longman, Rees, Orme, Brown, Green & Longman, 1835), p. 83.
36 '1382 Bible (Wycliffite, E.V.) Deut. xxviii. 29, "Thou shalt graasp [a1425 L.V. grope] in mydday, as is woned a blynd man to graasp in derknissis"'(*OED*).
37 Peter Vassallo gives some examples of this in *Byron: The Italian Literary Influence* (Basingstoke: Macmillan 1984), p. 159.
38 A. Pope, *Essay on Man*, in *The Poems of Alexander Pope*, ed. John Butt (London: Methuen, 1963), Epistle II, line 3.

7

The politics of the unities: tragedy and the Risorgimento in Byron and Manzoni

Arnold Anthony Schmidt

Scholars have traditionally stressed the influence of Vittorio Alfieri on Byron's plays, particularly in regard to Byron's attraction to the dramatic unities.[1] At the same time, however, Alessandro Manzoni's tragedy *Il conte di Carmagnola*, which gained fame in its day for violating Aristotle's unities of time and place, also left its mark on Byron's *The Two Foscari*. Both plays illustrate the difficulties of accurately ascribing causes to historical events, showing the ways that private motivations colour and influence public actions. Manzoni's play centres on the title character, a fifteenth-century military leader, and his shifting allegiance between Milan and Venice in the context of the era's internecine Italian wars. Caution and insecurity drive the duke of Milan to fear overthrow from Carmagnola's growing popularity and military might, but was the warlord truly planning to betray Milan? Byron's *Two Foscari* presents these historical events from the Venetian perspective, sketching a power struggle between Doge Foscari and Senator Loredano. Foscari's rival uses the figure of Carmagnola as a weapon to bring down the doge and destroy his family, but how much responsibility does Foscari bear for Carmagnola's ultimate execution for treason? The unities play an important role in the ways in which Manzoni and Byron attempt to answer these questions, and the effect of those answers on their audiences.

Carmagnola, written between 1816 and 1819, and published in 1820, appeared in the midst of the literary debate between Italian neoclassicists and Romanticists.[2] At a moment in Italian history when the Austrian, papal and other governments in Italy censored political speech, writing about aesthetics became highly tendentious, a way to discuss politics while avoiding censorship. This debate took place primarily in two ideologically moderate Milanese periodicals: the conservative-leaning *Biblioteca italiana*, sponsored by the Austrian government, and the Romantic *Il Conciliatore*, whose contributors included Giovanni Berchet, Ludovico di Breme, Federico Confalonieri and Silvio Pellico, all of whom Byron knew and whose positions largely aligned with Enlightenment liberalism. According to Marvin Carlson, the contributors to *Il Conciliatore* gathered regularly at di Breme's box at Milan's La Scala opera house, which became 'a necessary visiting place for foreigners', including Byron.[3]

As a poet, Byron inadvertently found himself in the middle of this controversy. Italian neoclassicists considered him an ally for his defence of Alexander Pope and, later, for championing the unities in dramas such as his Venetian tragedies.[4] Not everyone read Byron's plays the same way, of course, and he gained admirers on both sides of the debate. As Marvin Carlson points out, the tragedies' 'politically [...] liberal republican message was precisely in tune with' the Romantics who 'accepted and even adulated' Byron, despite his neoclassicism.[5] Gerald Gillespie notes that the Italian Romantics admired Byron's politics, even if they disagreed with him about aesthetics.[6] Moreover, the Romantics saw Byron's formal experiments, as in *The Giaour*, alongside the psychological individualism and Italian imagery of *Childe Harold's Pilgrimage*, as rejecting the stultified poetic strictures of the past and fostering nationalism. Significantly, Pellico reviewed *The Giaour* in *Lo Spettatore* in 1818, and, when the first Italian translation of Byron's Eastern tale appeared that same year, di Breme wrote a lengthy introduction to it that served as a polemical declaration of the tenets of Italian Romanticism.[7]

Though Manzoni did not contribute to *Il Conciliatore*, the periodical did review some of his writing. Teresa Guiccioli, in *My Recollections of Lord Byron and those of Eye-Witnesses of his Life*, also notes Byron's familiarity with the Milanese author's writings, commenting on Byron's 'esteem [...] for Manzoni'.[8] Federica Brunori Deigan believes that Manzoni's friendship with Berchet, Confalonieri and Ermes Visconti, who published an influential attack on neoclassicism, first brought Manzoni's work to Byron's attention.[9] However, while Byron knew the Italian poet's work, he had no intention of involving himself in Manzoni's anti-Aristotelian crusade. Rachel

A. Walsh observes that 'Byron wanted nothing to do with Italy's literary wars', though he did feel deeply about the issues at stake.[10] And those issues, political and aesthetic, gained prominence as insurrection stirred the Italian peninsula.

A few months before the 1820 uprising in Naples, Manzoni published *Carmagnola*, a Romantic – sometimes called Shakespearian or organic – tragedy that programmatically violates the dramatic unities. Just after that failed rebellion, Byron published *The Two Foscari*, which, in contrast, pointedly attempts to adhere to the unities. Both plays, composed at this historical moment when revolution filled the air, dramatise abuses of state power and conflicts between the individual and the collective, implying a connection between politics and the unities. Examining both playwrights' theatrical deployment of images of the fifteenth-century *condottiero* (mercenary leader) Francesco Bussone da Carmagnola brings this connection into focus. First, though, we need some sense of the historical context within which these plays were written.

Political upheaval increased in Italy after the spring of 1817, when a rebellion against the Austrians took place in Macerata in the region of the Marches in the Papal States. In 1819, General Guglielmo Pepe spearheaded the revolutionary Carbonari and elements of the Neapolitan army in a series of insurrections and attempted uprisings. Nationalists rebelled against Ferdinand I of the Kingdom of the Two Sicilies in Naples and Palermo in 1820.[11] Reformers in Naples won a liberalised constitution based on the Spanish one of 1812, while Sicily – for a while, at least – gained independence.[12] By the time Austria responded with troops in 1821, revolution had erupted in several parts of Italy.

In their own ways, Manzoni and Byron both supported this revolution. As Michael J. Curley notes, Manzoni composed his famous poem 'Marzo 1821', 'in expectation that Piedmont rebels would [...] liberate Lombardy from Austrian oppression'.[13] The poem visibly shares many themes with *Carmagnola*, voicing hopes for liberty, for cooperation among Italy's various regions and, according to Alberto Rizzuti, supporting 'the basic qualities of the insurrectionists' programme'.[14] The revolt failed, however, and, in the months that followed, Manzoni lived through what he described as 'ces jours néfastes' ('these sinister days') of Austrian repression.[15] He only published 'Marzo 1821' after the 1848 rebellion against Austria known as the *Cinque giornate di Milano* (Five Days of Milan), in which his son Filippo participated and suffered arrest. As for *Carmagnola*, Austrian censorship shows that the government recognised the tragedy's controversial nature. Austrian officials initially prevented the performance of Manzoni's play in Milan, published only months after censors pressed for the closing of *Il Conciliatore*, though the play still influenced public opinion as it circulated in print.[16]

As Carlson points out, the play 'was widely read and quoted, especially the patriotic chorus', which became an anthology piece and perhaps the best-known section of the play.[17] The chorus, set after the climactic battle of Maclodio (1427), emphasises the price paid for the peninsula's disunity, underscoring the common roots and heritage of all Italians. Nature itself created Italy as a unified land, connecting its various parts and protecting the peninsula with seas and mountain ranges, but foreign powers that have divided and conquered Italians profit from their disunity. This situation can change, the chorus suggests, if Italians would only recognise their shared history and culture, bringing the peninsula's fragmented regions together to form a unified nation.

Byron supported the rebellion more directly. In love with Teresa Guiccioli in Venice, he followed her to Ravenna and increasingly involved himself in the revolutionary activities of the Carbonari. His circle in Ravenna included Teresa's father, Count Ruggero Gamba, who later spent six years in a Ferrara jail as a political prisoner, and her brother Pietro, who, after supporting Italian nationalist causes, accompanied Byron to Greece, where both would die for its independence.[18] Both Gambas were prominent Carbonari, and Byron met others such as Vicenzo Gallino, who followed him to Greece and remained with him at his deathbed.[19] In time, Byron joined the secret society himself, stored weapons for the group and prepared to lead a troop of Carbonari in the planned rebellion against Austria. However, in the wake of insurrections against the Bourbons in Naples in May 1820, and in Sicily in July, the Habsburg government took pre-emptive action against revolutionaries in the north. In August 1820, in Austrian-controlled Lombardy-Venetia, Carbonari membership became a capital offence. Austrian police arrested di Breme, Confalonieri (like Byron, a Carbonari leader) and Pellico, sentencing the latter two to the notorious Spielberg prison, and forced Berchet into exile.[20] The nationalist feelings of the times find their expression in Manzoni's tragedy. Let us return, then, to Manzoni's and Byron's dramatic treatment of Francesco Bussone.

Carmagnola presents Bussone, a peasant who rises to power as a *condottiero*, loyally serving the duke of Milan and winning battles for him. The duke, however, rejects Carmagnola, possibly because of the mercenary's increasing popularity and the duke's consequent fear that, like other mercenary leaders of the era (such as Francesco Sforza), he might overturn his rule and seize power. Carmagnola, his pride wounded, meets with Doge Foscari to discuss fighting for Venice. Ignoring the fact that the Venetians do not trust him completely, even after surviving an assassination attempt by the duke of Milan, Carmagnola ultimately agrees to fight for Venice, winning battles and conquering territory. At the end of the battle of Maclodio, though, Carmagnola's officers follow the traditional mercenary practice of freeing captured soldiers. The *condottiero* justifies this as a professional courtesy and a step towards peace, arguing that leniency shown to conquered Milanese soldiers would encourage them to join him and fight for Venice against his old employer. The Venetian delegates see things differently and consider it a violation of their agreement. From their point of view, Venice has paid Carmagnola to win the battle and so deserves the right to dispose of prisoners as it sees fit. The delegates characterise Carmagnola's actions as a self-serving way to continue the conflict, to the profit of himself and his troops. Possibly, however, they also believe – and fear – the *condottiero*'s claim that, if he could amass both Venetian and Milanese soldiers into a large army, his forces would threaten Venice itself. After subsequent engagements in which Carmagnola performs without enthusiasm, the Venetians treat his actions as betrayal. Foscari and the Council of Ten trick Carmagnola, calling him to the doge's palace on the pretext of discussing peace, and then beheading him.

Was the warlord simply proud, but loyal, or did he genuinely betray Venice? While Manzoni in many ways idealises Carmagnola, Machiavelli offers a more balanced appraisal. He observes that Venetians saw Carmagnola 'fighting very virtuously when he was under the government of the Duke of Milan', but by the time he fought for Venice, 'he had cooled to the war. They decided that they could not win with him, because he did not want to win, nor could they dismiss him without losing again that which he had acquired. Thus it was necessary to kill him to secure themselves' – and the territories that he had conquered.²¹ Whether or not the historical Carmagnola acted treasonously, it is clear that his skill in leading an army did not translate into the political acumen necessary to thrive – indeed, even to survive – in the perfidious world of early modern Italian government.

The implications of this story resonated in Austrian-dominated Italy, as did Manzoni's decision to present Carmagnola's tragedy in both patriotic and anti-neoclassical form. Dramatic form, and especially its adherence to the classical unities, was a hot issue. In 1819, *Il Conciliatore* published Ermes Visconti's thoughtful, if polemical, analysis of the unities in a two-part article entitled 'Dialogo sulle unità drammatiche di luogo e di tempo' ('Dialogue on the Dramatic Unities of Place and Time'). Conceding the importance of the unity of action, Visconti focuses his critique on the central neoclassical assumption of verisimilitude. He denies that audiences experience plays that follow the unities of time and place as more real than those which violate them, rejecting the neoclassical notion that having actions take place over time, in several places, breaks the audiences' belief in the narrative itself. Defending Shakespeare not for his verisimilitude but for presenting audiences with what appears natural, Visconti observes that *Macbeth*'s violation of the unities of time and place to show incremental changes as they occur in the mind of the title character makes him seem more, not less, real. Ultimately, Visconti rejects the unities of time and place, seeing only the unity of action as necessary.²² However, in Romantic-period Italy, as in Britain, the use of the unities also had political valence. In Italy, those intellectuals who supported tradition in the arts also supported traditional government structures and Austria's imperial policies, while others likened rejecting the unities to rejecting the *ancien régime* restored after Napoleon's downfall. Those advocating literary reform often advanced nationalist positions on Italian unification and independence from foreign powers.

The politics of both the form and subject matter of Manzoni's *Carmagnola* are very visible. The *London Magazine*, for instance, noted the play's treatment of 'the discords of the Italians in the fifteenth century, and their internal wars, waged between various provinces – wars to which the slavery of this fine but unhappy country may be traced'.²³ We can also see how Manzoni's choices of form and content are very much of their European moment when we consider them within the broad context of European Romanticism. Following a path blazed by William Shakespeare – whose works John Hennig describes as 'the Magna Carta of liberty from the three unities'[24] – the structure of Manzoni's tragedy also evidences the influence of Schiller and Goethe, who praised the play. By looking to Shakespeare as a model, Manzoni also heeds the call made by Madame de Staël in her 1816 essay 'Sulla maniera e l'utilità delle traduzioni' ('On the Manner and Usefulness of Translations'), which has been 'credited with launching the Italian Romantic Movement'.[25] In this essay, which appeared in the first issue of the *Biblioteca Italiana*, de Staël calls on writers to look beyond their own shores, not simply to copy international authors but to free themselves of the narrow range of traditional national models. Friedrich Schlegel addresses a related sort of myopia, rejecting tragedies based on mythology and the misty past, and instead urging the creation of a national theatre and treatment of more relevant historical subjects.[26] Manzoni, who read Schlegel, does exactly that,[27] also aligning himself with ideas about the importance of historical subjects discussed in *Il Conciliatore* by Pellico, who urged Italians to write dramas not about the age of romance or antiquity but about their own national history.[28]

For these reasons, in his review of Manzoni for the *Foreign Quarterly* of July 1827, George Moir notes that 'amidst the innovations which the stirring spirit of speculation and experiment, now at work in Italy, has introduced, we have to hail the commencement of a dramatic revolution'. The reviewer also praises Manzoni's tragedies for avoiding the 'very highly overrated [...] mythological and classical subjects' typically adopted by Italian authors and instead writing on 'subjects of a national character'.[29] Joseph Luzzi characterises the decision to write about Italian history and Carmagnola as a deliberately political act: Manzoni, he observes, 'devoted himself to reporting historical events because he believed that the Italian drive for unification could not afford the luxury of make-believe'.[30] Manzoni's play, in other words, advanced the political agenda articulated by the authors of *Il Conciliatore* – indeed, according to Carlson, *Carmagnola* was 'the most successful attempt so far in Italy to fulfil the ideals' of that periodical, namely 'progress, patriotism, and liberty'.[31]

Manzoni, of course, chooses for his tragic hero a historical *condottiero* whose uncertain loyalty was a vexed historical question. In *Carmagnola*, he attempts to vindicate the warlord, shifting the tragedy's emphasis from charges of treason to the dangers of Venetian – and contemporary Austrian – realpolitik. Although Manzoni's play proves a vehicle for communicating Venice's treachery, Carmagnola's status as a *condottiero* warrants examination – after all, Venetian distrust of the warlord echoes Italy's long-standing distrust of mercenaries generally, seen by authors such as Francesco Guicciardini and Machiavelli as destructive to its people and politics. *Carmagnola* makes an implied contrast between mercenaries, paid to fight for any cause, and soldiers who, like Cincinnatus, fight for their country and liberty before returning home. Carmagnola surely falls into the first category, but Manzoni's play suggests that, given the opportunity, his conscience might lead him to fight for Italian unity. The warlord's personality does not lead audiences to believe that, should he make such a conquest, he would then reduce his own power by establishing a republic. Still, even ruling as an enlightened monarch over broad areas of Italy would bring different regions together and unify their peoples, dialects and cultures, almost paving the way for the Risorgimento by creating the germ of a national state as English and French monarchies had done. Most importantly, in fighting for pay, Carmagnola reminds audiences of the peninsula's many soldiers and officers who during the Napoleonic wars – through choice or coercion – fought in the *Armée d'Italie* and other French military units. Generals such as Pepe, who led anti-Austrian rebellions in 1820 and 1848, as well as many of his men and officers, received training and experience from fighting for France. After Napoleon's fall, many of those same soldiers used their military skills to fight for Italian nationalism. Carmagnola, then, like Pepe and so many others, fought for pay when he had to, but now, perhaps, would fight for a cause in which he believes – that of Italy. In presenting the warlord in this way, Manzoni transvalues traditional views of mercenary fighters, representing Carmagnola as a potential patriot, which would explain why the playwright goes out of his way to redeem a historical figure seen by so many as flawed.

Manzoni's play draws attention to leadership and the roles of individuals within government institutions, presenting a conflict between two visions of power – one heroic, the other political – and illustrating the failings of each. Manzoni's Foscari, as doge and symbolic head of government, embodies not individual but institutional authority. Venice's republican structure, with its Polybian separation of powers, balances the doge's ability to act with his obedience to various other public bodies. Carmagnola acts alone; Foscari cannot. The play also contrasts two forms of government – the duke of Milan's aristocratic regime and Venice's imperfect, but long-standing, republican rule, ideal in theory, despotic in practice. In their current configurations, neither form suggests a model for a future unified Italy, the tyranny of both surely reminding contemporary audiences of Austrian oppression.

What then does Carmagnola symbolise for the Risorgimento? In the tragedy, the *condottiero* is an ideologically nationalistic, if proud, leader, the play raising issues related to Italian regionalism, infighting and foreign influence. While not a patriot anachronistically fighting for an Italian nation state, the *condottiero* does recognise the bonds among the Milanese, Venetians and other inhabitants of the peninsula who cling to regional identities instead of seeing themselves as Italians. The warlord mourns the fate of 'questa / Divisa Italia' – 'this divided Italy' (I, iv, 326) – whose fragmentation and weakness make it a prize to be plucked by the strong.[32] He therefore acknowledges the futility of Italy's internal strife, which in the fifteenth century as in the nineteenth, served only to benefit foreign powers. As Curley observes, what Manzoni's tragedy denounces as 'the concept of *ragione di stato* [reason of state]' is 'the same principle followed by the Doge of Venice in his persecution of Carmagnola' and by the Austrian government in Italy.[33] In that sense, 'the play is of greater value as a work of art informing us about [...] the state of Italy in Manzoni's own time, than about the state of Italy in the early fifteenth century'.[34] Italy needs heroes like Carmagnola, but individuals must fit into the collective, and the warlord's military prowess and personal popularity appear to threaten both Milan and Venice. Like Napoleon, whom he resembles in his military skill and pride, if not his political judgement, Carmagnola holds promise as a saviour, but a promise that remains unfulfilled.

Both *Carmagnola* and *The Two Foscari* highlight the betrayal of Carmagnola by the doge, but in Byron's tragedy the warlord serves a very different function from the one he serves in Manzoni's play. Obviously, as their titles indicate, *Carmagnola* focuses on the warlord, *The Two Foscari* on the doge. While in Manzoni's play viewers observe Foscari behaving treacherously, Byron's tragedy presents the doge ambiguously, failing to create for the audience a clear portrait, making the tragedy's treatment of Carmagnola central to what viewers believe they know about the doge's personality and psychology. Byron never shows Foscari's actions regarding the *condottiero*, leaving it to the audience to determine, on the basis of what other characters say about the doge, the extent of his culpability in Carmagnola's fate. Moreover, through its neoclassical form, *The Two Foscari* pointedly controls information about the doge, limiting the audience's ability to make that determination.

In these two plays, following or abandoning the unities fundamentally affects the ways in which audiences perceive and interpret the *condottiero*. The essential difference here is between showing and telling. Manzoni features Carmagnola as a character in his play, bringing him to life on stage for viewers to evaluate, while the *condottiero* never appears in Byron's tragedy, functioning only as the subject of dialogue between other characters, which changes him from a tragic hero into an ethical enigma. *Carmagnola* urges Italians to unite and cast out foreign powers. Instead of stirring patriotic activism, as Manzoni's play does, Byron's tragedy seems cautionary, presenting Italy's past in ways that provoke analysis and offer essential warnings about great men and events, politics and historical processes. In *Carmagnola*, the *condottiero*'s tale serves as an admonition, an inspiration and an object lesson, whereas in Byron's work Carmagnola, who is never seen on stage, acts as a vehicle to complicate the personality of Foscari, a different sort of flawed leader. The warlord becomes a litmus test used to evaluate the veracity of Loredano's accusations of murder against the doge, and, in doing so, to justify or undermine the legitimacy of Foscari's rule and that of the Venetian republic.

To see the difference in the way these two authors utilise the *condottiero*, compare their Romantic and neoclassical representations of Foscari's behaviour towards Carmagnola. In the last act of his tragedy, Manzoni brings the doge face to face with the warlord, directly accusing him of treachery. The Venetians, unmoved by his rebuttal to their accusations, try, condemn and execute him. Byron treats the same actions, but in markedly different ways, using Foscari's interactions with Carmagnola to suggest, rather than directly state, information about the doge's actions and motivations. This becomes evident during a conversation in Act IV, when Senator Barbarigo expresses disbelief after hearing Loredano accuse the doge of poisoning his relatives. The audience never sees Foscari's interactions with Carmagnola and Venetian officials, as it does in Manzoni's play.

Instead, viewers hear the following conversation as characters discuss Carmagnola's guilt and punishment in scenes that primarily paint a portrait of the doge, a portrait whose accuracy the audience cannot readily ascertain. Barbarigo asks: 'And art thou sure [...] / And yet he seems / All openness'; Loredano replies: 'And so he seem'd not long / Ago to Carmagnuola'. Foscari and the Ten decided to execute the *condottiero*, whom Barbarigo describes as 'The attainted / And foreign traitor' (considered, as a subject of the duke of Milan, a foreigner), eight months before actually doing so, but said nothing about it. Instead, Loredano observes that, 'the old Doge, who knew him doom'd, smiled on him / [...] Eight months of such hypocrisy as is / Learnt but in eighty years' (IV, i, 285–303). This dialogue implies that the doge, able to deceive Carmagnola, could also deceive others and appear innocent. Here Carmagnola's story serves as a touchstone: if believed, it shows Foscari as treacherous, calculating and capable of murder.

Clearly, Byron's images of Foscari differ greatly from Manzoni's. At first glance, Manzoni's doge appears direct and forceful, while Byron's Foscari seems duplicitous. However, this depends on how we read Byron's play in relation to the history it represents. Those familiar with early modern Venetian government practices could not interpret Carmagnola's history the way Loredano does. His conversation about the *condottiero* makes Foscari's concealing the actions of the Ten seem particularly devious. Rather, Venetian government policy required the Ten to keep all debates and decisions secret, and severely punished their disclosure.[35] None could alert Carmagnola of the vote to execute him without appearing disloyal. Moreover, the historical Loredano actually attended the meetings of the Ten that decided the *condottiero*'s fate; in fact, Loredano urged Carmagnola's execution, while Foscari sought exile as a punishment to save the mercenary's life. Forbidden to disclose that decision to Carmagnola, Loredano would also have spent eight months concealing his death sentence from the warlord.[36] These facts change the ways viewers interpret the doge's secrecy and Loredano's veracity: in the light of them, we see that the doge must remain silent on Carmagnola's sentence, while Loredano appears hypocritical in condemning that silence, which he himself also observed. Significantly for the play's themes of individual and institutional treachery, however, the ways in which viewers learn this historical information proves as important as the information itself.

Adhering to the unity of time prevents Byron from presenting the audience with earlier scenes that would illustrate key aspects of the doge's personality, such as his guilt or innocence in the murder of Loredano's relatives. Instead, viewers learn of these events through conversations among interested parties, interested enough to distort the truth, though the play does not indicate for certain that they do so. Instead, Byron's neoclassical presentation compounds the doge's guilt and lends credence to, if it does not justify, Loredano's image of Foscari as murderer, based on circumstantial evidence. In the opening of the play, Loredano reminds Barbarigo that 'My father and my uncle are no more' (I, i, 33). Barbarigo replies that he has 'read their epitaph, which says they died / By poison' (I, i, 34). Loredano then commits a logical fallacy (*post hoc ergo propter hoc*) by concluding that what came before must have caused what followed. He says: 'When the Doge declared that he / Should never deem himself a sovereign till / The death of Peter Loredano, both / The brothers sicken'd shortly: – he *is* sovereign' (I, i, 35–8). Loredano considers Foscari, who has become doge, the murderer of his father and uncles. While possible, no evidence in the play supports this accusation: certainly the simple fact of Foscari becoming doge after the deaths of Loredano's relatives does not prove murder, as he believes. Here the information presented to the audience through Byron's fidelity to the unities undermines the status of the doge as heroic individual in particular, but also diminishes the stature of those capable of the patriotic intervention so essential to Manzoni's Risorgimento agenda.

Based on distortions of Venetian history (ignoring the doge's plea for the *condottiero*'s life) and of legal procedure (the Ten's secrecy), images of Carmagnola in *The Two Foscari* paint a particularly harsh view of Venice in general and of Foscari in particular. Byron's play, however, resists easy interpretation as it tends to demonstrate the pitfalls of leadership. A dramatic structure that prevents audiences from witnessing these events as they take place compels viewers to evaluate the personalities, motivations and actions involved solely through the words of others. The difficulties of ascertaining the true course of events (was Carmagnola a traitor and did Foscari poison his rivals?) undermine faith in history and the possibility of using the past to guide future actions, a long European tradition rooted in the parallel biographies of *Plutarch's Lives*.

Byron's own doubts about these things emerge more clearly if we study his tragedies in light of his own political actions, which reveal tensions between his sceptical political pronouncements and idealistic deeds, particularly regarding his attitudes towards leadership in government and towards revolution in Britain, Italy and elsewhere. Fearful of democracy, Byron believed that leadership should come from a society's educationally and socially elevated classes. This becomes evident when we try to reconcile Byron's Carbonari activities in Italy, leading a group called 'the *Turba* (Mob), composed mostly of workmen', with his condemnation of John Cam Hobhouse's successful campaign as a radical candidate for Westminster in the 1819 Parliamentary election.[37] Upon learning of 'Hobby-O's' imprisonment in Newgate for a political pamphlet he had written, Byron sent his lifelong friend a cruel satiric squib. Hobhouse's positions, however, turned out more moderate than Byron feared, having precedents at least as early as John Wilkes' 1771 Bill of Rights manifesto, which demanded electoral reform, elimination of electoral bribery and closer supervision of public monies.[38] Still, condemning Hobhouse for running as a radical, Byron wrote, 'I am and have been for *reform* always – but not for the *reformers*.'[39] He does not equate reform with democracy (and, frankly, neither did Hobhouse, who opposed the First Reform Bill). Thus, Byron applauds his own working with social inferiors when leading the Carbonari while simultaneously condemning Hobhouse, during his Parliamentary campaign, for treating as equals those whom Byron does not consider gentlemen. Byron's actions stem, in part, from his Whig attitudes towards liberty.

According to the Whig version of history, beginning in the medieval and early modern periods, liberty for the people, especially the masses of gentry, middle and working classes, came about because of those few, like Byron, at the top of society – the aristocracy. As Abraham D. Kriegel explains, feudal liberties 'were bestowed from above by the crown, often with reluctance [...] in response to demands of the nobility'; in this sense, and significantly for understanding Byron's politics, 'modern liberty was in its origins an aristocratic idea', and Britons generally saw 'the nobility as the source of liberty'.[40] Byron's neoclassicism, a manifestation of Whiggism, justifies his condemnation of Hobhouse: Jonathan Gross connects Byron's support of Pope with the aesthetics of the Holland House Whigs, whose neoclassical tastes separated 'Whig aristocrats and the upper classes' from 'the middle class or Cockney school of Hunt and Keats'.[41] Hobhouse violated this social hierarchy by mingling on equal terms with democrats in England. Byron, as a Whig aristocrat, in conjunction with other nobles such as Count Gamba, occupied his natural position as a leader opposing arbitrary power – this time that of Austria – and supporting liberty for his fellow aristocrats, as well as social inferiors.

The neoclassical structure of Byron's Venetian tragedies echoes this connection between Whig ideology and hierarchy. Intriguingly, plays that follow the dramatic unities also lead, using character dialogue to control information by describing from those characters' own perspectives actions unseen by the audience. Following the unities, and particularly the unity of time, forces dramatists to emphasise telling theatre-goers about what has happened rather than showing them those events. Neoclassical productions have characters relate past actions in dialogue, instead of dramatising actions on stage that audiences witness and can evaluate for themselves. Actors need not deliberately lie to distort the meaning of the events they recount; they must only discuss them subjectively, in character. Indeed, they cannot do otherwise – the information they present comes from their point of view. This contrast between telling and showing undergirds the politics of the unities and specifically affects the ways viewers might respond to Byron's two Venetian tragedies, both of which hinge on key events that occur before the stage action begins. This is, in large part, why criticism of these plays generally focuses on two issues that strain credibility: in *Marino Faliero*, the title character's decision to rebel because of an insult to his wife, and, in *The Two Foscari*, Jacopo Foscari's love of Venice that leads him to prefer death there to life elsewhere.

William Gifford's 1822 article on Byron's plays in the *Quarterly Review* raises these issues, attacking the logic of the unities in terms similar to those used earlier by Visconti in *Il Conciliatore*. As Gifford points out, audiences have difficulty accepting these motivations in Byron's plays in part because they cannot evaluate them. Viewers learn what drives the action – Foscari's rebellion, Jacopo's return – from characters telling what happened, delivering information. Audiences do not see Steno as he premeditates and commits his insult. Nor do they see Jacopo Foscari's dealings with foreign powers that might compromise his loyalty to Venice or dramatic moments showing his attachment to the city that might explain his return even on pain of death. If audiences witnessed these scenes, they might understand the characters' responses to them and, more crucially, accept those responses as legitimate. Perhaps, writes Gifford, if Byron had dramatised Faliero's long-suffering abuse at the hands of his contemporaries, then viewers might see Steno's insult as sufficient motivation for rebellion, the 'very slight addition of injury' that 'might make the cup of anger overflow'. Later, Gifford raises a similar objection to Jacopo's predicament and offers a similar solution. Regarding Jacopo's love of Venice, Byron should have 'set before our eyes the intolerable separation from a beloved country, the lingering home-sickness [...]. He should have shown him to us, first, taking leave of Venice [...] next pining in Candia' and finally conspiring with foreign powers to get home.[42]

Consider, then, the difference between Romantic and neoclassical approaches to drama. Obviously, both styles assume that authors organise the action in specific ways to achieve particular dramatic goals, but, for the moment, think only of the stage experience. Both show the audience present-tense scenes, allowing theatre-goers to evaluate them objectively. In Romantic plays such Manzoni's, the story evolves over time, the past seen, not narrated. Manzoni shows to the audience the character of Carmagnola, the good and the problematic, for the viewers to evaluate. Seeing him on stage, spectators decide if they believe the *condottiero* a hero or a traitor. Audiences see Foscari and the senators discuss Venetian concerns and learn of Carmagnola's motivations, often from the warlord himself, and witness the events leading up to his death. More importantly, seeing his actions and hearing his words, viewers have the means to decide for themselves his guilt or innocence. Neoclassical plays, instead, in their adherence to the unities, narrate rather than dramatise significant past episodes. In Byron's drama, Carmagnola is the subject of conversation, figuring in the tragedy only as others – and, in particular, others with specific agendas – portray him. Consequently, audiences experience these past moments only by way of information gathered through dialogue filtered through the priorities and experiences of the characters who narrate them. As figures such as Loredano present Carmagnola's story, possibly distorting it for their own purposes, audiences believe or disbelieve these narratives based on their attitudes towards the speakers, not based on first-hand knowledge gained from witnessing the incidents discussed. Byron's neoclassical approach, not trusting audiences to evaluate key past events for themselves, tightly controls information to colour interpretations of those events.

In terms of content, Byron uses the *condottiero*'s biography to delineate character, particularly that of two historical figures, Foscari and his nemesis James Loredano, in order to explore his own anxieties about leadership and the legibility of history. In terms of form, the play's neoclassical structure echoes the connection between Whig ideology and social organisation. Thus, in Byron's Italian tragedies, following the unities has political implications. Political actors in hierarchical societies limit the decision-making power of those below; authors who adhere to the dramatic unities limit the audience's ability to make decisions regarding the play's actors and actions by restricting the information available to viewers, inhibiting the scope of their interpretation. At a moment when Byron presents himself as an aristocratic leader in Italy, his plays, because of their neoclassical rather than Romantic structure, encourage doubts about all leaders. In the end, the dramatic structure of Byron's Venetian tragedies makes it difficult to accept the plays' leaders – rebellious Doge Faliero or establishment Doge Foscari – as worthy rulers. Both appear, at best, as flawed politicians. Indeed, Byron's Faliero seems far more flawed than the character of Faliero in Manzoni's *Carmagnola*, though he too participates in processes leading to the warlord's death.

If Manzoni's portrait of Carmagnola paints him as proud, but patriotic, Byron's image reveals a general scepticism about leadership and an uncertainty about social and political change, in Britain or on the Continent. If Manzoni distorts history by painting the *condottiero* too heroically, he does so to advance a Risorgimento ideology, to condemn the peninsula's infighting and to cultivate national unity. Byron's Venice shows people motivated by self-interest and other psychological impulses, as well as institutions acting for self-preservation. While *Carmagnola* pointedly inspires patriotic activism in its chorus and elsewhere, Byron presents Italian history as a warning about great men and momentous events and urges analysis of politics and historical processes. Perhaps most importantly, Byron's tragedy fails to present anyone as heroic. The play shows actual Venetian heroes, Foscari and Loredano, not as the formidable military and political leaders that they were in their youths but as feeble, vindictive and ineffectual old men. If both playwrights tell Italians about their past,

Manzoni's critique fires patriotism while Byron's version of history leaves audiences sceptical about the possibility of expelling foreign powers and creating a unified nation. He portrays the Venetian government's failings as a system of law without justice, and underscores the fallibility of all leaders. After all, if tyranny existed in Venice, a republic for centuries celebrated for possessing the world's most reasonable system of government, what hope remained?[43]

Byron, of course, still hoped. The Venetian plays express his internal conflict between idealism and scepticism. Vexed as to the relative importance of individuals, situations or accidents in making historical events come to pass (something satirised by his treatment of heroism in *Don Juan*), Byron longed for political and social improvement but doubted, given material circumstances and flawed human nature, that it would happen. People and events had corrupted Revolutionary and Napoleonic ideals, causing the failure of such potentially transformative developments as the Neapolitan revolution. However, that did not prevent Byron from acting, and he followed the ideals of liberty to Greece, where again, at least during his lifetime, people and events made progress impossible.

Acknowledgement

This chapter benefited from discussions with Mark Schoenfield, as well as with participants in the December 2014 'Byron in Italy' conference at the University of Manchester, including Bernard Beatty, Peter Cochran, Julia Markus, Alan Rawes and Diego Saglia.

Notes

1. For a discussion of Byron and Alfieri, see P. Cochran's 'Byron, Alfieri, and the writing of plays', in P. Cochran (ed.), *Byron at the Theatre* (Newcastle: Cambridge Scholars, 2008), pp. 36–59.
2. See M. J. Curley, *Alessandro Manzoni: Two Plays* (New York: Peter Lang, 2002), p. 7.
3. M. Carlson, 'The Italian Romantic drama in its European context', in G. Gillespie (ed.), *Romantic Drama* (Amsterdam: John Benjamins, 1994), pp. 233–48 (p. 243).
4. James Chandler discusses Byron's polemic with William Lisle Bowles in 'The Pope controversy: Romantic poetics and the English canon', *Critical Inquiry*, 10:3 (1984), 481–509.

5 M. Carlson, 'Nationalism and the Romantic drama in Europe', in G. Gillespie (ed.), *Romantic Drama* (Amsterdam: John Benjamins, 1994), pp. 139–52 (p. 149).

6 G. Gillespie, 'The past is prologue: the Romantic heritage in dramatic literature', in G. Gillespie (ed.), *Romantic Drama* (Amsterdam: John Benjamins, 1994), pp. 429–64 (p. 443).

7 See G. Muoni, *La fama del Byron e il Byronismo in Italia* (Milan: Società Editrice, 1903), p. 9.

8 T. Guiccioli *My Recollections of Lord Byron and Those of Eye-Witnesses of His Life* (New York: Harper & Bros., 1869), p. 274.

9 F. B. Deigan, 'Byron's, Shakespeare's, and Manzoni's Venice', in *Alessandro Manzoni's The Count of Carmagnola and Adelchis*, trans. F. B. Deigan (Baltimore, Md.: Johns Hopkins University Press, 2004), pp. 47–51.

10 R. A. Walsh, *Ugo Foscolo's Tragic Vision in Italy and England* (Toronto: University of Toronto Press, 2014), p. 93. For more on these 'literary wars', see N. Havely, 'Francesca frustrated: new evidence about Hobhouse's and Byron's translation of Pellico's *Francesca da Rimini*', *Romanticism*, 1:1 (1995), 106–20.

11 See A. Scirocco, *L'Italia del Risorgimento 1800–1871* (Bologna: Il Mulino, 1993), pp. 80–105; C. Duggan, *The Force of Destiny: A History of Italy since 1796* (London: Allen Lane, 2007), pp. 3–217; J. A. Davis, *Italy in the Nineteenth Century* (Oxford: Oxford University Press, 2000).

12 See Davis, *Italy in the Nineteenth Century*, p. 284.

13 Curley, *Alessandro Manzoni*, p. 5.

14 A. Rizzuti 'Viganò's "Giovanna D'arco" and Manzoni's "March 1821"', *Music and Letters*, 86:2 (2005), 186–201 (p. 194).

15 Quoted in Curley, *Alessandro Manzoni*, p. 19.

16 See Carlson, 'Nationalism and the Romantic drama', p. 148.

17 Carlson, 'Nationalism and the Romantic drama', p. 148.

18 Guiccioli, *Recollections*, pp. 555–6.

19 See M. T. C. Stagni, *Con Byron tra Bologna e Ravenna* (Bologna: Pendragon, 2001), p. 62.

20 See E. Holt, *The Making of Italy, 1815–1870* (New York: Athenaeum, 1971), pp. 57–8.

21 N. Machiavelli, *Il principe: politica e questione morale*, ed. Marcella Vasconi (Bussolengo: Demetra, 1995), p. 88, my translation.

22 E. Visconti, 'Dialogo sulle unità drammatiche di luogo e di tempo', *Il Conciliatore: foglio scientifico-letterario* (Bologna: Arnaldo Forni Editore, 1981), pp. 165–72 (p. 170).

23 Anon., '*Il Conte di Carmagnola*, an Italian tragedy', *London Magazine*, 2 (November 1820), 499–509 (p. 508).

24 J. Hennig, 'Goethe and an English critic of Manzoni', *Monatshefte*, 39:1 (1947), 9–16 (p. 12).

25 Carlson, 'Nationalism and the Romantic drama', p. 147.
26 Carlson, 'Nationalism and the Romantic drama', p. 147.
27 See Curley, *Alessandro Manzoni*, p. 8.
28 See Carlson, 'Nationalism and the Romantic drama', p. 148.
29 G. Moir, 'Italian tragedy', *The Foreign Quarterly Review*, 1 (July 1827), 135–71 (pp. 136, 135).
30 J. Luzzi, *Romantic Europe and the Ghost of Italy* (New Haven, Conn.: Yale University Press, 2008), p. 175.
31 Carlson, 'Italian Romantic drama', p. 243.
32 A. Manzoni, *Tragedie*, ed. G. Bollati (Torino: Einaudi, 1965).
33 Curley, *Alessandro Manzoni*, p. 15. The *OED* defines 'reason of state' as 'a purely political ground of action on the part of a ruler or government, esp. as involving expediency or some departure from strict justice, honesty, or open dealing'.
34 Curley, *Alessandro Manzoni*, p. 13.
35 For an extensive but readable introduction to the *Serenissima*'s complicated government structure and processes, see R. Finlay, *Politics in Renaissance Venice* (New Brunswick: Rutgers University Press, 1980).
36 D. Romano's *The Likeness of Venice: A Life of Doge Francesco Foscari, 1373–1457* (New Haven, Conn.: Yale University Press, 2007) sheds particular light on the historical doge, with more general information found in his *Patricians and Popolani* (Baltimore, Md.: Johns Hopkins University Press, 1987). For another insightful source on the era's people and politics, see G. Benzoni, *I Dogi* (Milan: Electa, 1982).
37 L. A. Marchand, *Byron: A Portrait* (Chicago: University of Chicago Press, 1979), p. 330.
38 See A. Cash, *John Wilkes: The Scandalous Father of Civil Liberty* (New Haven: Yale University Press, 2006), p. 295.
39 Letter to John Cam Hobhouse of 26 June 1819, in *BLJ*, vol. VI, p. 166.
40 A. D. Kriegel, 'Liberty and Whiggery in early nineteenth-century England', *The Journal of Modern History*, 52:2 (1980), 253–78 (p. 256).
41 J. Gross, *Byron: The Erotic Liberal* (Lanham, Md.: Rowman & Littlefield, 2001), p. 103.
42 W. Gifford, 'Lord Byron's *Dramas*', *The Quarterly Review*, 27 (July 1822), 476–524 (pp. 488, 506).
43 For a discussion of Venice's highly influential role as a model in political theory, see J. G. A. Pocock, *The Machiavellian Moment: Florentine Political Thought and the Atlantic Republican Tradition* (Princeton, NJ: Princeton University Press, 2003), particularly chapters 4, 7, 8 and 9.

8

Parisina, *Mazeppa* and Anglo-Italian displacement

Peter W. Graham

Parisina and *Mazeppa* are oddities among Byron's tales. Neither is 'Eastern' in the sense of being located at the Ottoman-dominated end of the Mediterranean, as the other tales are. *Parisina* is set in the Italian duchy of Ferrara, at the fifteenth-century court of Niccolò III d'Este. The frame story of *Mazeppa* takes place in the aftermath of Charles XII of Sweden's defeat by Peter the Great of Russia at the battle of Poltava in the Ukraine (1709), while the body of the poem, a retrospective tale told by seventy-year-old Mazeppa, begins at the Polish court of John Casimir and ends somewhere in the Ukrainian wilds. *Parisina* is an anomaly among the tales in featuring a heroine who is actively amorous and a hero who, apart from being ardently adulterous, is too conventional in his values to be a Byronic hero as that archetype is generally understood. *Mazeppa* for its part is too humorously ironic to blend with Byron's other tales and in many ways fits better with *Beppo* and *Don Juan*, the *ottava rima* masterpieces roughly contemporaneous with its period of composition. But, considered separately and together, *Parisina* and *Mazeppa* can help readers understand the intricate fabrication of Byron's Anglo-Italian identity – and being juxtaposed in dialogue throws new light on these two tales generally sidelined in the Byron canon.

The construction of Romantic identity as a complex interplay of space, culture, history, politics, poetry and personal contingency has for some decades now been a compelling interest of literary historians and cultural geographers. In the twenty-first century this critical approach to Romantic constructions of places, sensibilities and texts has produced such studies as Diego Saglia's *Poetic Castles of Spain: British Romanticism and Figurations of Iberia* (2000), Stephen

Cheeke's *Byron and Place: History, Translation, Nostalgia* (2003), Maria Schoina's *Romantic 'Anglo-Italians': Configurations of Identity in Byron, the Shelleys, and the Pisan Circle* (2009) and Jane Stabler's *The Artistry of Exile: Romantic and Victorian Writers in Italy* (2013). The following speculative chapter profits by the insights and approaches of these scholars and others, but its way of proceeding will be somewhat different from theirs. Here, as in Cheeke's book, the main focus will be on personal and poetic aspects of Byron's cosmopolitanism rather than its political resonances. But *Parisina* and *Mazeppa*, in addition to their outlier status as Eastern tales, run against a strong prevailing current that Cheeke identifies in Byron's poems – the necessity of 'being there' or 'having been there': 'Being there on the spot having been there on the spot, composing on the spot, having made observations on the spot – the word registers the authority of direct personal knowledge and experience of a place, as well as suggesting a particular concentration of perception.'[1] And, as Cheeke rightly claims, 'place was central to Byron's fashioning of himself, and Byron's places were constantly changing'.[2] In *Parisina* and *Mazeppa*, however, it is the man of mobility's constant change or displacement, his *not* being on the spot, that proves crucial to Byron's poetic and self-fashioning purposes.

In *Parisina* he obliquely voices or vents emotions specific to his life in contemporary England through reviving and revising an old Italian story. *Mazeppa*, composed in Italy but not located there, both echoes his Italian life and art and prophesies their next phases. Both tales are distinguished by prolonged and perplexed periods of composition and by a shared theme of transgressive love taking the form of a *ménage à trois*. Both tales are displaced narratives, Anglo-Italian in different ways that seem distinctively suitable to Byron's personal circumstances during their respective periods of composition. *Parisina* and *Mazeppa* variously reveal Byron's literary notions of Italy, his empirical understanding of the congenial milieu he entered as an expatriate and came truly to inhabit, and his famous mobility, 'a thing of temperament and not of art' as he put it in *Don Juan* (XVI, 97) and 'an excessive susceptibility of immediate impressions – at the same time without *losing* the past', as he defines it in that poem's notes.[3] Taken together, the two tales complicate the way readers can understand Byron's self-locating, embedding and acculturating himself in Italian culture.

A 29 November 1813 letter to Annabella Milbanke offers a richly suggestive way of understanding *Parisina* through Byron's now famous volcanic metaphor for his poetry: 'the lava of the imagination whose eruptions prevent an earth-quake'.[4] As the date indicates, the comment to Annabella comes from the period when Byron was writing his Eastern tales, but it is an idea he articulated in varying forms, aloud and on paper, in prose and in verse, throughout the rest of his life. No mere means of blowing off steam, the 'lava of the imagination' connects Byron's life and his art in an intriguing way – especially in the case of *Parisina*, a tale where recounting incidents based in, but not faithful to, history gives Byron a discreet way of talking about himself.

Published in February 1816 along with *The Siege of Corinth* and, like that poem, apparently composed in a sporadic, complicated patchwork way between 1812 and 1815, *Parisina* appeared when Byron's marriage, finances and reputation were all in ruins and his self-exile from England was imminent. The poem comes at the end of a rapidly composed sequence of six Eastern tales, effusions Byron sometimes deprecated as sub-artistic toss-offs, though, as previously in *Childe Harold's Pilgrimage*, he was serious in a gentlemanly, cosmopolitan way about accuracy in matters of fact. He was also gentlemanly about payment, regularly instructing John Murray to give copyright money to others – until *The Siege of Corinth* and *Parisina*. Murray generously offered £1,000 for these copyrights. Byron turned down the offer on his own behalf but asked to have the sum distributed to William Godwin, Coleridge and Charles Maturin. Murray balked at that; and Byron, in fairly desperate financial straits at the time, pragmatically accepted payment himself, thereby fording an economic Rubicon he never recrossed.[5] Byron's change of policy on payment eventually combined with the lower cost of living on the Continent and the receipt of his share of the Wentworth fortune that had devolved upon Lady Byron to allow him to cut a figure as an Anglo-Italian milord that he could not have afforded in England during his 'Years of Fame'.

As its prefatory paragraphs indicate, *Parisina* is based on Edward Gibbon's account of an incident from the life of Niccolò III d'Este, a fifteenth-century duke of Ferrara who on discovering that his second wife, Parisina Malatesta, had been unfaithful with his illegitimate son, Ugo, had the guilty lovers executed. In Byron's retelling of the story, Hugo and Parisina had been engaged before Niccolò (whom Byron rechristens Azo, the name of the first Este to rule Ferrara) married her. When Byron's Azo discovers the adulterous affair, he has only Hugo killed. But he obliges Parisina to witness the beheading, and she descends shrieking into what looks like madness, though the narrator leaves her subsequent fate mysterious, whether it be 'blighted and remorseful' years of penitence in a convent (517), murder by 'bowl or steel' (519) or death on the spot at the loss of 'that dark love she dared to feel' (520).

Jerome McGann's editorial notes on the poem's composition, publishing history and literary and historical background show how complicated both the writing process and Byron's selective, semi-accurate appropriation of Italian historical fact for poetic fiction are in *Parisina*. As McGann argues from manuscript sources, it seems that *Parisina* and *The Siege of Corinth* may originally have been a single tale of Alp and Francesca, who respectively remain the renegade protagonist and the love interest in the latter work.[6] Byron's choice of the name 'Francesca' for an illicit lady love can be read as both Italian literary allusion and English covert confession. Byron's own Regency 'Francesca' was Lady Frances Wedderburn Webster, wife of a husband whom Byron held in contempt and 'Platonic' object of country-house flirtations amusingly chronicled in Byron's letters to Lady Melbourne at a time when Byron might have needed romantic distraction from both Augusta Leigh and Annabella Milbanke. Lady Frances was Byron's subject in such other roughly contemporary personal lyrics as the 'Genevra' poems and the bitter 'When We Two Parted', which, without naming names, deplores Lady Frances's notoriety as the duke of Wellington's mistress, most infamously at Brussels around the time of Waterloo.

The comic Regency love triangle of Byron and the Wedderburn Websters has a tragic Italian counterpart in the adulterous story of Francesca da Rimini, famous thanks to Dante's *Divina Commedia*. The thirteenth-century Francesca da Polenta, daughter of the lord of Ravenna, had been given in a peace-brokering political marriage to Giovanni Malatesta, son of the lord of Rimini. She betrayed her crippled husband with his younger brother Paolo. Along with Paolo, she died at her husband's hand. Dante consigns the guilty pair to the windblown second circle of hell, where the lust-driven are punished. Byron, who alludes appreciatively to Dante's treatment of Paolo and

Francesca in prose and verse alike, would later, around the time when he was writing *The Prophecy of Dante* and was in the early days of his own adulterous relationship with an aristocratic native of Ravenna, translate this episode from *La Divina Commedia* and publish it as 'Francesca of Rimini'.

Why did a tale that Byron might have called *Francesca* morph into one called *Parisina*? One possible explanation, of course, is the bifurcation of the original project that would have featured Francesca and Alp. But another potential reason has to do with the somewhat older poet Leigh Hunt, whose acquaintance Byron made during the period of *Parisina*'s composition and of Hunt's imprisonment in Surrey Gaol for libelling the prince regent. At this time, Hunt was himself writing a version of the story of Francesca and Paolo that would appear in 1816 as *The Story of Rimini*. Byron, who had personally brought Italian books relevant to the *Rimini* project to Hunt in prison, was instrumental in persuading Murray, whose offer to contribute to the *Quarterly Review* Hunt had spurned for political reasons some seven years earlier, to be the publisher of this work – and the grateful Hunt, without asking permission, effusively dedicated the poem to Byron, beginning 'MY DEAR BYRON, You see what you have brought yourself by liking my verses.'[7]

It seems likely that Byron would not have wanted to bring out a version of the Paolo and Francesca story that would directly compete with the Hunt poem he had sponsored and professed to admire. The name change from Francesca to Parisina, however, signals more than a polite desire not to compete in the literary marketplace – it points to a desire on Byron's part to distance his own portrayal of Italy from the governing aesthetics of Hunt's. *Rimini* and *Parisina* share a number of overall themes – most notably the adulterous, quasi-incestuous love triangles featuring brother against brother in the former and father against son in the latter – while specific details signal Hunt and Byron's ongoing conversation during the time when they were finishing their poems, including the anachronistic presence of Azo and Hugo in the opening scene of Hunt's *Rimini* and the sleep-talking through which the cuckolded husband learns of his wife's betrayal in each poem. But whereas for Byron the historicity of Italy is far more important than are its potentially picturesque qualities, Hunt's figuration of Ravenna and Rimini entails a good deal of atmospheric scene-painting that gives his narrative a pretty backdrop. Byron and Hunt also part company as to the aesthetics of poetic diction. As Nicholas Roe has pointed out, Hunt's loosened couplets enact a Romantic repudiation of neoclassical precedent with which Byron, a defender of Pope and Dryden, would disagree.[8] Furthermore, Byron's generally positive response to Hunt's draft of the third canto objects to 'occasional quaintness – & obscurity – & harsh & yet colloquial compounding of epithets – as if to avoid saying common things in the common way', a stylistic criticism that would be echoed and intensified in published form by William Gifford, John Wilson Croker and other foes of the 'Cockney School of Poetry'.[9]

However, three issues further complicate this intertextual conversation with *Rimini*, all of which surface when one thinks about how *Parisina* both uses and departs from Italian historical precedent to serve Byron's conscious purposes or subconscious needs in a sometimes dark and always hectic time of his life. These issues are incest, fatherhood and cant. On the score of cant, Byron's favoured term for the hypocrisy he detected, detested and denounced in Regency England, it is important that in Byron's version of the story of Duke Niccolò (Byron's Azo), Parisina and Ugo the love bond between the young pair precedes Azo's marrying Parisina. This altered sequence of events makes it easier to sympathise with the lovers and even to conclude that the emotional and ethical offence, if not the legal crime, is Azo and Parisina's marriage rather than Hugo and Parisina's adultery. In consequence, Azo's professed reason for having refused to let Parisina wed Hugo can be read as the height of cant. As Hugo forthrightly states after being condemned to death by his father,

> 'Tis true, that I have done thee wrong –
> But wrong for wrong – this deemed thy bride,
> The other victim of thy pride,
> Thou know'st for me was destined long.
> Thou saw'st, and coveted'st her charms –
> And with thy very crime – my birth,
> Thou taunted'st me – as little worth;
> A match ignoble for her arms,
> Because, forsooth, I could not claim
> The lawful heirship of thy name.
>
> (252–61)

In other words Azo, who had seduced and abandoned the noblewoman who bore Hugo out of wedlock, now has had the canting moral effrontery to use the illegitimate status his own sexual villainy bestowed on Hugo as the pretext for denying the blameless bastard the lady who loves him and has promised to marry him. This strategic departure from historical fact might be seen as enhancing a stereotypically sinister notion of Italian morals and marriage familiar to English novel-readers, accustomed as they were to Italy providing diverse sorts of Cisalpine wickedness drawn from what Diego Saglia has termed a 'Gothic archive'.[10] But that does not mean that promiscuity, coerced or thwarted marriages, revenge for cuckoldry and other crimes of the heart are to be seen as safely distant, in place or in time, from Regency society. Later, in *Beppo* and especially *Don Juan*, an Anglo-Italian Byron will draw explicit, ironic contrasts between sexual and marital hypocrisy as variously practised in the 'sunny South' and the 'moral North'. In these poems, hypocrisy is a transcendent human vice that takes contingent cultural forms. In *Parisina*, a Byron who as yet has experienced Italy only through literature and history leaves the intercultural conclusion-drawing implicit.

Besides presenting the young adulterers as an engaged pair broken up by a coerced marriage, Byron departs from Italian anecdotal accounts by making Hugo, in so far as we can tell, the only son Azo has yet sired, when there were reputed to be bastards aplenty. As McGann's editorial notes point out, according to a Ferrara proverb, on 'both sides of the river Po, they are all Niccolò's sons'.[11] In *Parisina*, however, Hugo is not just Azo's apparent sole male issue; he is also a remarkably fine son for a soldier-prince, no Byronic renegade but a stout, reliable and proven defender of his father's regime, a warrior who, as his forthright speech before death makes clear, has 'shed more blood in cause of thine, / Than e'er can stain the axe of mine' (239–40). Whatever the technicalities of pedigree, Hugo has clearly inherited his father's best qualities:

> Albeit, my birth and name be base,
> And thy nobility of race
> Disdained to deck a thing like me –
> Yet in my lineaments they trace
> Some features of my father's face,
> And in my spirit all of thee.
>
> (282–7)

Although Azo professes to scorn him as a product of guilty love, Hugo is nonetheless so noble a specimen of manhood that it is his execution rather than the loss of the lovely but expendable Parisina that becomes the vengeful father and husband's true punishment. Even in a cant-ridden patriarchal milieu, Azo comes to learn that legitimate sons are not adequate replacements for the noble yet illegitimate one he condemned and executed:

> And Azo found another bride,
> And goodly sons grew by his side;
> But none so lovely or so brave
> As him who withered in the grave;
> Or if they were – on his cold eye
> Their growth but glanced unheeded by,
> Or noticed with a smothered sigh.
> (530–6)

This cautionary tale of fathers and sons may take place in fifteenth-century Italy, but its lesson is relevant to, and written for, Regency England.

Parisina's variation on the theme of incest plays with a literary topic that preoccupied the tale-telling Byron between 1812 and 1816, from the passionate love between apparent half-siblings (but actual cousins) Salim and Zuleika in *The Bride of Abydos* to the mysterious but all-consuming love between actual siblings Manfred and Astarte in *Manfred*. *Parisina*, unlike the earlier tale and the later drama, offers an explicitly consummated incestuous love. But, as mentioned above, the incest is merely technical, a legal or cultural construction. He is Azo's son, she Azo's wife – but that does not make them blood kin. Incestuous love, and the need to tell tales that both expressed and sanitised it, seems to have run hot and strong through Byron's imagination in the years of *Parisina*'s inception, growth and publication. These were the years of his most intense closeness with his married, older half-sister Augusta Leigh, whom he had hardly known until adulthood and by whom he very likely fathered a child, Medora, born on 15 April 1814.

If personal varieties of incestuous experience and their practical consequences were much in Byron's mind, though, he could hardly articulate and explore them candidly and directly in his published poems. But thanks to the 'lava of the imagination', pent-up thoughts, displaced (in this case to Italy) and historicised (here, in the Ferrara court of Niccolò d'Este) could find an outlet. Italy is, at this point in Byron's career, a place where he can imagine and poetically release what must remain publically suppressed in England.[12] Once Byron found himself 'on the spot' in Venice, however, this release would become possible in life as well as art.

Towards the end of *Parisina*, Byron generalises and perceptively articulates the need to express and displace feelings too powerful for Wordsworth's 'spontaneous overflow'. The narrator muses on the outward composure but inward agony of Azo, who has doomed himself in condemning his son to death: 'The deepest ice which ever froze / Can only o'er the surface close – / The living stream lies quick below, / And flows – and cannot cease to flow' (553–6). That flow has to go somewhere. During the years of *Parisina*'s composition, Byron seems to have conceived of as-yet-unvisited Italy, like other Mediterranean places and cultures he had actually experienced, as a channel into which that lava could flow more freely than it could into a British outlet.

Displacement works rather differently in *Mazeppa*, a poem written in Italy, saturated with Byron's sensibility during his time there but set in other places and times. Begun in April 1817 and published in June 1819 with the 'Ode on Venice', *Mazeppa* had a comparatively lengthy, interrupted period of composition during which Byron, self-consciously cultivating his role of Anglo-Venetian, also wrote the fourth canto of *Childe Harold's Pilgrimage* and *Beppo*, and began *Don Juan*. The first two of these works treat Italian subjects. The last two employ an Italian metrical form, *ottava rima*. The first two cantos of *Don Juan*, published barely two weeks after *Mazeppa*, immediately and completely overshadowed the belated tale.

Metrically, *Mazeppa* may be the last leaf on the tetrameter tree of the Eastern tales, but its style, tone and narrative are less easily characterised. Jane Stabler views the poem's 'knowing hybridity' as proto-postmodernist. Reading in a different way to make a similar point, Bernard Beatty sees *Mazeppa* as a 'transition point' between the two halves of Byron's poetic career.[13] The hybrid or transitional nature of the tale has in great measure to do with displacement, cosmopolitanism and Byron's evolving Anglo-Italian identity. Here, as in *Parisina*, the displaced feelings are Byron's. But in contrast to the earlier poem's way of proceeding, Byron's personal contingencies – some of them retrospective, some comparative, some uncannily proleptic – are displaced from Italy rather than to it.

As McGann's annotations to the Oxford edition of *Mazeppa* make clear, the allusive nature of the poem makes reading it in dialogue with other texts particularly valuable. Considering *Mazeppa* in light of Byron's other projects of the period, *Beppo* and *Don Juan*, reveals the literary side of his evolving Anglo-Italian persona, disclosed and displaced through a tale involving a Polish protagonist, a Swedish audience and a *mise en scène* that sweeps from Polish court to Ukrainian wilderness. *Mazeppa* resembles *Don Juan* in having a complex time-scheme juxtaposing distinct historical periods. Mazeppa's recollected tale is said to have taken place fifty years before the battle of 'dread Pultowa' (1709), and the external narrator's description of 'Moscow's walls' being 'safe again' implicitly grounds the poem's outer layer of narrative in a post-Napoleonic age, after the Russian winter of 1812 had put an end to Napoleon's ambitions for eastward conquest:

> And Moscow's walls were safe again,
> Until a day more dark and drear,
> And a more memorable year,
> Should give to slaughter and to shame
> A mightier host and haughtier name;
> A greater wreck, a deeper fall,
> A shock to one – a thunderbolt to all.
> (8–14)

Similarly, but more subtly, Mazeppa's comment on the uninhabited landscape over which the untamed steed carried him can be seen as a kind of chronotope fusing that eastern 'wild plain of far extent' (430) with the scarred, still-littered field of Waterloo, over which Byron had recently passed in April 1816, only nine months after the great battle: 'The year before / A Turkish army had march'd o'er; / And where the Spahi's hoof hath trod, / The verdure flies the bloody sod' (435–8).

Mazeppa also resembles both *Beppo* and *Don Juan* in having a philosophising, conversational narrator, though with a difference. Because the bulk of the poem is narrated in Mazeppa's voice – from the first line of section 5 until the nine lines of section 20 that conclude the poem – the tale mostly fuses the roles of philosophising narrator and enduring protagonist, the former being Mazeppa at seventy, the latter

Mazeppa half a century younger. In its own way, *Mazeppa* shows many of the hallmarks of the distinctive modes of writing Byron developed through his intense engagement with Italian writers, perhaps most especially Casti, whose *Novelle galanti* made him 'long to go to Venice to see the manners so admirably described',[14] and Pulci, who had significantly influenced *Beppo* and with whom Byron pairs himself using Cardinal Wolsey's phrase 'Ego et Rex meus' ('I and my king') in a letter describing the packet containing the first canto of *Don Juan*, *Mazeppa* and the 'Ode on Venice' that he has just posted to England.[15]

But if *Mazeppa* offers a geographical displacement of Byron's Italianate modes of writing, it also displaces other matters linked to Byron's life, writing and developing identity in Italy. Although Voltaire's *Histoire de Charles XII* describes Mazeppa's romantic conquest only vaguely as 'la femme d'un gentilhomme Polonais' ('the wife of a Polish gentleman'), Byron invents specifics linking the love triangle to both *Beppo* and *Don Juan*.[16] The cuckolded husband in *Mazeppa* is 'a count of far and high descent' (156), which makes him a nobleman holding the same rank as Laura's lover and thus inverts the respective social positions of the betrayed husband and the betraying lover portrayed in *Beppo*. The Count Palatine's being thirty years older than his wife corresponds to Don Alfonso's seniority to Donna Julia in *Don Juan*; and the beauty of the Count Palatine's young wife is, like Donna Julia's, an apparent consequence of ethnic mixture: 'She had the Asiatic eye, / Such as our Turkish neighbourhood / Hath mingled with our Polish blood' (208–10).

The lady's name, Theresa, coincidentally relates her to Byron's life rather than to his contemporary *ottava rima* poems; for Byron's Anglo-Italian identity would soon acquire one of its best-known attributes, his status as the '*cavalier servente*' of a middle-aged Italian count's much younger wife.[17] But although Byron had met the newly wed Teresa Guiccioli at the Contessa Albrizzi's salon in January 1818, during the period when he was writing *Mazeppa*, he fell in love with her only when they met again at the Contessa Benzoni's *conversazione* in April 1819, months after he had dispatched both *Don Juan* and *Mazeppa* to Hobhouse as announced in his letter of 11 November 1818. Thus connecting Byron's real-life Italian liaison with the legendary Polish one recounted in *Mazeppa* is a matter of life curiously coming to reflect art rather than art deriving from life.

While the poem was written in Italy and converses with the *ottava rima* poems Byron was writing at much the same time as he was discovering how perfectly the Italian conventions of the *improvvisatore* suited his poetic sensibility, it also looks back to his last years in England, most notably through resemblances to *The Rime of the Ancient Mariner*. The years 1815–16 were the period of Byron's personal acquaintance with Coleridge. These years also marked the high point of Byron's opinion of Coleridge as a writer, a time when Byron was thinking of the older man not as the metaphysician he mocks in *Don Juan* but as a poet and playwright whose work he admired. As a member of the Drury Lane Committee, Byron had championed the production of Coleridge's tragedy *Remorse*, successfully staged in 1813. Having heard Walter Scott recite the then-still-unpublished *Christabel* at John Murray's on 30 June 1815, Byron was struck with admiration of the 'fine wild poem' – and among his last literary favours before leaving England in April 1816 was his securing Murray as Coleridge's publisher for *Christabel*, 'Kubla Khan' and 'The Pains of Sleep'.[18] Byron recited *Christabel* to his Diodati circle in Switzerland, thereby galvanising the famous ghost-story competition that would eventually result in Mary Shelley's *Frankenstein*. But, as is the case with *Frankenstein*, *Mazeppa*'s most conspicuous literary debt to Coleridge comes not from *Christabel* but from *The Ancient Mariner*.

McGann's editorial notes point out specific verbal echoes and situational parallels between *The Ancient Mariner* and *Mazeppa*.[19] More broadly and organically, the entire tale can, like *Frankenstein*, be seen as following the *Ancient Mariner* model of storytelling: an external narrative frames a tale spun by its world-wandering protagonist for a didactic purpose – although in Byron's ironic text the moral is lost on the sleeping Charles XII. Like *The Ancient Mariner* and *Frankenstein*, *Mazeppa* tells the tale of a painful, lonely journey inflicted on the protagonist as the consequence of or penance for sin. Coleridge's rime and Byron's tale are also linked by the crucial presence of animals in the narrative and a comparably humane appreciation of the dignity of animal life. The crime precipitating the Mariner's punishment is his random killing of a companionable Albatross; the Mariner's moment of gracious redemption comes through his appreciation of the beauty of marine water-snakes he has previously seen as loathsome and his blessing them; and the didactic conclusion the Mariner offers his mesmerised audience, the Wedding Guest, is:

> He prayeth best, who loveth best
> All things both great and small;
> For the dear God who loveth us,
> He made and loveth all.
> (614–17)[20]

The lesson that sleeping Charles XII fails to hear as Mazeppa ends his tale is secular and existential rather than pious: 'What mortal his own doom may guess? – / Let none despond, let none despair!' (853–4). But another practical moral that the external narrator and Mazeppa variously affirm through words and deeds pervades the text: a compassion for horses every bit as respectful of non-human animal life as even the Ancient Mariner could wish for, especially in the aftermath of battle, where 'danger levels man and brute, / And all are fellows in their need' (50–1). However, the practical care of and sympathetic concern for horses evident throughout *Mazeppa* also seems connected in a compelling way with some specific aspects of Byron's life in Italy.

Although a love of horses and of the sports associated with them has for centuries been an enduring trait of the English country-house class, and Byron was certainly able to sit a horse before he went to Italy, it is intriguing that he seems to have become seriously devoted to recreational riding only after settling in Venice, where such exercise would be relatively troublesome, involving as it would have to a boat ride to the Lido. Why might rides of the sort described by Shelley in 'Julian and Maddalo' become important to Byron in Venice and remain part of his subsequent life both in Italy, where he rode at evening, first in the pine forests of Ravenna and later in Pisa and later still in Greece, right up to the last weeks of his life in Messolonghi? Answering such a question involves speculation, but Byron's penchant for contrarian figure-cutting might offer one portion of a hypothetical explanation.[21] Perhaps he was inclined to cultivate recreational horsemanship in Venice after having avoided it in London partly because riding had been so typical an activity of someone of his class in his native city. Here, Byron's well-known scorn of another currently fashionable, gaited London pastime – waltzing – might offer an illuminating comparison. Byron refused to waltz partly because so many other fashionable people were intent on doing so but mostly because, given his deformed foot, he could not have waltzed gracefully. Similarly, it seems possible that another reason for Byron not being a sport rider in England was that although his riding skills were perfectly adequate for practical purposes his technique was not polished enough to allow him to shine among Hyde Park equestrians. Unlike fellow aristocrats born to their estates, he had not been instructed in the fine points of dressage from his earliest days. Unlike army officers, he had not been obliged to perfect horsemanship for professional reasons. And his physical disability would have limited the ease with which he could ride formally: posting would have been particularly difficult. Thus, in Venice Byron might have found it liberating to gallop freely on the Adriatic shore, where keeping a horse was comparatively cheap and the judgemental eyes of well-schooled English riders were generally absent.[22]

Human feats of fine horsemanship are not an issue in *Mazeppa* either. The young Mazeppa has to be strong in body and spirit to survive his excruciating passive horseback ride across eastern Europe, but the steed to which he is tied is the poem's magnificent athlete in a tale more concerned with the treatment of horses than with the heroism of equestrians. Granted, the 'slaughter' attendant on the battles of Pultowa and Moscow, alluded to early in the narrative, involved cavalry action – and when an older, harder Mazeppa returns to 'to thank / The Count Palatine for his discourteous ride' by destroying the castle where the 'bitter prank' began, his Cossack force is a cavalry: 'twice five thousand horse' (411–13). But throughout the poem, the narrator and Mazeppa focus more on the innate nobility of horses and the responsibility of humans to treat them well than on human heroics on horseback. Indeed, one of the best things we can know of old Mazeppa is his kindness to his mount, a 'wearied courser' (64) more loyal and serviceable than most human companions would be. Charles recognises the remarkable bond between the hetman and his Cossack horse: 'On the earth / So fit a pair had never birth, / Since Alexander's days till now, / As thy Bucephalus and thou' (101–4). This hyperbolic praise prompts Mazeppa's wry rejoinder – 'Ill betide / The school wherein I learn'd to ride!' (107–8) – that in turn spurs Charles's request for the story of Mazeppa's epic bareback ride. The punitive, inextricable connection of youth and untamed stallion, a complete inversion of the frame tale's bond between the old hetman and his faithful warhorse, serves as a flagrant example of man's inhumanity to man and beast alike.

The freedom-loving Byron was likewise no fan of the metaphorical bit or whip hand, whether deployed by 'mobs or kings', as he puts it in *Don Juan* (IX, 25, 1). It is easy to see how Byron's English sensibility could imagine, in Italy, that *Mazeppa*'s noble vision of unmastered Ukrainian horses would share the liberal and liberating impulses that in the months ahead would draw him into the revolutionary Carbonari movement. In fact, Byron, as an outsider serving causes to which he was not born, came to have a role to play not unlike like Mazeppa's among the Cossacks. First he supported Italian freedom and unification; later he financed, helped organise and eventually died for the Greek struggle for independence from the Ottoman Empire. Byron's relationship with the Carbonari brotherhood, into which he was drawn by the Gambas, father and brother of his mistress Teresa Guiccioli, involved a complicated mix of engagement and scepticism. Byron believed in the cause and was willing to risk personal danger to serve it, even to the extent of storing Carbonari weapons in his Ravenna lodgings – but his gentlemanly English sense of human decency and his penchant for mockery kept him from being the sort of unquestioning believer revolutionary groups find most reliable and congenial.

A high-born resident alien who mixed empathy and cynicism much as did the sardonic yet kindly Mazeppa he figured in his tale, Byron committed himself to the revolutionary Carbonari society – but with a distinctive Anglo cast to his Italian partisanship. In a 10 December 1820 letter to Lady Byron and in other near-contemporary letters to other correspondents, Byron describes the ambush of Ravenna's Austrian commandant 'on account of his having been severe against the Carbonari' and details his own response of bringing in the dying commandant and giving him what care was possible. Reflecting on the murder of a brave man who had been a powerful political adversary, Byron both deplores the '*wild* Justice' of assassination and recognises that it is 'the consequence of a negligent administration of the laws, or of a despotic government'.[23] Months later, in a 28 April 1821 letter written to Thomas Moore around the time of the Gambas' exile from Ravenna after the failed revolt, Byron calls Italy 'this Inquisition of a country' and observes, as 'a very pretty woman said to me a few nights ago, with the tears in her eyes, as she sat at the harpsichord, "Alas! the Italians must now return to making operas". I fear *that* and maccaroni are their forte, and "motley their only wear". However, there are some high spirits among them still.'[24] The disappointed revolutionary neither subdues his stereotype-perpetuating humour nor fails to recognise that admirable Italian freedom-fighters coexist with ineffective ones. Still later, Byron's Ravenna letter to Murray dated 4 September 1821 encloses what he calls an 'Italian scrap', an anonymous assassination threat against him as *capo* or chief of the so-called 'Mericani', a Romagna term for 'the *popular* part, the *troops* of the Carbonari'. Representing himself as brave enough to laugh at a death threat and petty-minded enough to mock illiteracy, Byron dismisses the 'Italian scrap' with cool, fastidious English amusement: 'it will make you laugh – and him [Hobhouse] too – the *spelling* particularly'.[25]

My approach to understanding how these two tales show Byron's evolving and ever-protean Anglo-Italian identity both being shaped by what he wrote and shaping his writings has been eclectic: sometimes formalist, sometimes comparative, sometimes speculative, often based in biographical or historical contextualising, occasionally using a theoretical lens to show how, for a cosmopolitan of Byron's sort, placement and displacement, being there and not being there, productively interact. Byron, who wished more insular English poets would trade their lakes for ocean, had the curiosity, courage, formal and informal education, material assets and socio-political privilege to travel widely, both in space and in time – to Italy and elsewhere. *Parisina* and *Mazeppa* are, in their different ways, poetic consequences of his distinctive actual and mental ways of 'being there'.

Notes

1 S. Cheeke, *Byron and Place: History, Translation, Nostalgia* (Basingstoke: Palgrave Macmillan, 2003), pp. 18–19.
2 Cheeke, *Byron and Place*, p. 20.
3 *CPW*, vol. V, pp. 649, 769.
4 *BLJ*, vol. III, p. 179.
5 See P. W. Graham, 'Byron and the business of publishing', in J. D. Bone (ed.), *The Cambridge Companion to Byron* (Cambridge: Cambridge University Press, 2004), pp. 27–43 (p. 34).
6 See *CPW*, vol. III, pp. 479–80, 489–90.
7 Quoted in N. Roe, *Fiery Heart: The First Life of Leigh Hunt* (London: Pimlico, 2005), p. 252. Timothy Webb has written insightfully on the friendship and mutual poetic influences of Hunt and Byron during this period of their lives. See, for instance, T. Webb,

'Leigh Hunt's Letters to Byron from Horsemonger Lane gaol: a commentary', *The Byron Journal*, 37:1 (2009), 21–32; and T. Webb, 'After Horsemonger Lane: Leigh Hunt's London letters to Byron (1815–16)', *Romanticism*, 16:3 (2010), 233–66.

8   Roe, *Fiery Heart*, p. 245.
9   Letter to Leigh Hunt of 22 October 1815, in *BLJ*, vol. IV, p. 320.
10 D. Saglia, 'From Gothic Italy to Italy as Gothic archive: Italian narratives and the late Romantic metrical tale', *Gothic Studies*, 8:1 (2006), 73–90.
11 *CPW*, vol. III, p. 490.
12 As *Parisina* was about to appear, Byron seems to have felt confident (if falsely so) that the personal circumstances and emotions vented in his imaginative eruption had not at least been detected by his wife: in a letter of 2 January 1816 to John Murray he writes of the fair copy in Annabella's hand that he is 'very glad that the handwriting was a favourable omen of the morale of the piece – but you must not trust to that – for my copyist would write out anything I desired in all the ignorance of innocence' (*BLJ*, vol. V, p. 13).
13 J. Stabler, 'Byron, post-modernism, and intertextuality', in J. D. Bone (ed.), *The Cambridge Companion to Byron* (Cambridge: Cambridge University Press, 2004), pp. 265–6; B. Beatty, 'Continuities and discontinuities of language and voice', in A. Rutherford (ed.), *Byron: Augustan and Romantic* (London: Macmillan, 1990), pp. 117–35 (p. 131).
14 Letter to Pryce Gordon of 'June? 1816', in *BLJ*, vol. V, p. 80.
15 Letter to John Cam Hobhouse of 11 November 1819, in *BLJ*, vol. VI, p. 76.
16 See *CPW*, vol. IV, p. 173.
17 For further discussion of the *cavalier servente* and Byron's adoption of this role with Teresa Guiccioli, see Diego Saglia's chapter in this volume.
18 Letter to John Murray of 30 September 1816, in *BLJ*, vol. V, p. 108.
19 See *CPW*, vol. IV, p. 494.
20 S. T. Coleridge, *Complete Poetical Works*, ed. E. H. Coleridge (Oxford: Clarendon, 1912).
21 I am indebted to Christine Kenyon Jones for some penetrating insights shared as we exchanged speculations on Byron and equestrianship.
22 In L. Hunt, *Lord Byron and Some of His Contemporaries* (New York: AMS, 1966), Leigh Hunt recollects riding with Byron in Italy and claims that 'he was a good rider, graceful, and kept a firm seat. He loved to be told of it; and it being true it was pleasure to tell him' (pp. 42–3).
23 Letter to Lady Byron of 10 December 1820, in *BLJ*, vol. VII, p. 249.
24 *BLJ*, vol. VIII, p. 105.
25 *BLJ*, vol. VIII, p. 197.

9

This 'still exhaustless mine': de Staël, Goethe and Byron's Roman lyricism

Alan Rawes

Three writers, in three hugely influential texts, led and largely defined the Romantic reinvention of Italy and, in particular, Rome: Madame de Staël in *Corinne, ou l'Italie* (1807),[1] Goethe in *Italienische Reise* (published in instalments in 1816, 1817 and 1829),[2] and Byron in Canto IV of *Childe Harold's Pilgrimage* (1818).[3] In Britain, naturally enough, Byron's text was the most influential of the three, and in ways that extended far beyond the world of literature and the arts: *Childe Harold* IV had perhaps its widest cultural impact through the explosion of mass tourism that so marked the nineteenth century, becoming 'the *Urtext* of the Italian experience for the British tourist, acknowledged as a normative model for the perception of Italy'.[4]

This was partly due to external factors. First, there was the phenomenon of thousands of new tourists heading to the Continent after the end of the Napoleonic wars, all hungry for guidance as to what to see, as well as how to look at what they saw: the popularity of all sorts of travel writing rose sharply in the early decades of the nineteenth century. Second, there was the birth of the modern tourist guidebook, in the form of John Murray's *Handbooks for Travellers* series, and Murray's extensive quotation from, but also his touristic reconstruction of, Byron in these handbooks, especially *Murray's Handbook for Travellers in Central Italy*. This commodification of Byron was in fact so successful that Murray went further to publish, in 1843, 'a pocket-sized travel edition of Byron's works, to be read – and rehearsed – on the spot'.[5] Third, of course, there was Byron's already established '"star quality"', which made him 'a moving tourist attraction' in his own right.[6] But there were internal features of *Childe Harold* IV that also readily lent themselves to touristic appropriation. One is the canto's 'theatrical tenor', which had a 'celebrated capacity to revivify' all kinds of 'well-known tourist haunts' through the performance of 'Byronic' feeling.[7] More fundamental, however, is the lyric mode of Byron's canto, which not only points out sights to see but also models a way of individually *experiencing* those sights. In this chapter I want to spotlight this lyric mode by contrasting it with the very different ways of approaching Rome – and Italy more generally – offered by de Staël and Goethe.

To some extent all three writers share a vision of Italy. They visit many of the same places (though de Staël's and Goethe's texts go to Naples, and Goethe's goes further still to Sicily, while Byron's text visits neither), but all put Rome centre stage. And, following in the wake of Johann Winckelmann's seminal 1764 history of ancient art, *Geschichte der Kunst des Alterthums*, each sees Rome as 'a museum' of 'antiquities', turning the living, modern city primarily into a means of engaging with these antiquities.[8] For all three authors, Italy's 'magnificent cultural residue from antiquity and the Renaissance overwhelmed any signs of cultural activity in modern Italy',[9] as each seeks out what Goethe calls 'the Everlasting Rome, not the Rome which is replaced by another every decade' (154).

However, these writers also seek – and find – very different things in this 'Everlasting Rome'. For de Staël, 'Rome's many monuments to the dead' teach us 'how ephemeral' past, present and future generations of human beings were, are and will be. And by teaching 'the observer' this, 'the presence in Rome of the remains of so many periods' encourages in that observer a 'resigned acceptance of' his/her 'own transitoriness', and thus a kind of 'resignation, even serenity' in the face of suffering and mortality.[10] Teaching historical perspective, de Staël's Rome becomes a place of 'solace' for both 'creative geniuses and ordinary people in times of suffering'.[11] Rome offers sufferers of all kind – personal, political, social, historical – comfort, solace, consolation, teaching resignation in the face of history, indeed of life itself.

According to Goethe, quoting Winckelmann, Rome is 'the "world's university"', 'a locus of education and self-exploration' that offers the possibility of personal transformation through exposure to the examples of artistic perfection that its ancient remains present:[12]

> Goethe is transported out of the present by the great Roman presences from the past, is transported with the sense that he is now at last moving 'into another simpler and greater world' [...]. At the end of the *Journey* Goethe [presents himself as] a young man whose future is beginning to unfold as he 'ventures upon something unusual'.[13]

Rome is, for Goethe, a vast demonstration of the human ability to achieve 'noble perfection' (148) in the arts. It trains him how to recognise and understand that perfection and inspires him to try and replicate that perfection himself, as a literary artist, in the future.

What Byron finds in Rome is different again, not least because he sees a great many things in the city's ruins. Byron's famous 'moral of all human tales', for example, written on the Palatine, teaches us that all is

> but the same rehearsal of the past,
> First freedom, and then Glory – when that fails,
> Wealth, vice, corruption, – barbarism at last.
> (108)

Rome's ruins make manifest the pointlessness of human endeavour. But Rome also manifests the working of time, 'the beautifier of the dead, / Adorner of the ruin, comforter / And only healer when the heart hath bled' (130). Rome's ruins teach this truth as much as the 'moral of all human tales': it is 'amidst' the 'wreck' (131) of the Coliseum that Byron conceives of his great 'forgiveness curse', to be worked out in, and by, time. And if the ruins of the Palatine point out the ultimate barbarity of human endeavour, Cecilia Metella's tomb inspires Byron to build 'a little bark of hope, once more / To battle with the ocean and the shocks / Of the loud breakers' (105). Indeed, the 'moral of all human tales' itself contains a kind of hope: while all human tales end in 'barbarism at last', they also produce, along the way, 'freedom' and 'glory'. The endless histories that are memorialised in Italy's ruins and art offer a record of repeated renewal as well as decline – in Florence, during the Renaissance, 'Was modern Luxury of Commerce born, / And buried Learning rose, redeem'd to a new morn' (48). There is, of course, a 'moral' for contemporary Italy in this.[14] Time, which 'hath wrong'd [Italy] with ten thousand rents /

Of [her] imperial garment', 'shall deny, / And hath denied, to every other sky, / Spirits which soar from ruin', but it also reveals the fact that Italy's 'decay / Is still impregnate with divinity, / Which gilds it with revivifying ray' (55).

The historical spectacle of Rome teaches Byron other things in *Childe Harold* IV, but it is not what these three texts take *from* Rome that I want focus on here so much as their ways of responding *to* Rome. What I want to suggest is that, while the fictional and autobiographical works of de Staël and Goethe appropriate the ruins of Rome for their own needs and purposes, *Childe Harold* IV presents us with an attentive lyric responsiveness to the ruins of Rome per se. De Staël's fiction seeks to offer the consoling solace of Rome's past in answer to the needs of a France – indeed a continent – ripped apart by the Napoleonic wars.[15] Goethe's autobiography subordinates Rome to its concern with the ways in which Rome's past achievements answer the 'immediate interest' and 'personal need' of its author, born of a 'crisis' in which Goethe needed to revitalise his own artistic life.[16] For de Staël, Rome is a consolation and a comfort; for Goethe it is a university. For Byron, Rome is an experience, and his lyric poem seeks to represent that experience. I am here partly disagreeing with Jerome McGann when he says that like 'everything else in Byron's poem, Rome is an expression and extension of himself'.[17] The poem does not always and only Byronise Rome – it also Romanises Byron.[18] But, of course, McGann is responding to something real about the poem: what *Childe Harold* IV adds to Romanticism's recreation of Rome – precisely because of its lyrical responsiveness – is Byron, a 'ruin amidst ruins', tracking 'fallen states and buried greatness' (25). *Childe Harold* IV's radically individualised, lyricised recreation of Italy, and especially Rome, is one of its most powerful legacies to the later nineteenth century and beyond, not least in terms of tourism. To bring this lyricisation into sharper focus, I want to compare its treatment of one particular place – the Palatine – with those of de Staël and Goethe.

The first of these to be published was *Corinne*. Byron knew de Staël personally, having met her at parties in London in 1813–14 and attended some of her salons at the Château de Coppet in Switzerland in 1816. He pays extended tribute to her in a long note to *Childe Harold* IV. He also obviously knew *Corinne* very well – he annotated Teresa Guiccioli's copy of the novel, though after he had written *Childe Harold* IV. He admired aspects of de Staël's book, but not its treatment of Italy. In Teresa's copy, for instance, he wrote:

> I knew Madame de Staël well – better than She knew Italy; – but I little thought that one day I should think with her thoughts in the country where she has laid the scene of her most attractive production. – She is sometimes right and often wrong about Italy and England – but almost always true in delineating the heart.[19]

De Staël's novel clearly 'guides much of Byron's thought' in *Childe Harold* IV,[20] but not, generally, in a positive sense – as Joanna Wilkes has put it, one 'illuminating way of interpreting *Childe Harold* IV is as an extended and sometimes critical response to the much read *Corinne*'.[21] We will certainly see some implicitly critical allusions to Corinne's response to the Palatine in Byron's, but let us look at de Staël's text first:

> Oswald and Corinne began their tour with the Palatine hill. The palace of the Caesars, called *the golden palace*, used to occupy it completely. Now, only the ruins of the palace remain on the hill. Augustus, Tiberius, Caligula, and Nero built its four sides, but stones, completely covered all over by proliferating plants, are all that remains of it today. Nature has regained its empire over the works of man and the beauty of the flowers is a consolation for the ruin of the palaces. Luxury in the eras of the kings and of the Republic consisted entirely of public buildings; private houses were very small and very simple. Cicero, Hortensius, the Gracchi, lived on the Palatine hill, which, in the days of Rome's decadence, had barely enough space for the home of one man. In later centuries, the nation was no more than an anonymous crowd, referred to only by its master's reign. There is no point in searching in these places for the two laurel bushes planted in front of Augustus' door, the laurel of war and the laurel of the arts cultivated by peace; both have disappeared.
>
> Some rooms of Livia's baths still remain on the Palatine hill. They show where precious stones used to be lavished on ceilings like an ordinary decoration, and you can see there paintings whose colours are still perfectly intact; the very fragility of the colours adds to our amazement at seeing them preserved and brings the past close to us. If it is true that Livia shortened Augustus' life, it was in one of these rooms that the crime was plotted, and the eyes of the sovereign of the world, betrayed in his profoundest affections, may have dwelt on one

of these pictures whose elegant flowers still survive. In his old age, what did he think of life and its pomp? Did he remember his proscriptions or his glory? Did he fear or hope for a world to come? And the last thought which reveals everything to man, the last thought of a master of the universe, does it still wander beneath these arches?[22]

Oswald is the tourist here, with Corinne as his 'tour guide', whose impulse is to interest her companion in, and educate him about, Rome.[23] Through Corinne's conversations with Oswald, de Staël also invites her (French) readers on a 'tour' of Rome, seeking to instruct those readers as to what there is to see in Rome, and why it might be worth seeing. Indeed, 'one could actually read *Corinne* to work out an itinerary for an Italian', and Roman, 'tour (and people did just that)', looking at each site in turn through Corinne's introduction of it to Oswald.[24] But in this passage, de Staël in fact first draws her reader's attention to lack, loss and absence – the palace of the Caesars 'used to occupy' the space, but 'only ruins [...] remain'. She then supplements these 'ruins' with information about what, or rather who, was there ('Augustus, Tiberius, Caligula and Nero'), while turning to 'the beauty of the flowers' as a 'consolation' for their absence now and the 'ruin' of their 'palaces'. Already we can see the essence of de Staël's Rome: mentally, Rome is a historical panorama that takes in its sweep the founding of empires (Augustus), supreme military victories (Tiberius), decadence and tyranny on a grand scale (Caligula) and the end of great dynasties (Nero); physically, Rome is a landscape of mere 'stones' ('all that remain'); experientially, these mental and physical landscapes directly clash to produce a sense of absence and loss, but Rome is also a fecund provider of consolation for that absence and loss.

The rest of the passage repeats this movement from (historical) plenitude to (present) dearth and then to (emotional) consolation. There is a further widening and peopling of the historical vista with classical 'kings', 'the Republic', 'small and simple houses', 'Cicero, Hortensius, and the Gracchi'. A deepened sense of loss follows the recollection of these things and people. Registering their absence from the scene now, the passage quietly laments their passing away, as 'the Republic' was replaced by 'the anonymous crowd' and 'master's reign' of the later Roman Empire. Corinne then confronts Oswald with the passing of the empire in its turn, represented by 'the laurel of war and the laurel of arts cultivated in peace' that were 'planted in front of Augustus' door', but which have now 'disappeared'. The first paragraph ends on this note of absolute absence.

The second paragraph, however, shows de Staël determinedly looking for consolation for this lack in the beauty of what 'remain[s]' on the Palatine of Roman art: the 'paintings' whose 'colours' are 'perfectly intact' and, in their 'fragility', enrich our 'amazement' at the Palatine ruins. The 'paintings' and their 'colours' also 'bring the past close to us', but not the daily life of Roman bathing, nor the beauty of Roman art, nor the comfort and luxury of a Roman emperor's life. Rather they 'bring' the betrayal and death of a 'sovereign of the world' to us: Augustus, 'betrayed in his profoundest affections', facing death alone. And it is in this 'past' that de Staël finds her greatest source of consolation on the Palatine hill.

Like us all, and despite his power, 'pomp' and 'glory', Augustus suffered personally and profoundly. Like us all, 'the master of the universe' had to confront death: even Augustus shows us human 'transitoriness', and just how 'ephemeral every generation of human beings' is. This already seems pitched at encouraging resignation in the face of suffering and mortality. But there is more comfort being offered here, directly drawn from the Palatine, and this comes in the final sentence of our extract. Encouraged to think about human mortality per se by the example of Augustus, de Staël rather beautifully imagines herself in a potential, and very intimate, communion with Augustus: is her own thought of death, and even her very thinking about it, as she contemplates the Palatine, actually Augustus's 'last thought' entering her consciousness as it 'wander[s] beneath these arches'? In this idea the ruins of the Palatine become not a monument to the universal fact of suffering and death but a point of access into the universal, shared experience of confronting death. This is the ultimate consolation offered by the Palatine in de Staël's reading of it: it teaches us that every human being suffers and dies, however powerful they may be, and it inspires in us the sense that what feel to be our most intimate, private 'fears and hopes' are, in fact, shared by everyone else who lives or ever lived. Goethe's response to the Palatine was very different.

Byron greatly admired Goethe, but never mentions *Italienische Reise*, the German writer's account of his 1786–8 journey to Italy, and almost certainly did not read any of it (Byron could not read

German).[25] However, he could conceivably have had some knowledge of the first two instalments, published in 1816 and 1817, or even the letters they are based on,[26] possibly via de Staël or one of her guests at the salons at Coppet – Schlegel, for example – that Byron attended in 1816, possibly via Percy Bysshe Shelley.[27] But it is not as an influence on Byron that I want to look at Goethe's text but as a roughly contemporary point of contrast. Here is how Goethe responds to the Palatine:

> Today I went to the pyramid of Cestius and in the evening climbed to the top of the Palatine, where the ruins of the imperial palaces stand like rocks. It is impossible to convey a proper idea of such things. Nothing here is mediocre, and if, here and there, something is in poor taste, it, too, shares in the general grandeur.
>
> When I indulge in self-reflection, as I like to do occasionally, I discover in myself a feeling which gives me great joy. Let me put it like this. In this place, whoever looks seriously about him and has eyes to see is bound to become a stronger character: he acquires a sense of strength hitherto unknown to him.
>
> His soul receives the seal of a soundness, a seriousness without pedantry, and a joyous composure. At least, I can say that I have never been so sensitive to the things of the world as I am here. The blessed consequences will, I believe, affect my whole future life. (137)[28]

This is by far the shortest of our three passages, and W. H. Auden and Elizabeth Mayer point out one reason for this: while the 'traditional method of description tries to unite the sensory perception of objects with the subjective feelings they arouse by means of a simile or a metaphorical image', Goethe 'very rarely does' this. 'On the contrary, he deliberately keeps the sensory and emotional apart [...] the adjectives he employs to express his emotional reactions are almost always vague and banal – words like *beautiful*, *important*, *valuable* occur again and again.'[29] Thus, while Goethe gives us a brief description of the 'imperial palaces' standing on the Palatine 'like rocks', he laments but also insists that it is 'impossible' to 'convey' either 'an idea of such things' in themselves or the 'feeling' they inspire in this particular viewer. The most we get of Goethe's 'emotional reactions' to what he sees are 'vague' gestures towards experiences of 'grandeur', 'great joy', 'a sense of strength', 'soundness', 'seriousness' and 'joyous composure' that seem deeply felt and deeply appreciated but are no more than named. This is in part, perhaps, because Goethe wants to 'convey' the profundity of such experiences – for him, in 'this place' – as beyond the reach of language. But while Goethe might seem unable to share the experience of 'this place' with those who have not been there themselves, there is also a sense that he does not especially want to. As a letter writer he does not seem to be trying to share his deep emotional experiences in Italy so much as report that he has had such experiences – 'one feels that much is happening to Goethe' in Italy 'which is of great importance to him, but which he declines to tell'.[30] He is, though, seeking educative and character-building experiences that will 'affect' his 'whole future life', especially as a literary writer – experiences that he can hoard for other, future writing projects.[31] And there are at least three aspects of the education offered by Italy that Goethe carefully points his reader towards, even if he does not entirely share his own experience of them.

The first is Goethe's insistence that Italy is 'training' (387) him 'to pay attention to the external world' – Goethe's descriptions of Italian sites (and sights) repeatedly climax not in a response to those sites but in an insistence that attending to them is educating, and will continue to 'educate', his 'eye'.[32] As he says, after less than two months in Rome: 'I am now starting to look at the best things for a second time. As my initial amazement changes to a feeling of familiarity, I acquire a clearer sense of their value' (152). Six weeks later he is still 'giving the best a second or third look' and 'everything is beginning to make a pattern' as his 'preferences' become 'clearer', and his 'emotional response to what is greatest and most authentic' becomes 'freer and more relaxed' (171). Five months after this, he can confidently assert, 'My eye is being well trained and in time I might become a connoisseur' (362). In the section on the Palatine above, we again see how Rome has 'educated', and continues to educate, Goethe, who, trained by Rome to be the kind of viewer who 'looks seriously about him and has eyes to see', now learns what the Palatine gives back to such a viewer. But Goethe's emphasis on the education offered by extended exposure to Rome's great monuments of classical antiquity does not have as its ultimate goal an ever greater appreciation of those monuments. Such appreciation is not an end in itself but a means, since the second aspect of the education offered by Italy that Goethe stresses is self-discovery.

As Goethe puts it early on in his account of his journey to Rome, 'my purpose in making this wonderful journey is […] to discover myself in the objects I see' (57). Eight months later, he is 'more and more finding out who I am' (345). For Goethe, looking at Rome 'with eyes to see' is a matter of challenging, exploring and developing one's self – of discovering what that self is and what it is capable of achieving. Attending to the 'noble perfection' of, for example, 'the Pantheon, the Apollo Belvedere, [...] the Sistine Chapel' means 'patiently' waiting to see if that 'noble perfection' will 'grow inside one' (148). The 'great joy' of attending to Rome 'with eyes to see' it is, for Goethe, the 'discovery' that, confronted with a phenomenon such as the 'noble perfection' of the Palatine's 'grandeur' (in which nothing is 'mediocre' and by which even 'poor taste' is elevated), something like that grandeur does indeed 'grow inside' him, as he 'become[s] a stronger character', 'acquires a sense of strength hitherto unknown' and achieves 'a joyous composure' 'in this place'. This is the self Goethe 'discovers' through the proper appreciation of Rome – a new, better, larger, stronger self that is only knowable in its response Rome's art and architecture – 'Only in Rome can one educate oneself for Rome' (133). Rome trains the eye to see, but in doing so it also empowers the self with a new sense of that self's own strength and scale. By learning to attend to the 'grandeur' of Rome, we 'discover' that, 'expanded by the genius of the spot', our minds become 'colossal', as Byron says of St Peter's (155). In other words, we might say, Goethe's Rome teaches humanity its own perfectibility – Goethe has 'never been so sensitive to the things of the world' as he is in Rome, but in Rome even 'the most ordinary person becomes somebody, for his mind is enormously enlarged' (150). Where de Staël's Rome communicates a fundamental vulnerability that is shared by classical and modern human beings, Goethe's Rome teaches shared power and potential.

The third aspect of the education offered by Italy for Goethe is a product of the first two. Like de Staël, Goethe finds in Rome something he can take away with him.[33] As he puts it in our passage on the Palatine, 'the blessed consequences' of being 'so sensitive to the things of the world as I am here' 'will, I believe, affect my whole future life'. However, while he hopes that 'the moral effect of having lived in a larger world will be noticeable' (150) on his return home, Goethe's main concern when it comes to his post-Italy future is his life as a writer – and with his pressing sense that, as a writer, he 'must cultivate [the] knowledge of the arts' he has acquired in Italy and 'reach some sort of maturity' (348). What he takes from his time in Rome is a revitalised confidence in his ability to achieve that 'maturity', and the later stages of *Italienische Reise* see Goethe mentally preparing himself for his return to Germany and returning to his own writing 'determined at least to attain the attainable and do what can be done' (347), 'hop[ing] to accomplish something' and eager to 'see what will come out of my efforts and how far I can go' (377), 'having so long' previously 'suffered the fate of Sisyphus and Tantalus' (347). And long before he leaves Italy, this optimism is already being justified – as he writes in a letter written during the summer before his departure for home: '*Tasso* will arrive soon after the New Year. *Faust* in his courier's cloak will announce my arrival' (374).[34] Indeed, as Joseph Luzzi puts it, 'scholars agree' that *Italienische Reise* 'charts the evolution of the mature aesthetic vision that transformed Goethe into a principal voice not only in German culture but general European culture'.[35] If, for Goethe, Rome can train the eye and mind 'to pay attention to the external world' and in doing so offer a way of testing, stretching and thereby discovering and expanding one's intellectual and imaginative capabilities, the third aspect of Goethe's Rome that *Italienische Reise* emphasises is that it is a 'school' in which one can learn how to be a great writer.

This is a long way from the way in which Byron responds to Rome. *Childe Harold* IV 'narrates Byron's trip (April–May 1817) from Venice by way of Ferrara and Florence to Rome; it was composed July–December 1817' in Venice.[36] Byron's text is not that of a resident Roman 'tour guide' who speaks from a deep and intimate knowledge of the place (like Corinne), nor that of a 'connoisseur' of Rome, trained by the long study of the city (like Goethe). As Jonathan Gross points out elsewhere in this volume, Byron does share with de Staël's Oswald the sense of being an exile in Italy – as Byron puts it just before the poem turns to the Palatine, there 'woos no home, nor hope, nor life, save what is here' (105). But Byron's speaker is also very much a first-time visitor to the city who is manifestly excited to be there in ways that Oswald is not,[37] and intensely eager to simply experience – to be in – Rome:

> Then let the winds howl on! their harmony
> Shall henceforth be my music, and the night
> The sound shall temper with the owlet's cry,
> As I hear now, in the fading light

> Dim o'er the bird of darkness' native site,
> Answering each other on the Palatine,
> With their large eyes, all glistening grey and bright,
> And sailing pinions. – Upon such a shrine
> What are our petty griefs? – let me not number mine.
>
> (106)

Byron's account of the Palatine begins with a tuning out and a tuning in. What is tuned out is the self and all its 'petty griefs'; what is tuned into is 'what is here'. Through an act of focusing the mind on what is directly present, the 'winds' that drive 'the ocean' and 'loud breakers' against which Byron's speaker must 'battle' (105) are first 'temper[ed] with' the 'cry' of the 'owlets' on the Palatine. We might even say that the Palatine is presented as a distraction from the self here (rather than a source of consolation or education for the self), but this is only one of the many things it becomes in Byron's poem.

Byron's attentiveness to the 'material realities of place' can be heard in the detail of 'owlet' rather than 'owl'.[38] His speaker's determination to maintain that attentiveness to what is directly in front of him can be heard in other details, especially at moments of potential movement forward in the stanza. The general idea of 'owlets' does not lead into a rift on 'the bird of darkness' per se, as it might well after the comma at the end of line 3, but back to the owlet cries as 'I hear [them] now'. Even as the location of these owlets is announced as the Palatine the stanza does rush to engage with the 'Imperial Mount' of Ancient Rome (107) but stays with the birds, noticing their 'large eyes', 'glistening grey and bright', and 'sailing pinions', simultaneously countering the reader's own curiosity about the Palatine with an invitation to imaginatively dwell in this 'now' instead of moving on. What we see here is a self-disciplined holding back and holding open of the self. The aim does not seem to be a specific emotional experience, nor an education but rather what Gavin Hopps has called a 'dilated openness' to the given.[39]

As Byron's determined openness to what is present on the Palatine carries over into the following stanza, his poem certainly seems to knowingly answer de Staël's focus on the 'flowers', both real and painted, that Corinne sees (but does not name) on the Palatine – the only plants de Staël notes as present, each time interpreting them as a source of, or a point of access to, 'consolation'. Byron notes flowers, too, but differently: 'Cypress and ivy, weed and wallflower grown /

Matted and mass'd together' (107). Corinne's 'flowers' here become 'wallflowers' as Byron's speaker replaces her act of interpreting and appropriating flowers with an attention to the individual specificity of the flowers he sees, and then by situating these wallflowers in their own world, rather than relating them to a human, emotional one – the wallflowers grow mixed up with 'cypress', 'ivy' and 'weed', with the other plants (with the exception of the 'weed') noticed again in their own specificity. None of these plants is made to 'mean' anything, offering only a manifestation of the fecundity and plenitude of 'what is here' in front of Byron's speaker, as they grow 'matted and mass'd together'. Similarly, 'hillocks' are 'heap'ed' in the same line. Only after all this material abundance is noticed and noted do we get to the ruins of the Palatine themselves.

But these, too, are looked at as they are, rather than read for what they were or might be. Both de Staël's and Goethe's first gesture is to tell the reader what these ruins used to be; Byron describes what they are, now, in a degree of detail that both de Staël and Goethe shy away from. For de Staël, 'all that remains' of 'the palace of the Caesars' are 'stones'; for Goethe, 'the ruins of the imperial palaces stand like rocks'; for Byron, the Palatine's 'hillocks' are 'heap'd' on

> what were chambers, arch crush'd, column strown
> In fragments, chok'd up vaults, and frescoes steep'd
> In subterranean damps, where the owl peep'd,
> Deeming it midnight.
>
> (107)

Even the return of the owl is important here, as part of an experience of the here and now that Byron is carefully orchestrating into a lyric apprehension of the actual that moves through, and relishes, a multiplicity of detail without prioritising any single detail – that seeks to directly experience everything that draws its attention, in whatever location it finds itself in. Experiencing the here and now as the here and now is certainly valued over knowing what the here and now was, in another seemingly direct answer to de Staël's account of the Palatine:

> Temples, baths or halls?
> Pronounce who can; for all that Learning reap'd
> From her research hath been, that these are walls –
> Behold the Imperial Mount! 'tis thus the mighty falls.
>
> (107)

De Staël's 'baths' and 'frescos' do not prompt Byron to feel that 'the past' is brought 'close to us'. The past remains absent in Byron's experience of the Palatine at this point. What is present is 'walls', and, in this stanza at least, cannot be read as more.

However, the last line of this quotation does signal an expansion of Byron's attentiveness to 'what is here', as he, like both de Staël and Goethe, does begin to read and interpret the ruins before him, both historically and existentially. This leads into the famous stanza on the 'moral of all human tales' we quoted earlier. Like de Staël and Goethe, then, Byron is manifestly interested in what ruins might tell us, over and above what they show us, about the past and future as well as the present, though his reading of these ruins is rather gloomier than that of either of his predecessors.[40] What is different about Byron's poetic response to the Palatine, however, is the fact that his reading of the ruins in front of him is not the climax or the point of that response but just one part of it. Indeed, this reading is summarily dismissed even in the stanza that articulates it, as Byron says, 'Away with words', silently sidestepping the inevitable irony of doing so while then going on to invite readers in the next stanza to somehow 'draw near' to the Palatine themselves and 'Admire, exult – despise – laugh – weep, – for here / There is such matter for all feeling' (108), not just the rather depressing one he has just communicated. And as Byron's speaker wilfully reopens the poem to the scene in front of him, we see the fundamental difference between Byron's approach to Rome and those of de Staël and Goethe, who certainly open themselves up to Rome but in search of a particular kind of experience. Rome is a beautiful consolation for suffering for de Staël, and, for Goethe, the greatest training course in the world for the writer who aspires to greatness. For Byron it is first and foremost a multifarious, endlessly varied encounter, an experience of, a meeting with, living realities – historic ('tis thus the mighty falls'), moral ('the moral of all human tales'), physical ('walls'), sensual ('the owlet's cry', 'subterranean damps') and emotional ('Admire, exult – despise – laugh – weep […] all feeling'). And to sustain this experience of 'what is here', Byron's speaker once again, in the next stanza, focuses himself on, and opens himself up to, the living reality, now, of what is in front of him:

> Tully was not so eloquent as thou,
> Thou nameless column with the buried base!

> What are the laurels of the Caesar's brow?
> Crown me with ivy from his dwelling place.
> Whose arch or pillar meets me in the face,
> Titus or Trajan's? No –'tis that of Time:
> Triumph, arch, pillar, all he doth displace
> Scoffing; and apostolic statues climb
> To crush the imperial urn, whose ashes slept sublime,
>
> Buried in air, the deep blue sky of Rome,
> And looking to the stars: they had contain'd
> A spirit which with these would find a home,
> The last of those who o'er the whole word reign'd,
> The Roman globe, for after none sustain'd,
> But yielded back his conquests: – he was more
> Than a mere Alexander, and, unstain'd
> With household blood and wine, serenely wore
> His sovereign virtues – still we Trajan's name adore.
>
> (110–11)

Byron's speaker focuses his attention here on both the 'nameless column' before him and the present moment in which he is encountering it; he does not ask 'what were' Caesar's laurels but what they 'are'. Similarly, he refuses to speculate as to whose the 'arch' or 'pillar' that meets him 'in the face' might have been, insisting instead on 'whose' it is now. Doing so leads to the rather unoriginal idea of 'Time', but Byron's speaker is not here looking for big ideas so much as ways of directly experiencing what is in front of him. The idea of time is a perfect way of doing this, since it allows him to see the ruins of the Palatine as a living process rather than inert 'stones' – he does not say time 'has displaced' 'arch and pillar' but that time 'doth displace' them, 'scoffing'. The Palatine makes manifest time doing precisely this, as he looks.[41] The seemingly dead 'nameless column', then, communicates a kind of vitality if one can tune into that vitality – this is how it is 'eloquent'.[42] Tully, eloquent as he was, 'was' eloquent; the 'nameless column' is, right now, even more eloquent than Tully because it expresses the process by which even Tully himself faded, and continues to fade further, into the past tense. Tully was history (then); ruins are temporality (now).

And so: owls, plants, arches, vaults, frescoes, damps, walls, 'the Imperial Mount', 'the moral of all human tales', 'all feeling', 'Time' itself – for Byron the Palatine is all this, but it is also more. Again, in the lines on 'Time' here, we reach a 'moral' that is not a climax: Byron's final example of time's displacement of 'triumph' goes on to manifest an attentiveness on the part of his speaker not just to what is before him but also to his own ever-shifting responses to what is before him – as the speaker's attention turns to the 'apostolic statues' that 'crush the imperial urn' we see his first direct (if implicit) identification of himself with what he sees on the Palatine.

Those statues are of St Peter and St Paul, which, in 1587, were put in the place of the urns of Trajan and Marcus Aurelius. Byron's final stanza rather poignantly responds to these statues with the idea that one of the urns they replaced (Trajan's) might, in fact, have 'contain'd / A spirit which with these [both the new statues and the Christian figures they represent] would find a home'. This thought points in at least two directions: first, to Trajan himself and his strange contribution to this particular speaker's response to the Palatine ('still we Trajan's name adore'); second to the speaker's own explicit desire to 'find a home' in Italy, and especially in Rome – this is, we should recall, a speaker for whom there is 'no home, nor hope, nor life, save what is here'. Once again, Byron's poetic attitude to Rome here is very different from the fictionalised and autobiographical attitudes of de Staël and Goethe. Goethe wanted to take Italy home with him. De Staël wanted to send home the consolations offered by the beauties and historical monuments of Italy. Byron wanted to do neither of these things. Unlike Goethe, who knew he would have to return to Germany eventually, and unlike de Staël, who hoped to return to France, Byron had no idea of what his future might be when writing *Childe Harold* IV. What the poem's attentiveness to the ruins of Rome per se presents him as is a 'spirit which with these would find a home'; a man who wants to 'stand / A ruin amidst ruins' (25) in 'Rome! my country!' (78). In the lyric mode of *Childe Harold* IV, in other words, Byron creates a highly 'distinctive poetics of exile' through which to articulate and perform a 'Romantic quest [...] for "home"'.[43]

Yet this quest is, like all such quests, 'endless'.[44] Byron might say that the 'orphans of the heart must turn to' Rome (78), but neither he nor his poem found a home there – *Childe Harold* IV does not offer Rome as a sanctuary for the homeless. What the exile's mindset of the speaker of *Childe Harold* IV does help the poem to do, however – born as it was in Italy as a means of responding to Italy – is to present its reader with a distinctive lyric persona that is highly attentive to – and directly, personally *experiencing*, indeed greedily consuming – 'all' the 'treasures' of 'eye', 'ear', 'heart' and 'soul' (108) that the experience of Rome might have to offer him as he tracks 'Fall'n states and buried greatness, o'er a land / Which *was* the mightiest in its old command / And *is* the loveliest' (25). This persona is one of the great achievements of *Childe Harold's Pilgrimage*, as is the creation of a wholly original lyrical poetic mode that could body forth that persona and its radically 'dilated' attentiveness. *Childe Harold* IV's lyric persona and mode allow Byron to recreate Rome as a city of ruins that, though 'long-explored', remains 'a still exhaustless mine' (128) not of consolation, as it was for de Staël, nor of educative models of 'noble perfection', as it was for Goethe, but of all kinds of moral, educative, aesthetic, historical, political, emotional, imaginative, spiritual and religious *experiences*. Rome is lyrically transformed into a city to be avidly consumed, relished and revelled in, and a city that rewards such self-immersion with special, personal, intimate, direct experiences of place that distract the self from all its habitual 'petty griefs'. Here we can perhaps begin to see more clearly what Anna Jameson means in *Diary of an Ennuyée* (1826) when she talks about the 'poetical interest' Byron 'supplied' to sites that 'could not have possessed [it] before'.[45] Throwing a spotlight on the Roman lyricism of *Childe Harold* IV certainly helps us to see why later tourists might have responded to the canto's invitation to 'draw near' to the ruins of Rome by following its author to the 'Eternal City' in hordes.

Notes

1 Quoted here in translation from Madame de Staël, *Corinne, or Italy*, trans. by S. Raphael (Oxford: Oxford University Press, 1998). Page numbers follow quotations.
2 Quoted here in translation from J. W. Goethe, *Italian Journey*, trans. by W. H. Auden and E. Mayer (Harmondsworth: Penguin, 1970). Page references follow quotations.
3 There are many other texts that contribute to the Romantic reimagining of Italy, of course, from Chateaubriand's 'Promenade dans Rome au clair de lune', through the poetry of Leigh Hunt, Percy Shelley and Felicia Hemans (among many others), the novels of Ann Radcliffe (and Gothic fiction more generally) and Mary Shelley, to Stendhal's *Promenades dans Rome* and *Rome, Naples et Florence* – indeed, we might reasonably extend our list of three defining figures to four

to include Stendhal, in whom 'the Romantic morphology of Rome achieves a final, ironic shift', according to Jerome McGann. However, as McGann goes on to show, Stendhal writes very much under the influence of, and in response to, the three earlier texts I focus on here, not adding a new paradigm to Romanticism's recreation of Italy so much as rethinking, re-exploring and realigning the paradigms he inherited from de Staël, Goethe and Byron to the point at which in 'Stendhal – and pre-eminently in Stendhal's experience of Rome – the Romantic Movement has summed itself up; has weighed itself in the balances of love and desire, and has found itself, as it had found all other things, finally wanting'. See J. J. McGann, 'Rome and its Romantic Significance', in *The Beauty of Inflections: Literary Investigations in Historical Method and Theory* (Oxford: Clarendon Press, 1985), pp. 313–33 (pp. 325, 333).

4 Barbara Schaff, 'Italianised Byron – Byronised Italy', in M. Pfister and R. Hertel (eds.), *Performing National Identity: Anglo-Italian Cultural Transactions* (Amsterdam and New York: Rodopi, 2008), pp. 103–21 (p. 113).

5 Schaff, 'Italianised Byron', p. 108.

6 J. Buzard, *The Beaten Track: European Tourism, Literature, and the Ways to Culture, 1800–1918* (Oxford: Clarendon Press, 1993), pp. 122, 117.

7 Buzard, *The Beaten Track*, pp. 116, 120. For a full discussion of the 'particular appropriations and reinterpretations to which Byron and his works were subjected, in order to serve the [...] interests of visitors to the Continent' in the nineteenth century (p. 114), see pp. 114–30.

8 McGann, 'Rome and its Romantic significance', p. 314.

9 J. Luzzi, *Romantic Europe and the Ghost of Italy* (New Haven and London: Yale University Press, 2008), p. 54.

10 J. Wilkes, *Lord Byron and Madame de Staël: Born for Opposition* (Aldershot: Ashgate, 1999), p. 108.

11 Wilkes, *Lord Byron and Madame de Staël*, p. 107.

12 Luzzi, *Romantic Europe and the Ghost of Italy*, pp. 54, 61.

13 McGann, 'Rome and its Romantic significance', p. 319.

14 According to Angelica Goodden, *Corinne* also has an implicit political message for Italians, offering Corinne herself as 'a symbol of the freedom and fulfilment they look forward to themselves, artistically great even if politically repressed' – 'the expression of a political state that may come to prevail in her country, for it is free, spontaneous, and governed by native rhythms.' A. Goodden, *Madame de Staël: The Dangerous Exile* (Oxford: Oxford University Press, 2008), pp. 159, 158. Goethe's text offers Italy no political 'moral' comparable to those offered by Byron and de Staël.

15 Here de Staël also 'aimed to recall to her French readers Europe's cultural debt to Italy, and thus show how unjustifiable Napoleon's conquest of the country had been' (Wilkes, *Lord Byron and Madame de Staël*, p. 103), promoting Italy (the land of the 'imagination', 'wonders of nature' and 'the masterpieces of art') as one of the three great national cultures of Europe, each with its own distinct qualities, alongside France ('where social life is everything') and Britain ('where political interests absorb nearly all others') (*Corinne, or Italy*, p. 18).

16 McGann, 'Rome and its Romantic Significance', p. 316; Auden and Mayer, 'Introduction', *Italian Journey*, p. 11.

17 McGann, 'Rome and its Romantic significance', p. 324.

18 As Jonathan Sachs puts it, 'if the poem is quintessentially Romantic, it is also quintessentially "Rome-antic"', generating 'its drama from the juxtaposition' of 'Romantic themes' to do with the mind, imagination, personal suffering and 'Rome-antic' themes such as 'relics and ruins' and 'the inevitability of decay'. J. Sachs, *Romantic Antiquity: Rome in the British Imagination, 1789–1832* (Oxford: Oxford University Press, 2010), pp. 134–5.

19 'Marginalia in de Staël's *Corinne*', in *CMP*, p. 223.

20 McGann, 'Rome and its Romantic significance', p. 324.

21 Wilkes, *Lord Byron and Madame de Staël*, p. 10. As Wilkes points out, responses to de Staël's novel can be heard in Byron's treatment of the Coliseum, St Peter's, the Pantheon and the ocean, among other many other things in *Childe Harold* IV. For Wilkes' full comparative reading of the two texts, see *Lord Byron and Madame de Staël*, pp. 100–31.

22 De Staël, *Corinne, or Italy*, p. 69.

23 For Diane Long Hoeveler's discussion of the 'tour guide' as one of the 'dominant performance[s] undertaken by Corinne', and one that manipulates the male 'grand tour' and 'appropriates the cultural capital that is Rome for Oswald's gaze', see D. Long Hoeveler, 'Germaine de Staël's *Corinne, or Italy* (1807) and the performance of Romanticism(s)', in F. Burwick and P. Douglass (eds.), *Dante and Italy in British Romanticism* (Basingstoke: Palgrave Macmillan, 2011), pp. 133–42 (pp. 139–40).

24 Wilkes, *Lord Byron and Madame de Staël*, p. 119.

25 'I look upon Goethe as the greatest genius that the age has produced', Byron reportedly told Thomas Medwin, and dedicated *Werner* to 'The Illustrous Goethe'. T. Medwin, *Medwin's Conversations of Lord Byron*, ed. E. J. Lovell (Princeton, NJ: Princeton University Press, 1966), p. 260.

26 *Italienische Reise* was published in three parts. The first in appeared in 1816 'as a continuation of [Goethe's] autobiography titled, *Aus meinem*

Leben. Zweyter Abteilung. Erster Teil (From My Life. Second Section. First Part)'. This recounts Goethe's journey from Karlsbad to Italy and his first stay in Rome, 'spanning the period 3 September 1786 to 21 February 1787' and is 'based on correspondence to Carl August, Frau von Stein, Herder, and others in Weimar'. The second part covers 'Goethe's journey from Rome to Naples, his stay in Naples, his trip to Sicily, and eventual return to Rome (22 February to 6 June 1787)' and was published as *Aus meinem Leben. Zweyter Abteilung. Zweyter Theil* (My Life. Second Section. Second Part) in 1817. The third part, covering Goethe's second stay in Rome (June 1787 to April 1788), was published in 1829 as the twenty-ninth volume of *Ausgabe letzter Hand*, the last authorised edition of Goethe's works. G. L. Hachmeister, *Italy in the German Literary Imagination: Goethe's 'Italian Journey' and Its Reception by Eichendorff, Platen, and Heine* (Rochester, NY: Camden House, 2002), pp. 19–20, 21.

27 'I have a great curiosity about every thing relating to Goethe, and please myself with thinking there is some analogy between our characters and writings. So much interest do I take in him, that I offered to give 100*l.* to any person who would translate his "Memoirs", for my own reading. Shelley sometimes explained part of them to me' (Medwin, *Medwin's Conversations of Lord Byron*, p. 261).

28 This is one of two passages on the Palatine in *Italian Journey*. In the other, Goethe walks through 'the gardens on the Palatine which have reclaimed the waste spaces between the ruins of the Imperial palaces and made them attractive', where 'fragments of ornamental capitals, smooth and fluted columns, bas-reliefs etc.,' are 'strewn all around [...] in a wide circle in the same way that tables, chairs and benches are arranged for a merry party out of doors' (p. 392).

29 Auden and Mayer, 'Introduction', *Italian Journey*, p. 9.

30 Auden and Mayer, 'Introduction', *Italian Journey*, p. 16. For Goethe, Rome 'is such a great school and each day here has so much to say that one does not dare say anything about it oneself. Even if one could stay here for years, it would still be better to observe a Pythagorean silence' (*Italian Journey*, p. 134).

31 On 'his birthday at Carlsbad on 28 August 1786, friends sent him greetings as from various unfinished works – *Faust*, perhaps, *Egmont*, *Torquanto Tasso*, *Wilheim Meister*? – asking why he had not completed them, a joke that would surely have been the last straw if his journey had not already been a settled thing.' T. J. Reed, 'Introduction', in J. W. Goethe, *The Flight to Italy: Diary and Selected Letters*, ed. and trans. T. J. Reed (Oxford: Oxford University Press, 1999), p. xi).

32 Auden and Mayer, 'Introduction', *Italian Journey*, p. 15.
33 As, when leaving Venice, Goethe claims to 'have absorbed the atmosphere of this city sufficiently, and I know that I shall carry a picture away with me which, though it may be incomplete, is clear and accurate so far as it goes' (p. 104).
34 'The journey did much to rouse Goethe from his nearly decade-long poetic silence. In Italy, Goethe first turned to *Iphigenie*, rewriting the prose version into blank verse. In 1788, during his second stay in Rome, he completed the drama *Egmont*. He spent much time thinking about the unfinished *Torquanto Tasso* and *Faust* (1808) for which, while in Rome, Goethe composed both the *Hexenküche* (Witch's Kitchen) scene and the monologue for *Wald und Höhle* (Forest and Cave) [...]. The *Römische Elegien* were first composed after Goethe's return to Weimar' (Hachmeister, *Italy in the German Literary Imagination*, p. 56).
35 Luzzi, *Romantic Europe and the Ghost of Italy*, p. 60.
36 J. J. McGann, 'Notes', in Lord Byron, *Lord Byron: The Major Works*, ed. J. J. McGann (Oxford: Oxford University Press, 1986), p. 1026.
37 On Oswald's first arrival in Rome, the 'name of Rome did not yet arouse a chord in his heart; he felt only the deep isolation that afflicts the soul when you enter a foreign town' (de Staël, *Corinne, or Italy*, p. 20).
38 S. Cheeke, *Byron and Place: History, Translation, Nostalgia* (Basingstoke: Palgrave Macmillan, 2003), p. 97.
39 G. Hopps, 'Byron and the linguistic sketch: nihilistic semiotics or truthful fiction?', conference paper given at the 41st International Byron Conference, 'Reality, Fiction and Madness', University of Gdansk, 1–7 July 2015.
40 Cheeke sees 'a deep tension in the canto between the sense of a living historical spirit', experienced at specific locations, and 'the contrary sense of "sad wonder" at the absorption of such a spirit into the brutal moral lessons' of history (*Byron and Place*, p. 102).
41 This is perhaps as close as the section on the Palatine gets to what Cheeke calls the canto's 'historical method', 'in which a strict literalism and material reality of place go hand in hand with a supernaturalism centred upon the notion of a "magic spot", and in which direct and practical experience is raised to the level of visionary insight' (*Byron and Place*, p. 104). Cheeke's own, much better, example comes from the section of the poem on the Coliseum.
42 Sachs interestingly adds that for Byron the 'eloquence' of ruins offers 'a message of [human] futility and despair' but also 'the possibility of transcendence and clarity' in the very fact that they 'survive – as ruins', and this enables Byron to pull back 'from the futility' of the 'wreckage of history' (*Romantic Antiquity*, p. 143).

43 J. Stabler, *The Artistry of Exile: Romantic and Victorian Writers in Italy* (Oxford: Oxford University Press, 2013), p. 224. In Stabler's words, 'a long, hard look at exile dominates *Childe Harold's Pilgrimage* Canto IV' (p. 244); M. O'Neill, 'Realms without a name: Shelley and Italy's intenser day', in F. Burwick and P. Douglass (eds.), *Dante and Italy in British Romanticism* (Basingstoke: Palgrave Macmillan, 2011), pp. 77–91 (p. 77).
44 O'Neill, 'Realms without a name', p. 77.
45 Quoted in Buzard, *The Beaten Track*, p. 118.

10

Playing with history: Byron's Italian dramas

Mirka Horová

> Gonzaga: And so in all arts and in all actions, fortune and talent contend?
> Annibale: In all.
> Gonzaga: Therefore life is a game, oh signor Annibale: so I said it well, what an admirable definition it is that you have defined life by. And if this is true, which I think can no longer be doubted, if it is commendable to play, what one doubts is whether it is commendable to live.[1]

This chapter is concerned with the ways in which Byron dramatically deploys Italy and Italian history in *Marino Faliero*, *The Two Foscari* and *The Deformed Transformed* to destabilise the traditional concept of Western culture and civilisation as a progressive process, and of the role that art plays in this process, building up to an increasingly satirised and inherently disillusioned understanding of history and a transgressive, eclectic conceptualisation of art. Italy itself, in Byron's dramas, thus becomes a complex synecdoche. While Venice and Rome represent Italy, Italy becomes *pars pro toto* for the Renaissance. On closer inspection, Venice represents republicanism while Rome stands for the entirety of human history. The Italian Renaissance instances the perpetual rebirth not just of 'civilisation' and the arts but also violence, becoming the *theatrum mundi* in all its creative and destructive contradictions. And in all of this, notions of 'play' underpin Byron's dramatic representations of Italian history at every turn – play in its performative sense but more specifically in its sportive, competitive and manipulative senses.

Combining in a fluid perspective the past histories and – in prophetic mode – the contemporary present of a particular historical spot, the play element in Byron's two Venetian dramas begins with the carnivalisation of history. As we shall see, this carnivalisation occurs on a number of levels – thematic, dramatic and discursive: in *Marino Faliero*, tragedy fulfils itself against the background of the traditional Venetian *carnevale*, in an intricate web of carnival strategies that lead to the failure of the old doge's coup against his own kind, and the state he represents is revealed as a carnivalised mockery of republican ideals. In *The Two Foscari*, the carnivalesque becomes the grotesque in an alarming portrait of Venetian history as a puppet show conducted by one of the Venetian *eminences grises* and based on the malevolent economy of revenge. Here events are orchestrated by the chief puppet master, Loredano, as he writes and then closes the history of the two trapped Foscari. Venice becomes a grotesque puppet theatre where the puppeteer rules all and where the evil puppeteer himself becomes Fate, the agent of traditional tragic denouement, as he channels the carnival element of Venice's topsyturvydom into the grotesque fulfilment of a personal vendetta. Both plays are here signalling towards the theatre of the absurd, as well as towards a Kafkaesque universe structured by the inscrutable force of the law, but, in both instances, play governs both the action and the outcome of the drama, becoming the symbol of the way of the world, in a self-referential, repetitive and disconcerting reinterpretation of the *theatrum mundi*. Byron's Venetian diptych presents a journey through a particular local history that moves from the carnivalesque to the grotesque with profound implications for our understanding of Byron's ideas about the nature of, and the forces ruling, not just Italian but all history.

On multiple levels, then, play defines history for Byron in these two dramas. And, while the Venetian dramas can be read as case studies of the play at the heart of the Venetian state, *The Deformed Transformed* represents a satirical study of the whole of Western civilisation 'at play' – playing itself out *ad absurdum*. Indeed, as Byron's dramatic art reflects on Italian history, Italian history reflects art, another kind of play. Recycling and redefining the *ars simia naturae* principle of mimesis, where art apes nature, Byron's last dramatic take on Italy ultimately mixes this with the proto-Wildean concept of nature aping art. In fact, poised between Germany and Italy, and the different humanisms of Faust and the Italian Renaissance, *The*

Deformed Transformed sees Italian history as a battleground that is forever absorbing, multiplying and destabilising the basic meanings, values and status of art. Departing radically from the lyricised 'city of the soul' of *Childe Harold* IV (78), Byron's Rome here becomes a trope that heralds the fluidity and fragmentations of modernity, indeed postmodernity. In this way, among others, Byron's dramatic Italy is an Italy for the twentieth and twenty-first centuries as much as an Italy of Byron's nineteenth, or of the *Cinquecento* and *Trecento* that frame the Italian Renaissance, the backdrop to Byron's three dramatic plots.

As well as depicting and playing on the convoluted intricacies of Renaissance Italian politics, these dramas further resonate with the contemporary political scene – British and Continental – of Byron's own time,[2] as has been demonstrated by a number of critical responses to *Marino Faliero* and *The Two Foscari* in particular, ranging from Malcolm Kelsall's influential essay, 'Venice Preserved',[3] to the recent edited collection of essays, *Byron and the Politics of Freedom and Terror*.[4] These studies reveal all sorts of additional levels to the dramas' engagement with history. In this chapter, however, we shall begin with the story of Marino Faliero, as scripted by Byron, against the specific backdrop of the Venetian carnival.

Here, Michel Steno's bawdy graffiti scribbled on the ducal throne is a dramatic incendiary device that sets in motion the intricate turns of events by literally carnivalising the ducal throne, being a drunken carnival-night jest. Faliero feels that the offence to the ducal office and his very person is 'the last drop that makes the cup run o'er – and [his] was full already' (V, i, 244–5) and consequently carnivalises his own office by siding with the *arsenalotti* (Arsenal workers) uprising against the patrician ruling class, his own kind. History's own carnivalisation of events comes full circle outside the scope of the drama, when Steno, in a historical *coup de théâtre*, becomes doge seven doges down the line.

However, Faliero has long recognised that he ultimately serves only as a perpetual carnival king, 'a pageant' (I, ii, 271): the ducal office is presented to us as a hollow mask, the doge a mere puppet at the mercy and disposal of the ruling patrician councillors. Faliero describes his being made a plaything of the state. With the ducal cap an 'idle, gilded, degraded toy' (I, ii, 263), others, too, see the 'Doge is a mere puppet, who can scarce / Obtain right for himself' (II, ii, 32–3).

And as the drama unfolds Faliero's rhetoric gains bitter momentum, emphasising over and over the carnivalesque dupery of the ducal office. Increasingly self-denigrating, Faliero sees himself as a nonentity, 'a thing of robes and trinkets' (III, ii, 188). Yet the idea of innocent, powerless passivity soon gives way to an unsettling catalogue of this puppet's acts in the hands of his puppet masters, with the puppet no longer innocent in his passivity but actively participating in the oppression dictated by the ruling patrician power structure – 'a stickler for the Senate and "the Forty"', 'a council-fawner' (III, ii, 191–3). He is not just 'a tool' and 'a puppet' but also 'a fool' (III, ii, 194).

It is to escape this carnival world, and his part in it, that he embarks upon his doomed coup. But this itself is only another kind of play, merely a dice-throw, a *coup de dés*: 'I have set my little left / Of life upon this cast; the die was thrown / When I first listen'd to your treason' (III, i, 54–6). The doge deliberately plays the momentous lottery of fate in order to escape the games dictated by the patrician rulers of Venice. All he manages to do, however, is curse Venice. In this famous curse, the city, stripped of all its prized assets, will live on as a carnival, though emptied of its vital essence of pleasure and only kept alive by the 'coarse lusts of habitude' (V, iii, 87). The carnival that is Venice is here debilitated in all but its iterability, with smiles 'without mirth, and pastimes without pleasure' (V, iii, 91). The road to this future is 'but' a continuation of the 'game' we have seen played out in the drama, 'a game of mutual homicides' who have both 'cast lots for the first death', but which is 'won with false dice' (IV, ii, 289–91).[5]

The whole affair is not an impartial turn of fortune, then, but a corrupt game. The Venetian state, inevitably, wins because it fixes the game from the outset, as Faliero's aborted coup ends like a true carnival, reinstituting the power structures that it sought to subvert – with the disobedient carnival king, the doge, decapitated and the jester's cap, the *corno ducale* (ducal hat), passed on to some compliant player chosen in an election staged by the patricians drawing lots. The carnival of Venice goes on interminably, with Faliero's rebellion simply an episode of it. The state's handling of Faliero's execution determinedly sets itself against Faliero's suggestion that the Venetian state 'record the facts' of his rebellion so that 'the contemplator might approve, / Or at the least learn from whence the crimes arose'. 'When the beholder knows a Doge conspired', says Faliero, 'Let him be told the cause – it is your history' (V, i, 508–12). Faliero's reproof is ineffectual in the face of Venice's official masquerade. Yet history's own endlessly carnivalising propensity to distort, re-play (and play with), re-mask and re-perform itself has the last word. Though Faliero was sentenced to *damnatio memoriae*, defaced for eternity in the *Sala del Maggior Consiglio* as a faceless traitor covered by a black veil, that same black veil immediately commands attention as the most intriguing portrait of the whole ducal gallery, though portrait there be none – centuries later prompting Byron to write his play. The punitive act of erasure through masking works against its intended meaning, commanding attention and inspiring interest. In a final demonstration of history's playful carnivalisation of 'the facts', rather than condemning Faliero's memory to oblivion its mask keeps that memory alive.

If in *Marino Faliero* a slanderous graffiti serves as the excuse for setting in motion events that lead to the protagonist's tragic downfall, with Byron dramatising an act of erasure and censorship that seeks to get Venetian history 'back on track', in *The Two Foscari* he is also concerned with the writing – and rewriting – of history.[6] Here bank books and genealogies play a key role. They are the instruments of the grey eminence of Venetian history, the patrician rulers, and the drama begins with one particular patrician, Loredano, writing in his tablets, specifying the motive for his personal vendetta against the father and son Foscari. It ends with Loredano once more writing in his tablets, recording that the debt he imagines the doge owes him has been settled. Loredano is, as it were, writing the history of both hapless Foscari while they are still alive, *in medias res*. And, by the end of the drama, Loredano has managed to make the official legal records comply with the private conjectures of his bank books. He truly is a man of the written word: once the debt is written in his bank books, he does not stray from his punitive path until both Jacopo and Francis Foscari are dead.

This sinister frame has crucial ethical implications that push the play beyond *Marino Faliero*'s carnivalisation of Venice. If we read *The Two Foscari* as a revenge tragedy, we might argue that its events are very much held within the confines of both the tragic and the historical. But tragedy and history are here combined with a discernible element of something that does not strictly belong to either so much as to the uncanny world of the grotesque, which pushes Byron's representation of the *Serenissima* in disturbing new directions. It is not the grisly details of torture that drive things towards the grotesque – these are, on the contrary, kept offstage. The terror of the grotesque here is structural, as Loredano effectively takes on the force of fate, the god of traditional tragedy, and channels the power play of the Venetian state through the cold execution of a revenge plot.[7] Venice is still a state of carnivalesque masks, as in the world of *Marino Faliero*, where the doge is nothing but a toy in the hands of a corrupt state machine, but in *The Two Foscari* this masking reveals the absolute impenetrability of state power to all outside it and the absolute subjection of the doge's personality to his role in Venice's masquerade – the persona no longer simply masks but now absorbs the person who holds the office. As Wolfgang Kayser points out, among 'the most persistent motifs of the grotesque we find human bodies reduced to puppets, marionettes and automata, and their faces frozen into masks',[8] and the tragic Doge Foscari has been 'frozen' into such a 'mask', presiding 'with Roman fortitude' (I, i, 24) over the tortures of 'his last and only son' (I, i, 26): '*Feels he,* think you?' / 'He shows it not' (I, i, 27). As Bakhtin remarks, the 'theme of the marionette plays an important part in Romanticism. This theme is of course also found in folk culture, but in Romanticism the accent is placed on the puppet as the victim of alien inhuman force, which rules over men by turning them into marionettes.'[9] Faliero is certainly such a victim of the 'alien inhuman force' of the Venetian state.

However, if *Marino Faliero* presents Venice as a game, albeit not exactly a fair one, where both sides of a power struggle can at least have their go, *The Two Foscari* presents Venice as a puppet theatre, where power rests entirely in the hands of a single, unscrupulous patrician puppeteer, Loredano, and the doge is utterly powerless against his moves and the punitive machinery of the state that Loredano so skilfully deploys. As Foscari powerlessly and silently presides over the repeated torture of his only living son, he is Loredano's victim as much as he is Venice's. Faliero feels like a puppet sitting in state, executing the will of the patrician council in whose hands the power of the state really lies, but Foscari's ducal ordeal as Loredano's puppet is infinitely worse, since he has no chance for rebellion, nor indeed any chance to act in any way whatsoever. With total control over Venice, Loredano has total control over the doge. This is the 'unheroic and intensely political' universe of Byron's second Venetian tragedy.[10]

When the ducal mask is taken from Foscari in rushed quasi-legal proceedings that represent the penultimate act of repression executed by the Loredano-led state machinery (trumped only by the Council of Ten's insistence on masking the inglorious act of deposition by the state-ordained pomp of glorious public obsequy), there is not even the possibility of any great oration, since there is no heroic surge of agonistic polemic waiting to rise and charge, however powerlessly, against the wrongs perpetrated by the patrician council. Foscari remains his mask. The deposition of Foscari is delivered as a 'last decree, / Definitive and absolute' (V, i, 164–5) of the Ten – a sudden power override that cancels the doge's (also state-ordained) holy oath to remain in office till his death – and marks a 'state of exception' whereby the existing laws are lifted and 'force' facilitates the use of the law to suit the current situation – the Council of Ten acts as the sole 'executive power', wielding the now essentially lawless 'force of law'.[11] Ironically, the doge's downfall is partly brought about by his absolute trust in the justice of Venetian law – his allegiance to the 'law he found [but] did not make' (II, i, 395). But his stoical belief in the impartiality of fortune is his second big mistake – as Faliero points out, the lottery of fate in Venice is rigged by the ruling patricians. Foscari believes 'all […] advantages' are fortune's 'accidents' (II, i, 340–1) and, crucially, that 'nothing rests / Upon our will' (II, i, 359). Yet the doge's one striking insight, marking his impassive attitude as something rather more philosophical than the automated acceptance of a puppet, is his dictum that 'when we think we lead, we are most led' (II, i, 361). This describes both the bravado of Faliero and the reserved acceptance of Foscari. Where the former 'leads' a carnivalesque rebellion against a carnivalised power structure, the latter is 'led' to his death by the shameless workings of a grotesque accentuation of that same carnivalised, and carnivalising, structure – behind this structure, in *The Two Foscari*, is the figure of Loredano, bending the law against Foscari and clandestinely manipulating the patricians. If one obvious manifestation of Venice's grotesque nature in *The Two Foscari* is the state's reduction of Francis Foscari to a 'puppet', 'marionette' and 'automaton', his face 'frozen into' a 'mask', the root cause of that grotesqueness is the fact that Venice is being played – and can be played – by an 'ineffably', 'legitimately vile' individual (*DJ*, Dedication, 8, describing Castlereagh).

The only active counter-player to Loredano's machinations is Foscari's daughter-in-law, Marina. Byron gives her the voice of transhistorical polemic, and she takes over the role of the critic and prophet that Faliero had played in the earlier drama. Marina's searing critique boldly and repeatedly takes issue with Venice's so-called republican power structures, with an agonistic bravado surpassing even that of Faliero as its pointed catalogue of recriminations is directed not at an allied audience or spoken in soliloquy but thrown at the doge and the state he represents in the presence of the antagonist and chief master of fates, Loredano:

> Keep
> Those maxims for your mass of scared mechanics,
> [...] your dumb citizens,
> Your mask'd nobility, your sbirri, and
> Your spies, your galley and your other slaves,
> To whom your midnight carryings off and drownings,
> Your dungeons next the palace roofs, or under
> The water's level; your mysterious meetings,
> And unknown dooms, and sudden executions,
> Your 'Bridge of Sighs', your strangling chamber, and
> Your torturing instruments, have made ye seem
> The beings of another and worse world!
> (II, i, 299–313)

Marina's critique here and elsewhere represents a rhetorically potent, if politically powerless, confrontation of the ruthless machinery of the Venetian state, so easily manipulated by Loredano. This catalogue of the state's criminal acts and masked operations recalls, in much clearer and more terrifying images, the carnivalesque power wielded by the 'mask'd nobility' consistently evoked throughout Byron's first Venetian drama. Here, however, Marina's catalogue of vice culminates in another grotesque transformation of the carnivalesque Venetian state in which Venice seems to be controlled by 'beings of another and worse world' wielding unlimited power and channelling it into oppressive measures.

Nevertheless, while Marina may confront the grotesque 'alien inhuman force' of the Venetian state that has turned her father-in-law into a puppet, she cannot challenge this force. Nor can Foscari, as Lansdown notes, 'abandon either the palace [...] or the political status quo'.[12] Venetian puppet-doges cannot break free of the constraints of the puppet theatre, with its ducal palace and prison 'on each hand' (*CHP*, IV, 1). Indeed, the doge's downfall is not the result of *hamartia* but of the state of Venice itself, 'a character, with whose nature the other characters must reckon', but which is hidden behind a veil 'of Orwellian state secrecy'.[13] Byron's second Venetian drama demonstrates at every turn the 'tyranny', 'secrecy, coercion and black ops at the heart of [Venetian] rule', the passivity induced by Venice's power structure – for example, in the robotic diction of the Chief of the Ten and the masked practices of the Ten themselves – but most of all the ease with which Venice can be manipulated – played with and played – to serve the personal ends of a single, ruthless patrician.[14]

By juxtaposing Byron's two Venetian dramas, we can clearly discern that Venice's power structure evolves from the corrupt arrangement that triggered Faliero's untimely rebellion into something much darker, more convoluted and less openly structured, the power of the state having fallen quietly into the hands of a biased individual – the atmosphere, the motives and the tragic loops the two Foscari are forced to undergo are truly Kafkaesque. If in *The Two Foscari*, set about a century after *Marino Faliero*, the Council of Ten are legally decimating the republic,[15] their oligarchic power structure virtually omnipotent, and the state of Venice 'is the Law and the Law is the State' while the 'two Foscari inhabit a world bereft of justice',[16] it is Loredano who shows most clearly how this corruption is possible – indeed all too easy.

Playing with the law to serve his private patriarchal vendetta, Loredano blatantly admits that if the law does not allow him to execute his vicious plan, he will remake the law so that it will:

> Barbarigo: But will the laws uphold us?
> Loredano: What laws? – 'The Ten' are laws; and if they were not I will be legislator in this business. (IV, i, 37–9)

The 'bald-heads' of the Ten, who are said to hold Venice 'in bondage' (III, i, 244) are revealed to be only another set of puppets in the hands of the master-mover Loredano, who is prepared to ruthlessly 'legislate' according to his own personal aims. As Barbarigo observes: they 'speak [his] language, watch [his] nod, approve / [His] plans, and do [his] work' (V, i, 142–3). Venice in its entirety is a grotesque puppet show, serving a single indomitable will. Any subversive, revivifying, carnivalising potential of play is subsumed by the debilitating horror of the grotesque. As Bakhtin puts it, in 'Romantic form the mask is torn away from the oneness of the folk carnival concept. […] the mask hides something, keeps a secret, deceives [...]. The Romantic mask loses almost entirely its regenerating and renewing element and acquires a somber hue.'[17]

In this sense, Byron's second Venetian drama offers a full-blown, Romantic negation of traditional carnival – while Faliero's coup (allying him across the social spectrum to the *arsenalotti* and thus making it a 'folk' event) was a carnival attempt to 'regenerate and renew' Venice, in *The Two Foscari*, all social and familial bonds are rendered void – as Jacopo Foscari aptly puts is, 'nothing can sympathize with Foscari / Not even a Foscari' (I, i, 172–3). The only community active in the drama remains the inexorable power structure, which bureaucratically proceeds with its decrees and reports, controlling all even as it is itself susceptible to manipulation by the vengeful motives of just one master-mover, the 'secret' behind the Venetian mask that pushes the state from carnival to grotesque extremes.

As Kelsall demonstrates, Byron's Venetian plays represent the process of 'learning about things as they are' and, as such, they are a lesson 'in disenchantment'.[18] In these dramas, Venice is a game – a game played out to the point at which it becomes a grotesque travesty of play. And it is a game that extends beyond history-making and into historiography too, where the victors' perspective prescribes the ethics of the official annals of Venetian history. In Anne Barton's words,

> Byron's Faliero is [...] stingingly conscious [...] of the fact that history will judge him not according to the honesty of his dealings or the justice of his cause, but simply on the amoral basis of failure or success. The calumnies of time 'never spare the fame of him who fails, / But try the Caesar, or the Catiline, / By the true touchstone of desert – success'.[19]

Barton clearly demarcates the crucial lines of Byron's critique of official Venetian history here, which judges 'simply on the amoral basis of failure or success'. History's victors write and rewrite history to suit their own ends and justify their own actions. As Byron has it elsewhere, 'Had Bonaparte won at Waterloo, / It had been firmness; now 'tis pertinacity: / Must the event decide between the two?' (*DJ*, XIV, 90). Richard Cronin adds: 'In the end what interests [Byron] is the riddle of it all. How can one decide what is right and then choose sides if it is only in the act of choosing sides that the rights and wrongs of the matter become fixed?'[20] The problem of this essential indeterminacy of historical matters, a game played with right and wrong, marks yet another level on which Byron's Venetian dramas evoke and resonate with the principle of play. Of Faliero, Byron writes at the end of Appendix III: 'Had the man succeeded, he would have changed the face of Venice, and perhaps of Italy.'[21]

Instead, the Venetian carnival of power has become thoroughly grotesque by the time of *The Two Foscari*, which suggests both the extent to which, for Byron, the corruption of the state of Venice had progressed in the near-century after Faliero's fall and 'a Byronic recognition that republican sovereignty is doomed to the slaughterhouse of history'.[22] And it is to this slaughterhouse that Byron turns in *The Deformed Transformed*, where he extemporises and satirises the very foundations of humanism, history and indeed civilisation as such, with Renaissance Rome as its showcase.

History here becomes a bloody farce played out *ad absurdum* – Rome is reduced to a transhistorical, perverted trope of the *theatrum mundi* locked in a vicious circle of bloody rebirth, radically redefining our understanding of the term *Renaissance*. The 'game of living in imitation of Antiquity', as Johan Huizinga describes the Italian Renaissance, is one of 'violence, depth and purity'.[23] The Renaissance Italy that Byron seeks to bring to life, reinvent and simultaneously deconstruct in *The Deformed Transformed*, where he stages the event that marked the bitter end of the Italian Renaissance, the sack of Rome of 1527, focuses on precisely this Renaissance 'game' of imitation – highlighting the play of rebirth, in aesthetic and historical terms, but challenging the 'purity' of the Renaissance with its innate 'violence'.

From the beginning of the drama, and Arnold's first encounter with the Stranger, we bear witness to a critique, in the form of a playful travesty, of the idealistic Renaissance devotion to mimicking antiquity. As the Stranger parades a selection of classical heroes in front of Arnold, he reduces those idols to a kind of fashion collection:

> Fear not, my hunchback – if the shadows of
> That which existed please not your nice taste,
> I'll animate the ideal marble, till
> Your soul be reconciled to her new garment.
> (I, i, 261–4)

Aesthetics – taste – cancels ethics here, and the transformation of an unsightly rustic hunchback, with the help of classical forms, into a quintessential epic hero is effected under the sign of vanity alone. In the process of choosing a new body, the Stranger assures Arnold that if he indeed cannot decide on a form recalled from the real or mythical past, his necromantic powers will 'animate the ideal marble' to match the high demands of Arnold's 'aspiring' soul (I, i, 145). In the end, only the form of the demigod Achilles will suffice. The Stranger's promise to bring the idealised classical forms of chiselled marble to life thus parodies the Renaissance concern with rebirth through mimetic art. But the theme of the violence of mimetic representation, taken up especially in relation to sculpture, comes to the fore in the Olimpia and Cellini episodes, where the relationship between actual life and the 'ideal marble' it so often aspires to emulate is intricately explored.

The metaphorical masking of Olimpia as a marble statue of essential beauty contains a strong element of violence. The violence of art is demonstrated in the aesthetic objectification of the beloved. In a random encounter in the midst of the battle, Olimpia is unwillingly rescued by Arnold. Having seen her attempt to commit suicide by flinging herself from an altar in St Peter'son to the marble floor, Arnold instantly falls in love with her, exclaiming:

How pale! how beautiful! how lifeless!
Alive or dead, thou essence of all beauty,
I love but thee!
(II, iii, 142–4)

Here Byron shows Arnold locked in the aestheticising 'game of living in imitation of Antiquity' – 'beauty' surpasses 'life' and is the object of all 'love' as the potentially dying Olimpia is transformed into a statuesque image of the 'essence of all beauty' – her perilous state obscured by her objectification into a work of art. The woman is abstracted, transformed into an image and, as such, is herself negated in her entirety – made doubly lifeless, and essentially powerless. Arnold's wish can be read as an inversion of the Pygmalion myth: a wish to immobilise and objectify the beloved woman, moulding her into an 'ideal marble' version of herself – pale, beautiful, lifeless.

The violence of this aestheticising is distinctive and continues, but also changes, in the fragment of Part III of the drama, set in a post-war pastoral idyll, where the cohabitation of Arnold, Caesar and Olimpia is increasingly troubled since Olimpia does not return

Arnold's ardent affections. Here, too, Olimpia is rhetorically cast in marble, this time by the Stranger, whose tone, however, is far from admiring:

> This precious thing of dust – this bright Olimpia –
> This marvellous Virgin – is a marble matron –
> An Idol – but a cold one to your heat
> Promethean – and unkindled by your torch?
> (III, 86–9)

The Stranger's speech is penetrating and mischievous, and symptomatically unsympathetic to Arnold's classicising idealisation of Olimpia. The speech again employs the conceit of marble that haunts Olimpia throughout the text, satirising Arnold's objectification of her. In a smart twist of the continually subversive satirising of the Renaissance game of classical imitation that runs through the drama, Olimpia never escapes the marble altar from which she jumps when Arnold first sees her in St Peter's; her subsequent life in the drama becomes that of a mute monument, her metaphorical mask of 'ideal marble' moulding her into 'an Idol', 'a marble matron'.

In the Cellini episode, the Renaissance 'game of imitation of Antiquity' and its inherent connection to violence is foregrounded in the figure of Cellini, a 'cunning sculptor' but also a 'dealer in arms':

> Caesar: Thou hast in hand
>   A famous artizan, a cunning sculptor;
>   Also a dealer in the sword and dagger;
>   Not so, my musqueteer; t'was he who slew
>   The Bourbon from the wall.
> Arnold: Ay, did he so?
>   Then he hath carv'd his monument!
> Roman: I yet
>   May live to carve your betters'.
> Caesar: Well said, my man of marble! Benvenuto,
>   Thou hast some practice in both ways; and he
>   Who slays Cellini will have work'd as hard
>   As e'er thou didst on Carrara's blocks.
> (II, ii, 32–42)

Art here is deadening – Cellini is a 'man of marble'. In the midst of the battle, he can therefore retain another kind of playfulness: witty repartee. Casting Cellini in stone, the Stranger attributes to him almost superhuman qualities – he is a man of Carrara marble, a kind of sculpted mannerist monster combining the gravity of the Commendatore's stone-cast form and the levity of a Don Giovanni in a monumentally haunting, yet agile and witty presence, in line with Cellini's similarly conceived *Autobiography*. But the deadening influence of the aesthetic goes further than this: 'Cellini's sculpture in all its grandeur embodies the abstract system of belief at the centre of Roman culture. The eternal laws it insists upon mystify actual experience – including the violence to which Cellini is partner – and thus mask the ugly machinations of the culture from which it grew.'[24]

The 'game' of imitating classical aesthetics is itself an imitation of a classical game of 'ugly machinations' that 'mystify actual existence'. The very idea of having 'carv'd' one's 'monument', or of becoming someone's 'man of marble' for one's 'deal[ings] in the sword and dagger', resonates with the drama's 'cold pastoral' theme in which art is seen to cast life as lifeless statuary art, and life, in Wildean mode, wears the masks of art and imitates its ideals.

Indeed, Byron's rebirth of antiquity in *The Deformed Transformed*, as in *Childe Harold's Pilgrimage*, presents history's repeated battles over Rome as a paradigm for the never-ending *Urspiel* of human history. And it is particularly the dehumanising, violent game-playing of classical culture which, through that rebirth, comes to define modernity. Byron resurrects the trope of violence-as-entertainment in ancient Rome and displays it as a historical model that extends across the ages. As Huizinga remarks, 'the play-element in the Roman State is nowhere more clearly expressed than in the cry for *panem et circenses*', and the idea of the 'bloody circus' in *The Deformed Transformed* applies no longer only to the ancient arena of the pagan games of antiquity, or even to Rome, but to the whole world throughout history.[25] Rome, pagan and Christian, is simply one example of this gory game. For the Stranger, the whole world of men is the gladiator dying in the Coliseum for the amusement of the Roman crowd, though the crowd has now gone and only he remains: 'I must play with these poor puppets; / 'Tis a spirit's pastime in his idler hours' (I, ii, 321–2). The figure of the puppeteer appears once again in Byron's dramas, but with potentially universal implications for all human history, not just one specific period in Venice's past (though this too has wider implications for republican politics per se). And 'play' is once again at the heart of Byron's reading of history. The entirety of earthly conflict, violence and warfare is here transformed into the Punch-and-Judy-style pastime of a slightly bored supernatural spectator/puppeteer. The ancient trope of *theatrum mundi* gains both gravity and levity as the 'strutting and fretting' of Shakespeare's version of the metaphor is transformed into a violent mayhem that is both carnivalised and grotesque and from which the 'poor player' (*Macbeth*, V, v, 17–28) exits into the folds and creases of a shabby pantomime curtain:[26]

> Now, priest! Now, soldier! The two great professions,
> Together by the ears and hearts! I have not
> Seen a more comic pantomime since Titus
> Took Jewry. But the Romans had the best then;
> Now they must take their turn.
> (II, iii, 30–4)

The Stranger's commentaries on the ubiquitous bloody chaos, like his reading of the plundering of St Peter's by Catholic and Protestant soldiers alike, are disturbing for a number of reasons. The absurd nature of the sack was well captured by Martin Luther who summed it up in an aphorism: 'Christ reigns in such a way that the Emperor who persecutes Luther for the Pope is forced to destroy the Pope for Luther.'[27] Most disturbing, however, is the fact that the idea of human history as a set of farcical, violent, 'comic pantomime' interludes manifestly subverts any sense of ethics. Reading history as violence and violence as pantomime transforms that violence into 'a tale / Told by an idiot, full of sound and fury, / Signifying nothing' (*Macbeth*, V, v, 27–8). Life and death, victory and defeat, are granted in turns, and it is only a matter of time before the wheel of fortune turns things topsy-turvy once more in yet another 'comic pantomime'. Human history results in a moral blank – a game played out for a doubtful, perhaps non-existent, audience.

This notion of the Renaissance as a violent 'game' of imitating the violent games of antiquity echoes throughout the text, as Byron traces it from the violent mythical birth of Rome, whose 'earliest cement was brother's blood' (I, ii, 83), to its continual rebirth throughout the bloody conundrum of history. The Eternal City is never entirely destroyed by recurring bloodshed, but, rather, perpetuates and reinvents itself through that bloodshed, in a red circle of ongoing renaissance and reinvention, never parting or indeed learning from its own vertiginous past – a 'never-ceasing scene of slaughter' (I, ii, 89).

This is true even as the imitation of classical culture is subordinated to the modern 'rebirth' of Christianity. This becomes part of the scene featuring Olimpia's attempted suicide in St Peter's. As we have seen, Arnold reads Olimpia as a representation of essential beauty, cast in stone. The models informing Arnold's thinking are classical and statuary. Yet her suicide attempt is a rather somatic, subversive and violent mix of Christian and pagan rituals of rebirth – a 'bloody baptism' into martyrdom. Having killed one of her pursuers with a heavy crucifix, she throws herself off the high altar, declaring:

> I see thee purple with the blood of Rome;
> Take mine, that's all thou e'er shalt have of me,
> And here, upon the marble of this temple,
> Where the baptismal font baptized me God's,
> I offer him a blood less holy
> But not less pure than the holy water
> The saints have sanctified.
> (II, iii, 124–31)

Suicide is one of the cardinal sins, but Olimpia's heroism is essentially pagan, as she equates her blood with that of Renaissance Rome, and thus Rome's classical past, though in a very different way from Arnold's objectification of her. There can be no doubt as to her Christian virtues, however, and her violent attempt to transform herself from victim to martyr recasts Arnold's classical objectification of her, semantically painting over in crimson both idealised classicism and the ritual purification of baptism.

As a matter of fact, the theme of bloody baptism recurs throughout the entire drama. Crucially, it resonates within the larger scope of the drama's experimentation with, or deconstruction of, Italian Renaissance principles, painting in blood the very name of that era, the 'rebirth' of antiquity it represents and its classical ideals and artistic forms. If human history is a world of births and rebirths, of change and transformation, in *The Deformed Transformed* it is also a world of perpetual violence and death. And it is in its focus on the Renaissance 'game' of imitating the idealising forms of antiquity – and especially on that recurring emblem of Renaissance culture, sculpture – that Byron most powerfully presents that 'game' as a mimetic life-in-death, as an uncanny spectral presence invoking the violent 'games' of that classical perfection the Renaissance so eagerly sought.

Huizinga's analysis of the ways in which the Italian Renaissance itself 'played' helps us to see the full extent of Byron's intricate playing upon and twisting of the entire Renaissance ethos in *The Deformed Transformed*:

> The spirit of the Renaissance was very far from being frivolous. The game of living in imitation of Antiquity was pursued in holy earnest. Devotion to the ideals of the past in the matter of plastic creation and intellectual discovery was of a violence, depth, and purity surpassing anything we can imagine [...]. This striving, at once sophisticated and spontaneous, for beauty and nobility of form is an instance of culture at play.[28]

This 'culture at play' comes alive in Byron's drama, staged in all its complexity. In crucial contrast to Huizinga, however, Byron draws attention to the subversive, violent potential of these idealised principles. As Daniel P. Watkins remarks, 'the desperate struggle for love, honor, glory, and beauty – for a permanently ennobling ideal – totally deadens Arnold and the warring soldiers to genuine human compassion [...] and makes them contributors to public chaos and madness'.[29] If Olimpia represents a set of classical ideals while simultaneously instancing the 'earnestness', 'depth and purity' of the Renaissance 'game' of imitating those ideals inspired by an essentially nostalgic impulse to resurrect an idealised past, this game ultimately issues in the fragment of Part III where the Stranger mockingly sees her as a 'marble matron'. All artistic representation is here exposed as fundamentally violent. Cellini's 'cunning' art, on the other hand, involves the death of the Bourbon king shot dead while leading the attack on the walls of Rome. And in so far as we can speculate from the fragment of Part III, Olimpia ends the drama as a victim of the classicist Renaissance and its 'earnest' game of imitation, while Arnold serves as a critique of classical heroism and its 'permanently ennobling ideal'.

The Stranger, however, anticipates the raw future of modernity and indeed postmodernity, and their very different legacy of classical 'play'. In distinctly Byronic fashion, *The Deformed Transformed* as a whole is looking both back and forward – back in its critique of the idealised classical norms of the Italian Renaissance, and forward in its staggeringly postmodern conceptualisation of both history and artistic representation that tells us much about our world of agonistic superhero cinema and survival reality shows. In this sense, *The Deformed Transformed* points us to something that is also true of, but perhaps less obvious in, Byron's Venetian dramas, though Faliero's curse points us in this direction too. Byron's Italian dramas, concerned as they are with the specifics of Italian history, are interested in the working out of history per se. They are an extended exploration of that 'moral of all human tales' and 'same rehearsal of the past' that Byron sees written on the Palatine in *Childe Harold* IV: 'First Freedom, then Glory – when that fails / Wealth, vice, corruption, – barbarism at last' (108).

Therefore, though Byron's Italian dramas are perhaps in some ways difficult to group together – *The Deformed Transformed* is formally a very different kind of play from *Marino Faliero* and *The Two Foscari* – continuities connect these texts, and the evolution of certain fundamental Byronic ideas about history runs through them all. They all use Italian history to think about historical 'progress' more generally, and in them Italian history points to key paradigms. Italian history, Venetian and Roman, is dominated by political game-playing in which ethics are altogether absent. The results are the carnivalisation of politics to grotesque extremes where violence predominates. Renaissance Italy's attempts to revive classical republican and aesthetic ideals only revive antiquity's addiction to bloodshed. Humanism is ultimately dehumanising. And Italian history is, in Byron's dramas, a synecdoche for all history. As Faliero tells Venice, so Byron tells the world at large: 'it is your history'.

Notes

1 T. Tasso, *Il Gonzaga secondo, overo del giuoco, dialogo del signor Torquato Tasso* (Venice: Bernardo Giunti & fratelli, 1582), p. 5; my translation.

2 'Albion [...] in the fall / Of Venice, think of thine despite thy watery wall' (*CHP*, IV, 17). As A. A. Schmidt remarks, the 'plays' social and political elements call to mind contemporary Italian and British politics'. A. A. Schmidt, *Byron and the Rhetoric of Italian Nationalism* (Basingstoke: Palgrave Macmillan, 2010), p. 99.

3 M. Kelsall, 'Venice preserved', in R. Gleckner and B. Beatty (eds.), *The Plays of Lord Byron: Critical Essays* (Liverpool: Liverpool University Press, 1997), pp. 33–67. See also C. Franklin, '"My hope was to bring forth heroes": *The Two Foscari* and the fostering of masculine *virtù* by

[a] stoical heroine', in R. Gleckner and B. Beatty (eds.), *The Plays of Lord Byron: Critical Essays* (Liverpool: Liverpool University Press, 1997), pp. 163–80; and A. Rawes, '*Marino Faliero*: escaping the aristocratic', in B. Beatty, T. Howe and C. Robinson (eds.), *Liberty and Poetic Licence: New Essays on Byron* (Liverpool: Liverpool University Press, 2008), pp. 88–102.

4   M. J. A. Green and P. Pal-Lapinski (eds.), *Byron and the Politics of Freedom and Terror* (Basingstoke: Palgrave Macmillan, 2011).

5   J. Christensen reads Faliero's death as 'sacrificial', bringing 'the game of mutual homicides' 'to an end', in J. Christensen, '*Marino Faliero* and the fault of Byron's satire', *Studies in Romanticism*, 24:3 (1985), 313–33 (p. 324).

6   As Carla Pomarè observes, 'Byron's play does allude to an original crime, but in such concise and elliptical terms that one is obliged to refer to the Appendix to have a clear view of the events.' C. Pomarè, *Byron and the Discourses of History* (Farnham: Ashgate, 2013), p. 86.

7   See W. Kayser, *The Grotesque in Art and Literature*, trans. U. Weisstein (New York and Toronto: McGraw-Hill, 1966), p. 184.

8   Kayser, *The Grotesque in Art and Literature*, p. 183.

9   M. Bakhtin, *Rabelais and His World*, trans. H. Iswolsky (Bloomington, Ind.: Indiana University Press, 1984), p. 40.

10 R. Lansdown, *Byron's Historical Dramas* (Oxford: Oxford University Press, 1992), p. 185.

11 G. Agamben, *State of Exception*, trans. K. Attell (Chicago, Ill.: University of Chicago Press, 2005), p. 38.

12 Lansdown, *Byron's Historical Dramas*, p. 197.

13 Lansdown, *Byron's Historical Dramas*, pp. 185, 188.

14 J. Gonsalves, 'Byron's Venetian masque of the French Revolution', in M. J. A. Green and P. Pal-Lapinski (eds.), *Byron and the Politics of Freedom and Terror* (Basingstoke: Palgrave Macmillan, 2011), pp. 47–63 (p. 54).

15 This 'body became the key power in the Venetian republic, the power against which the protagonists in both Byron's plays battle'. Schmidt, *Byron and the Rhetoric of Italian Nationalism*, p. 106.

16 Lansdown, *Byron's Historical Dramas*, pp. 197, 196.

17 Bakhtin, *Rabelais and His World*, p. 40.

18 Kelsall, 'Venice preserved', p. 66.

19 A. Barton, '"A light to lesson ages": Byron's political plays', in J. D. Jump (ed.), *Byron: A Symposium* (London: Macmillan, 1975), pp. 138–62 (p. 150), quoting *Marino Faliero* (I, ii, 594–6).

20 R. Cronin, *In Search of the Pure Commonwealth: The Politics of Romantic Poetry* (Basingstoke: Palgrave Macmillan, 2000), p. 172.

21 *CPW*, vol. IV, p. 539.
22 Gonsalves, 'Byron's Venetian masque of the French Revolution', p. 55.
23 J. Huizinga, *Homo Ludens* (Bungay: Paladin, 1970), p. 206.
24 D. P. Watkins, 'The ideological dimensions of Byron's *The Deformed Transformed*', in R. Gleckner and B. Beatty (eds.), *The Plays of Lord Byron: Critical Essays* (Liverpool: Liverpool University Press, 1997), pp. 347–63 (p. 357).
25 Huizinga, *Homo Ludens*, p. 202.
26 Here the *theatrum mundi* is no longer 'a site' that offers 'a moral lesson which can help the observer to establish continuity between generations, avoid ancestral errors and act wisely in the present', as Martin Procházka puts it in 'Imaginative geographies disrupted: representing the other in English Romantic dramas', in *European Journal of English Studies*, 6:2 (2002), 207–20 (p. 208).
27 M. Luther, *Luther's Works*, 55 vols, ed. J. Pelikan and H. T. Lehmann (St Louis, Miss.: Concordia, 1955–85), vol. XLIX, p. 169.
28 Huizinga, *Homo Ludens*, p. 206.
29 D. P. Watkins, *A Materialist Critique of English Romantic Drama* (Gainesville, Fla.: University Press of Florida, 1993), pp. 205–6.

11

'Where shall I turn me?': Italy and irony in *Beppo* and *Don Juan*

Diego Saglia

> Where shall I turn me not to *view* its bonds?
> For I will never *feel* them – Italy! (*DJ*, Dedication, 16)

With this couplet Byron interrupts the flow of his reflections, in the unpublished dedication to *Don Juan*, about the forms of enslavement imposed on post-Napoleonic Europe by the Congress of Vienna and the Holy Alliance. Leaving behind the effects of Castlereagh's policies in Ireland, and his subservience to the allied powers, Byron turns with decision towards his newly adopted country, a satellite of the Hapsburg Empire.

Malcolm Kelsall reads these lines as one of 'those outbursts which seem so typically Byronic as he gestures broadly across the whole of Europe and the Congress system', and that determined his early nineteenth-century image as 'champion of the oppressed and freedom fighter'.[1] From another perspective, Jane Stabler suggests that their style encapsulates Byron's conviction that Italy could be 'the answer to all ills, literary and political', and the 'perfect backdrop' for adopting the expressive mode of 'the backward-looking poetry of exile'.[2] Alternately envisaging it in terms of political posturing or exilic writing, these interpretations define the couplet as a significant fragment of Byron's literary, political and existential self-positioning in Italy. They also highlight its multiple and potentially contradictory meanings, so that, if the couplet expresses the poet's discovery of 'the liberating possibilities of translation and acculturation' and 'the prophetic possibilities of speaking another language', it does so in a strikingly ambivalent way.[3]

The two lines from the *Don Juan* dedication stand out both graphically and syntactically because of the question and exclamation marks, the use of italics and the hiatus introduced by the dash. Yet they also belong in the flow of *ottavas* and their political discourse, as appears from the lexical chiming of 'bonds' with the earlier 'bind' and 'chain' (15), and of 'Italy' with the 'It' that sums up Castlereagh's crimes (15). Their ambivalence reflects the problematic nature of Byron's position within Italy's political and cultural jigsaw. He selects the country as a safe vantage point, from which – so he believes – he may be an unaffected observer of the ravages caused by Castlereagh and the effects of the Congress system. In actual fact, as we know, he was spied upon during his stay in Ravenna,[4] whose papal legate was subservient to Austria, and, more generally, his was only a half-hearted embrace of Italy, since he never turned away completely from England and Britain, or European politics and culture more broadly.

In the couplet, this interplay of positions and attitudes pivots on the word 'turn', a charged word in *Don Juan*. In the dedication, for example, it marks the difference between the turncoat Lakers and Milton, who did not 'turn his very talent to a crime' (10). It also carries metatextual implications when it describes Byron's mutable poetical moods, intimating an imaginative restlessness rooted in the constant dissatisfaction with a poetic language that does not 'express one half what I should say' (*DJ*, V, 132). 'Turning' thus amounts to a physical action, a political gesture, a poetic operation ('verse' comes from the Latin *vertere*, 'to turn') and a trope (from the Greek *trepein*, 'to turn'). In terms of rhetoric and delivery, it is also related to the moment known as 'parabasis' in Attic Old Comedy, in which the chorus steps aside and, breaking the scenic illusion, turns away from the main action to address the audience.[5]

Friedrich Schlegel famously defined irony as 'permanent parabasis', and, in 'The Rhetoric of Temporality', Paul de Man identified parabasis as the basis for a 'revelation of discontinuity' crucial to the emergence of the 'reflexive disjunction' of Romantic irony.[6] In his recent revisionist reading of de Man, Paul Hamilton has cast parabasis as the foundation of a type of irony that is not modelled on 'foreclosures of an infinite linear progress' but rather shaped by 'a branching out into lateral connections, a sideways rolling expansion', so that, as he goes on to suggest, parabasis tends to promote a kind of 'lateral or comparative inclusiveness'.[7] What de Man terms the 'discontinuity' vouchsafed by parabasis provides an essential key to Byron's version of satire and its distinctive 'exposure of a disparity between professed norms and actual behaviors', while the idea of the 'inclusiveness' of parabasis helps us to highlight the precise nature of Byron's ambivalent 'turn' to Italy.[8]

Parabasis is not a new concept in Byron Studies. Peter Graham employs it to examine those moments in which the poet 'addresses the reader or audience with the author's own views and concerns' so that parabasis constitutes an 'essentially theatrical device' capable of explaining the narrative digressions and shifts of *Don Juan*.[9] From a related perspective, Paul M. Curtis reads Byron's parabasis as a technique aimed at 'unframing' narrative and exposing 'the tenuous relationship between the real world and the narrated one'.[10] Expanding on these suggestions, I envisage this device or practice as a combination of textual movement and physical gesture that generates multiple viewpoints and potentially heterodox meanings. More specifically, I will show how parabasis is fundamental to Byron's use of irony and satire in relation both to his contradictory acts of self-positioning in Italy and to what we might call his Italian 'aesthetics of the turn'.[11]

Byron's veering towards Italy in the couplet from *Don Juan*'s dedication is a discursive and performative act endowed with historical and political significance, one that illuminates how his imagining of Italy is inextricable from the satire of his 'medley' poems in *ottava rima*, especially *Beppo* and *Don Juan*, which critics have repeatedly considered inherently Italian.[12] By focusing on Byron's parabasic 'turn' to Italy in *Beppo* and *Don Juan*, we gain a deeper understanding of how his complex self-positioning in Italy lies behind the innovative poetics of these works and their delineation of an unprecedentedly multiform world view.

Textual turns: the *tre corone* of Italian literature

Byron began his linguistic and literary self-positioning in Italy soon after his arrival in 1816. He became quickly acquainted with what he called the 'Venetian modification' of Italian, which he described to John Murray as 'like the Somersetshire version of English', though he also continued to cultivate 'the more classical dialects', by which he presumably meant Tuscan.[13] Similarly, his knowledge of Italian literature expanded. A clear sign of this was his purchase of

Pierre-Louis Ginguené's *Histoire littéraire d'Italie* (1811–19), which was also instrumental in acclimatising the English to *ottava rima*, since both John Hookham Frere and Byron read the French critic's pages on Luigi Pulci's *Morgante Maggiore* and drew inspiration from them.[14] Moreover, Byron experienced Italian literature both in book form and as part of his daily life. In Venice, as Philip Martin notes, he could hear the *ottava rima* 'in streets, in gondolas, after dinner, extempore or memorized', its comic mode thus becoming part of a whole mosaic of 'living associations'.[15]

Nevertheless, Byron's immersion in Italian literary culture was inextricable from the ambivalences and contradictions of his turn to Italy, as demonstrated by two emblematic prefatory writings – those to *Childe Harold* IV and *The Prophecy of Dante*. The former offers a list of exemplars of contemporary Italian achievements in 'Art, Science, and Belles Lettres', many of whom are literary figures: Vittorio Alfieri, Vincenzo Monti, Ugo Foscolo, Ippolito Pindemonte, Angelo Mai, Giuseppe Mezzofanti and Andreas Mustoxides (an Italian-educated Greek historian and philologist). Disproving arguments about Italian decadence, these names testify to the country's cultural fecundity, which Byron sees as a token of its solid cultural identity and longing for the 'immortality of independence'. The preface to the *Prophecy* also presents the poem as a politically charged homage to the Italians by way of their own literature. Yet, at the same time, Byron notes realistically that literature is 'all that is left them as a nation'. This altogether more mixed praise contrasts with the 'immersive' approach to Italy, reinforced by quotations in the original Italian, found in the preface to *Childe Harold* IV. Eventually, the separation of Byron's voice and text from Italy's context becomes unmistakable when, in the preface to the *Prophecy*, he states that he should not be 'deviating into an address to the Italian reader, when my business is with the English one'.[16] An expression of Byron's vacillating turn towards Italy, this volte-face characterises his treatment of Italian literature in *Don Juan*, where its greatest authors are not merely emblems of Italy's cultural identity or tokens of a cultural capital compensating for a non-existent state structure. They are also the targets of the poem's satirical play, instancing a simultaneous turn towards and away from Italy that demonstrates Byron's fundamentally parabasic relation to it.

This ambivalence is visible in the coded or explicit references to Italian authors in Cantos I–V – that is, the portion of *Don Juan* Byron wrote uninterruptedly between 1818 and 1820 before the lull in composition lasting until early 1822. To be sure, intertextual references in these cantos are not limited to Italian writers. Yet, of all the hints and echoes resonating in them, those about Italian literature stand out as the most numerous to be consistently drawn from one national tradition, and because they concern the three pillars of that tradition (Dante, Petrarch and, to a lesser extent, Boccaccio) alongside such stalwarts as Pulci and Ariosto.

References to Italian authors in the early cantos of *Don Juan* also stand out because of their textual distribution. Though Pulci and Ariosto are the most obvious authorities for Byron's new satirical medley mode, they appear relatively late in the poem. The first reference to Pulci is in Canto III, stanza 45, which, as Byron explains in a footnote, rewrites Canto 18, stanza 151 of *Morgante Maggiore*.[17] In the next canto, he introduces his well-known celebration of Pulci as the 'sire of the half-serious rhyme' (IV, 6), and later still he jocularly rhymes 'Pulci' with the Horatian 'dulci' (XIII, 81). Ariosto first features in a metadiscursive aside in Canto III about the digressions, omissions and ellipses of his new mode, all of which he defines as 'a loss to / The world, not quite so great as Ariosto' (96).

While Byron does acknowledge his most immediate Italian models for *Don Juan*, these authors, who so influenced his adoption of the *ottava rima* and its satirical tone, are nevertheless only sparingly cited in the opening cantos of *Don Juan*. In addition, these cantos contain no mention of Tasso by name, whose relevance to Byron's refashioning of the epic, as Nicholas Halmi convincingly argues, was as decisive as that of Ariosto.[18] This, of course, does not diminish the impact of these authors on Byron's definition of his ironic voice and satiric imagination. Their limited visibility, however, highlights the countervailing emphasis he lays, in Cantos I–V, on the founding fathers of Italian letters (the '*Trecentisti*' or '*tre corone*' – Dante, Petrarch and Boccaccio) and their ambivalent treatment, consonant both with Byron's turn to Italy and his self-positioning in relation to it. If the epic poets of the Renaissance provide him with a generic framework, a metrical form and a style, the *Trecentisti* have a different function in *Don Juan*. In the early cantos, they are both poetic medium and subject matter, revered cultural symbols and satirical butts, and are thus fully integrated into the poem's construction of a multifaceted and contradictory Italian reality and correspondingly Italianised poet-figure.

In the case of Dante, Canto I features a tongue-in-cheek echo of the Paolo and Francesca episode from *Inferno*, Canto V, in which Byron's narrator hints at the consummation of Juan and Julia's affair by remarking that 'That night the Virgin was no further pray'd' (76). Canto II offers a humorous reference to Count Ugolino (*Inferno*, Canto XXXIII) in a comment on Pedrillo's fate as the castaways' dinner (83). Canto III contains a diverting remark about the fact that Dante's Beatrice and Milton's Eve were enchanting figures because they were 'not drawn from their spouses' (10). In a more serious vein, the well-known 'Ave Maria!' section in Canto III (102–8) features a translation of lines 1–6 of *Purgatorio*, Canto VIII (stanza 108). Here, Byron resorts to Dante to intensify the evocativeness of a highly lyrical passage that sharply contrasts with, but, by the same token, throws into relief, the predominantly irreverent treatment of Italy's bard in the poem's opening cantos.[19]

Byron also weaves into Canto III several facetious remarks at the expense of Petrarch, which, contesting the poet's conventional status as one of Italy's literary glories, are more in line with eighteenth-century critical censure than Romantic-period re-evaluations of the country's foremost lyrical poet.[20] Anticipating the Dante/Beatrice quip cited above, Byron's narrator asks: 'Think you, if Laura had been Petrarch's wife, / He would have written sonnets all his life?' (8). This couplet re-echoes the ironic remarks about Juan's excess of Platonic sentimentalism in Canto I and the narrator's definition of Plato as 'no better than a go-between' (116). At the same time, though, the 'Ave Maria!' section references Petrarch much more respectfully, since the lyrical pathos of 'blessed be the hour! / The time, the clime, the spot, where I so oft / Have felt that moment in its fullest power' (III, 102) rewrites the opening of Petrarch's celebrated sonnet 'Benedetto sia 'l giorno e 'l mese et l'anno' ('Blessed be the day and the month and the year').[21] Usually overlooked by Byron's textual editors, this is an intriguingly coded use of Petrarch as a source of inspiration and not merely a target for flippant asides. As such, it highlights Byron's vacillating approach to Italy's greatest authors, expressing a veneration that also emphasises their deeply ironic treatment in *Don Juan*'s opening instalments. And in Canto V Byron reverts to the latter and predominant mode in a digression against the mischief-making 'amatory poets' of all times and nations, where, in ruthlessly alliterative fashion, he depicts Petrarch as 'the Platonic pimp of all posterity' (1).

The presence of Dante, Petrarch and, though less obvious, Boccaccio[22] in the early cantos of *Don Juan* bears witness to the centrality of the Italian literary canon to Byron's creation of his unprecedentedly multitonal work, as well as to the way in which the poem addresses its (British) recipients through the medium of another literary tradition. If this constitutes a reprise of the reference to the *tre corone* in *Childe Harold* IV (stanzas 56–9) and its lament over the absence of their tombs from the national shrine of Santa Croce in Florence, it is an undeniably subversive reprise, which works through a distinctly Janus-faced poetic method.[23]

As they celebrate the *Trecento*'s national significance and international impact, the references to the *tre corone* import into the poem the patriotic debates that Byron would have heard in Italian salons and literary circles, and that Madame de Staël magisterially represented in the discussion of Italy's dramatic tradition by a set of *cosmopolites* in Book VII, Chapter 2 of *Corinne*. The references in *Don Juan* also draw upon the knowledge of the *Trecentisti* Byron had gathered from J. C. L. Simonde de Sismondi's *De la littérature du Midi de l'Europe* (1813) and Ginguené's *Histoire littéraire de l'Italie* (which dedicates a significant amount of space to the *tre corone* in its overall plan). Thus, in the poem's initial cantos, Byron designs an intertextual network of prestigious forbears, a gallery of those 'poetic precursors' that contribute to the poem's version of what Jane Stabler terms the 'artistry of mixture and contrast' typical of exilic poetics, here manifested by way of explicit citations and other more indirect forms of ventriloquism.[24] In addition, as with the much more frequently explored references to the Renaissance epic tradition, those to the *Trecentisti* indicate how Byron programmatically links *Don Juan* to Italian literary culture through dissonant gestures emphasising its polemical relation to English and British literature.

The references to the *Trecentisti* also accord with Byron's turn to Italy more generally, as they show him both embracing and stepping back from the country and its culture in what, with Ralph Pite, we might term a paradoxically 'dispassionate involvement'.[25] Engaging with the greatest names of Italian literature through his subversively Pulcian style, Byron abandons the idea of this tradition as a venerable national heirloom and perversely employs an Italian-inspired style to laugh at one of the mainstays of Italy's identity. In doing so, he turns his adoptive country and culture into targets for the carnivalesque mode that, though already perceptible in earlier works such as *Manfred*, he inaugurated fully in his Italian satires.[26]

This approach to Italy is consonant with that 'dialectic of making and unmaking' that Frederick Garber identifies as foundational to Byron's output, since the nation's literature (especially the Renaissance epic) serves to construct Byron's medley mode even as that literature (in particular the *tre corone*) falls prey to the mode's own subversive discourse.[27] It is a handling of Italy's heritage that confirms how Byron's Italian turn is pervaded by an ironic attitude modelled on the logic of parabasis, his approach to the *tre corone* reworking the kind of ideological and gestural turn contained in the couplet from the dedication to *Don Juan* examined above. The lateral shift in the couplet translates more generally here into an ambivalent approach to Italy, its history, literature and current patriotic efforts through a constant recourse to the possibility of 'viewing' but not 'feeling' – an operation in which, nevertheless, the former action is ironically impossible without the latter. As I argue in the next section, Byron's parabasic relation to and construction of Italy is not just a question of 'turning' in discursive, literary and textual terms. It is also a performative gesture that draws upon, and plays with, the sense of theatricality that characterised his experience of Italy and influenced the representations of the country, its culture and its people in his satirical writings.

Serventismo and the performative turn

If Byron experienced Italy not only as an archive of texts but also as an unfolding spectacle of backdrops, gestures, costumes, sounds and voices, theatre effectively provided him with a lens through which he could view and understand the country. According to Stendhal, in Milan Byron began to explore Venetian society and customs by reading Pietro Buratti's satiric poems (originally intended as stage comedies) and Carlo Goldoni's plays.[28] As I explain in the following paragraphs, this perception and construction of Italy as inherently theatrical underpins his parabasic approach to the country and its culture.

An emblematic expression of Byron's alertness to Italy's inherent theatricality, *Beppo* emerged out of an Italian admixture of spectacle, voice and gesture. In part, its origins were vocal and performative, as Hobhouse recorded in his diary on 29 August 1817. On this occasion, Pietro Segati, the husband of Byron's fiery lover Marianna and a gifted raconteur, narrated an anecdote about a Turk in Venice, the long-lost husband of a wife to whom, on his return to Venice, he gave the choice of '"either quitting your *amoroso* [lover] and com[ing] with me, or stay[ing] with your *amoroso* or accept[ing] a pension and liv[ing] alone"'. Marianna interrupted the narration to announce: '"I'm sure I would not leave my *amoroso* for any husband" – looking at Byron.' Hobhouse concluded: 'This is too gross even for me.'[29]

The setting was Byron's palace at Mira, on the river Brenta. By this time, the poet had been Marianna's lover for a year, Segati being aware of this arrangement and accepting it. A man of the world himself, he had stopped at Byron's residence on the way to visiting his own mistress. His anecdote has long been recognised as one of the sources for *Beppo*, together with other, more respectably literary ones (Pulci, Berni, possibly Forteguerri and Casti).[30] What has been less frequently stressed, however, is that its significance as a source lies partly in the fact that it constitutes what Jerome McGann has termed a 'scene', one that must be read in the light of Byron's fascination with Italy's theatricality.[31]

Theatrical and performative features pervade Hobhouse's vignette, which centres on an act of narration before an audience, develops a tale that reads like the blueprint for a comedy, and presents the occasional snippet of dialogue. Moreover, if Marianna's interruption and commentary break the illusion of the husband's stage-like performance, they also replace the scene he is creating with another centred on herself and her meaningful look at her *amoroso*, which Hobhouse finds unbearable to watch. Further theatrical nuances and complications are then introduced by Segati and his role in this Venetian spectacle. For, as Hobhouse suggests, Segati seems to be knowingly inducing his listeners to take part in that spectacle, manipulating them in order to elicit a reaction and, evidently, succeeding – first with Marianna and Byron, then with Hobhouse himself.

Though the theatrical streak in *Beppo* is familiar to Byron scholars, it is worth stressing further that the poem repeatedly turns Venice itself into a theatre and a spectacle.[32] This is particularly visible in the description of Venetian women in stanzas 11 and 15. Here Byron's narrator first draws the reader's attention to the way women in Venice look as if they have just 'stepp'd from out a picture by Giorgione' when 'leaning over' a 'balcony' (11). He then reprises this comparison in stanza 15, where it leads into a more elaborate description:

> I said that like a picture by Giorgione
>   Venetian women were, and so they *are*,
> Particularly seen from a balcony,
>   (For beauty's sometimes best set off afar)
> And there, just like a heroine of Goldoni,
>   They peep from out the blind, or o'er the bar.

A combination of Italian lexis and English phonetics, the Giorgione/Goldoni rhyme throws into relief the spectacular features of Venice in *Beppo*: its women are objects of vision. Yet they are not only framed as in a picture but also exposed to sight by the raised and projected – stage-like – balcony. And Laura in the poem is a similarly spectacularised figure, especially in stanzas 65–7, which describe her movements around the masquerade as if she were on a stage:

> Now Laura moves along the joyous crowd,
>   Smiles in her eyes, and simpers on her lips;
> To some she whispers, others speaks aloud;
>   To some she curtsies, and to some she dips.
>   (65)

Laura's theatrical qualities are then emphasised further in her final exchange with the returned and 'Turkified' Beppo:

>   Beppo! what's your pagan name?
>   Bless me! your beard is of amazing growth!
> And how came you to be away so long?
> Are you not sensible 'twas very wrong?
>   (91)

Peter Cochran points to this passage as perfectly illustrating Byron's ability to abandon 'the declamatory mode he finds natural in his theatre-writing' in order to let a character speak freely in such a way that the 'density and volatility' of her 'way of varying her angle of attack, coupled with the naturalness of her manner, shows an ability to dramatise character which is equal to anything in Shakespeare or

Molière'.[33] Put differently, the theatrical comedy of *Beppo* emanates from the inextricable link between the poet's knowledge of the traditions of European drama and his exposure to Italian social *mores* and institutions.

Byron's parabasic reading of the theatricality of Venice begins to appear clearly in a couplet in stanza 56, where he explains the *Ridotto* to his readers, especially those familiar with London's entertainments. To do so, he asks them to imagine that the masquerade in the poem resembles what they would enjoy if they went 'To-night to Mrs. Boehm's masquerade, / Spectator, or partaker in the Show'. In the style of a guidebook, Byron glosses and 'translates' this Italian entertainment through an English equivalent, and in doing so invites his readers to enter the narrative, don a mask and become a 'spectator, or partaker' of the show – both roles are made available by the theatricality of masquerade. To be part of the masquerade of Venetian life is to blur the distinction between on stage and off stage, actor and observer.

This couplet also harks back to the well-known episode in which Byron, Douglas Kinnaird and other members of Watier's Club took part as extras in the stage version – in Thomas John Dibdin's *Harlequin and Fancy* performed at Drury Lane in 1815 – of a real masquerade held at Watier's on 1 July 1814. Returning to this experience in his 1821 'Detached Thoughts', Byron describes it through a complex series of mirrorings and inversions, for example where he notes that his aim was 'to see the effect of a theatre from the Stage' and that it 'was odd enough that D. K. & I should have been both at the *real* Masquerade [in 1814] – & afterwards in the Mimic one of the same – on the stage of D. L. Theatre'.[34] Intermixing a genuine and a staged masquerade, his words complicate any clear-cut distinction between reality and illusion, 'performance' and 'life'.[35] Even more significantly, as in the case of stanza 56 of *Beppo*, Byron's remarks hint at his ambivalent position inside the action and beside it, offering an instance of parabasis in accord both with the nostalgic streak characterising his early 1820s writings and the doubleness of his Italian turn.

Beppo most strikingly relates this parabasic perspective to the inherently theatrical nature of Italy through the figure of the *cicisbeo* or *cavalier servente* – a 'lady's escort who, in accordance with a custom which developed in the eighteenth century, was expected, with the husband's consent, to be in attendance on the lady, accompany her and assist her in all her activities'.[36] As with other foreign travellers and residents in Italy, Byron was fascinated by this figure, who embodied 'socially acceptable polygamy allowing sexual variety' and was contradictorily endowed with a clear yet also an indeterminate social position that the poet found both congenial and uncomfortable.[37] In Byron's time, *cicisbeism*, or *serventismo*, had a more limited social impact than in previous decades. As Roberto Bizzocchi observes, by the early nineteenth century, though traces of it remained, this practice was more significant as a cultural memory and was therefore especially useful to foreign commentators who tended to associate it with the progressive decadence of Italian *mores* since the Renaissance, as, for instance, Sismondi does in his influential *Histoire des républiques italiennes du moyen âge* (1807–15).[38] Of particular importance for Byron's re-elaboration of, and identification with, the *servente*, however, were its treatments in eighteenth-century Italian poetry and, more significantly, drama.

In poetry, this figure played a central role in the 1763 masterpiece of Italian neoclassical verse satire, Giuseppe Parini's *Il giorno*, which Ugo Foscolo examined in the 'Essay on Italian Literature' he wrote for John Cam Hobhouse's *Historical Illustrations of the Fourth Canto of Childe Harold*, published in 1818. The poem narrates the typical day of a vain and feckless young aristocrat, whose first waking thought is for his *servita* (lady) and whose routine is mostly taken up by his *servente* activities.[39] However, and crucially for my argument, *serventismo* was also a recurrent theme of eighteenth-century Italian theatre, and of social comedy in particular. Even the century's greatest Italian writer of tragedies, Byron's much admired Vittorio Alfieri, introduced the *cavalier servente* into one of his rare and not very successful comedies, *Il divorzio*. Intriguingly, between 1773 and 1775, the young Alfieri had been the *cicisbeo* of an older, married woman, Gabriella Falletti, an experience he described in an early diary and later described in detail, and abjured, in his celebrated autobiography.[40] Alfieri was a recalcitrant and therefore unsatisfactory *servente*, who preferred writing plays – he was then working on his first tragedy, *Cleopatra* – to keeping up with his round of frivolous duties.[41]

Nevertheless, it was Goldoni who gave this exemplary type its most extensive and nuanced treatment, one that often diverged from condemnatory representations such as Parini's, in numerous plays, written and performed between 1749 and 1760, including *Il cavaliere e la dama*, *La famiglia dell'antiquario*, *Le femmine puntigliose*, *La dama prudente*, *La moglie saggia*, *Il festino*, *La sposa sagace* and *I Rusteghi*. Offering a multifaceted picture of the *ménages* to which the *serventi* belonged, these works did not merely employ this figure as a stock comic type but also delved into its social and psychological features. In play after play Goldoni interestingly cast the *cicisbeo* as an indeterminate character whose meaning, in semiotic terms, is a function of other *dramatis personae*. In *La famiglia dell'antiquario*, the *cicisbei* Cavalier del Bosco and Dottor Anselmi are caught up in the war of jealousy between a mother- and daughter-in-law, who manipulate them for their own plots so that the two men end up defeated and humiliated. In *La dama prudente*, a woman is given two *serventi* by her jealous husband as a way of testing her constancy, though, in doing so, he merely increases his own jealousy. In *I Rusteghi*, the *cicisbeo* Count Riccardo cannot speak Venetian but only standard Italian and is thus mostly silent and talked about in the third person, as if he were not present.[42]

Though we may not be sure that Byron read or saw any of these plays, Goldoni's approach to *serventismo* has several thematic and functional similarities to Byron's treatment of it in his 'Venetian story', where his *cavalier servente*, the count, is both central and marginal, a figure of disturbance who upsets societal and matrimonial balances but plays a key role in their eventual restoration through the mechanisms of comedy. As Cheeke suggests, Byron was fascinated by the 'power-balance and role-playing' associated with *serventismo*, which he found disconcerting, while also taking a Sismondian view of the *cicisbeo* as a synecdoche for Italy because of the conventional metaphorical association of this practice with political servitude.[43] Both concerns implicitly pervade Byron's descriptions of his own stint as Teresa Guiccioli's *servente*, written in the style of a comic character: 'I am drilling very hard to learn how to double a Shawl, and should succeed to admiration – if I did not always double it the wrong side out – and then I sometimes confuse and bring away two – so as to put all the Serventi out – besides keeping their *Servite* in the cold.'[44] More importantly, however, in this amusing vignette the *servente* is a figure of ambivalence, who, in carnivalesque fashion, inverts conventional distinctions even while obeying convention, is both ludicrous and serious, a master who becomes a servant and a man who submits to a woman.

Beppo registers this doubleness by noting that the *servente*, a 'supernumerary slave', 'stays / Close to the lady as a part of dress' but must also associate with domestics and accessories – 'Coach, servants, gondola, he goes to call, / And carries fan, and tippet, gloves, and shawl' (40). In *Don Juan* he is a 'strange thing' whose 'actual and official duties' can only be 'supposed' (IX, 51). In both cases, the *servente*'s indefinability is inseparable from his unstable position in both Italian society and Byron's poetic text, with its reworking of identities made available by Italy's social and cultural context. In other words, *serventismo* provides Byron with a fluid gestural and performative model for his Italian turn, a model he explored and performed in person in his role as Teresa's *servente*, in which he was expected to be turned towards her adoringly, but also to turn away from her discreetly, in a complex ritual of proximity and distance. A nexus of textuality, theatricality and performance, the *servente* is as crucial to a full understanding of the Italian nature of comedy and irony in *Beppo* and *Don Juan* as the figure of the *improvvisatore*.[45] However, where the latter offers a model of impromptu versifying, the *cavalier servente* offers a different kind of paradigm as a figure of instability constantly bent on acts of parabasis. He stands centre stage and hovers in the wings, both scandalously visible and opportunely out of focus, implicitly commenting on a world he is both in and not in. A 'supernumerary' and 'a strange thing', he cannot be ascribed to any precise category and thus embodies an oblique point of view that in many ways encapsulates and, especially in *Beppo*, is used to perform, Byron's own turn to Italy, combining emplacement (his Italianised identity) and 'unplaceability' (his resistance, as an English lord and poet, to being altogether 'located' in Italy). An intersection of the ironic, the satirical, the hybrid and the theatrical, the *servente* reveals and illuminates essential facets of both Byron's complex poetic self-positioning in relation to Italy and the inherently Italian, parabasic nature of the poetry that resulted from that self-positioning.

'An Italian Carnival'

Written in Genoa in 1823, Byron's prose fragment, 'An Italian Carnival', gathers together the different strands of his turn towards

Italy, once again ascribing them to the context of masquerading. In a frequently quoted letter of 21 February 1820, Byron had declined Murray's invitation to write 'a volume of manners &c.' about Italy, while also stressing his own in-depth knowledge of its customs and highlighting the significance of 'the Carnival balls – and masquerades – when every body runs mad for six weeks'.[46] Yet, in a way, in the 1823 fragment, the poet seems to comply with Murray's request by drawing a picture of Italy, seen through the lens of carnival, that reprises the Janus-faced attitudes and approaches to Italy examined in this chapter.

The third-person narrative of 'An Italian Carnival' centres on a recognisable Byronic persona, 'a young Englishman' who 'had resided for some time in the Italian City of T.' (190).[47] Both an outsider and an insider, this character recalls that of the narrator of *Don Juan* as described in the unpublished prose preface to *Don Juan* – 'either an Englishman settled in Spain – or a Spaniard who had travelled in England'.[48] Sharing the same bicultural and displaced status, their complex relation to the place in which they find themselves makes them both figures of transition and 'in transit'. Their points of view are the slanted and ambivalent ones of both the 'Spectator, or Partaker in the Show' and the *cavalier servente* in *Beppo*. They are also politically akin. Just as the Spaniard/Englishman is possibly 'one of the Liberals' persecuted by Ferdinand VII upon his restoration to the Spanish throne,[49] so the Englishman in the 'city of T.' perceives 'the common disgust of Italy as well as Europe at the Holy Alliance – and the Austrian despotism – for – though nominally exempt from them they felt their influence in some measure – and indeed what Nation does not?' (191). And if the Spanish narrator is a victim of conservative repression, the character in 'An Italian Carnival' bears witness, with ironic equidistance, to the social stagnation and political disenchantment that Byron saw as endemic in post-Napoleonic Europe: 'Perhaps, the Italians would but ill exchange their Carnival for a Parliament, – but they long for the latter – and if England would barter with them – there might be no great loss to either – it would be a Masquerade for Masquerade – with the people represented for themselves' (193).

The insistence on feeling the influence of the political climate imposed by the Holy Alliance harks back to the use of 'feel' in the couplet from the dedication to *Don Juan* in which Byron announces his problematic Italian turn. Similarly, the shuttling between England

and Italy in 'An Italian Carnival' reworks the parabasic gestures typical of Byron's approach to the country. Moreover, the fragment mirrors *Beppo* and *Don Juan* by depicting a topsy-turvy reality where 'all ranks are jostled' in a 'mixture of mystery and hilarity' (192). Picturing a disjointed and cacophonous world, this piece neatly encapsulates the components of Byron's engagements with Italy already seen in *Beppo* and *Don Juan* – ambivalent references to Italian culture and literature (carnival and Goldoni), involvement and distance, performativity and theatricality, the comparative glance, ironic subversiveness and the formal admixtures characterising the poetry's medley mode. As it reworks the distinctive ambivalence of Byron's discourse on Italy, 'An Italian Carnival' amalgamates the contradictory foci that result from the parabasic turn to and away from Italy that is inseparable from Byron's development of the voice, style and persona of his Italian *ottava rima* poems.

Notes

1. M. Kelsall, *Byron's Politics* (Brighton: Harvester Press, 1987), p. 150.
2. J. Stabler, *The Artistry of Exile: Romantic and Victorian Writers in Italy* (Oxford: Oxford University Press, 2013), p. 18.
3. S. Cheeke, *Byron and Place: History, Translation, Nostalgia* (Basingstoke, New York: Palgrave Macmillan, 2003), p. 130.
4. See 'Appendix 1: Italian and Austrian Police Reports on Byron', in P. Cochran, *Byron and Italy* (Newcastle: Cambridge Scholars, 2012), pp. 321–45.
5. For further reflections on the 'turn' in contemporary literary studies, see H. Dubrow, 'Foreword', in V. Theile and L. Tredenick (eds.), *New Formalisms and Literary Theory* (Basingstoke: Palgrave Macmillan, 2013), pp. vii–viii.
6. L. Hutcheon, *Irony's Edge: The Theory and Politics of Irony* (London and New York: Routledge, 1994), p. 65. See also M. Redfield, 'Philosophy', in J. Faflak and J. M. Wright (eds.), *A Handbook of Romanticism Studies* (Oxford: Blackwell, 2012), pp. 327–38 (p. 336); P. de Man, 'The rhetoric of temporality', in C. S. Singleton (ed.), *Interpretation: Theory and Practice* (Baltimore, Md.: Johns Hopkins University Press, 1969), pp. 173–209.
7. P. Hamilton, *Metaromanticism: Aesthetics, Literature, Theory* (Chicago, Ill.: University of Chicago Press, 2003), pp. 20, 21. See also P. Hamilton, *Realpoetik: European Romanticism and Literary Politics* (Oxford: Oxford University Press, 2013), p. 89.

8   N. Halmi, 'The very model of a modern epic poem', *European Romantic Review*, 21 (2010), 589–600 (p. 598).
9   P. W. Graham, *Don Juan and Regency England* (Charlottesville, Va.: University Press of Virginia, 1990), p. 10.
10 P. M. Curtis, 'Byron and digression', in J. Stabler (ed.), *Palgrave Advances in Byron Studies* (Basingstoke: Palgrave Macmillan, 2007), pp. 60–80 (p. 68).
11 See Cheeke, *Byron and Place*, p. 14, and D. Saglia, 'Locating Byron: languages, voices, and displaced utterances', *Philological Quarterly*, 86:4 (2007), 393–414.
12 See, for example, J. J. McGann's references to 'the Italian medley style in *ottava rima*' and 'the Italian medley poets' in '"Mixed company": Byron's *Beppo* and the Italian medley', in D. D. Fischer and D. Reiman (eds.), *Shelley and His Circle, 1773–1822*, 8 vols (Cambridge, Mass.: Harvard University Press, 1961–2002), vol. VII, pp. 234–97 (pp. 243, 247).
13 Letter of 4 December 1816, in *BLJ*, vol. V, p. 138. See T. Webb, '"Soft bastard Latin": Byron and the attractions of Italian', *Journal of Anglo-Italian Studies*, 10 (2009), 73–100.
14 See P. Vassallo, *Byron: The Italian Literary Influence* (London: Macmillan, 1984), pp. 44, 140.
15 P. Martin, *Byron: A Poet before His Public* (Cambridge: Cambridge University Press, 1982), p. 180.
16 *CPW*, vol. II, p. 123; *CPW*, vol. IV, p. 215.
17 *CPW*, vol. V, pp. 698–9.
18 N. Halmi, 'Byron between Ariosto and Tasso', in F. Burwick and P. Douglass (eds.), *Dante and Italy in British Romanticism* (Basingstoke: Palgrave Macmillan, 2011), pp. 39–53.
19 On Byron's uses of Dante, see R. Pite, *The Circle of Our Vision: Dante's Presence in English Romantic Poetry* (Oxford: Clarendon Press, 1994), pp. 199–229.
20 On Petrarch's critical fortunes in eighteenth- and nineteenth-century England, see E. Zuccato, *Petrarch in Romantic England* (Basingstoke: Palgrave Macmillan, 2008), and pp. 126–30 on Byron's mostly hostile reception of Petrarch.
21 See F. Petrarch, *Petrarch's Lyric Poems: The Rime Sparse and Other Lyrics*, trans. R. M. Durling (Cambridge, Mass. and London: Harvard University Press, 1976), pp. 138–9.
22 Stanzas 105 and 106 of Canto III implicitly conjure up the figure of Nastagio degli Onesti from Boccaccio's *Decameron*.
23 On *Childe Harold*, IV, 56–9, see J. Luzzi, *Romantic Europe and the Ghost of Italy* (New Haven, Conn.: Yale University Press, 2008), pp. 56–7.

24 Stabler, *The Artistry of Exile*, pp. 24, 226.
25 Pite, *The Circle of Our Vision*, p. 229.
26 On *Manfred* as an anticipation of *Don Juan*, see Martin, *A Poet before His Public*, p. 117.
27 F. Garber, *Self, Text, and Romantic Irony: The Example of Byron* (Princeton, NJ: Princeton University Press, 1988), p. 211.
28 See 'Stendhal's account of Byron at Milan', in Lord Byron, *The Works of Lord Byron: Letters and Journals*, 6 vols, ed. R. E. Prothero (London: John Murray, 1902–4), vol. III, pp. 438–45 (p. 445).
29 Quoted in Cochran, *Byron and Italy*, p. 154.
30 See Vassallo, *The Italian Literary Influence*, pp. 43–6.
31 McGann, '"Mixed Company"', p. 246.
32 On *Beppo* and theatre, see Martin, *A Poet Before His Public*, pp. 177, 183; and McGann, '"Mixed Company"', pp. 252–3. On the theatricality of *Don Juan*, see D. Saglia, '"Don Alfonso" and the theatrical matrix of *Don Juan*, 1817–1821', in P. Cochran (ed.), *Aspects of Don Juan* (Newcastle: Cambridge Scholars, 2013), pp. 240–54.
33 P. Cochran 'Byron and Drury Lane', in P. Cochran (ed.), *Byron at the Theatre* (Newcastle: Cambridge Scholars, 2008), pp. 1–35 (pp. 2–3).
34 'Detached thoughts', No. 70, in *BLJ*, vol. IX, p. 37.
35 For a reconstruction and an interpretation of this episode, see J. N. Cox, *Romanticism in the Shadow of War: Literary Culture in the Napoleonic War Years* (Cambridge: Cambridge University Press, 2014), pp. 63–5.
36 Roberto Bizzocchi, *A Lady's Man: The Cicisbei, Private Morals and National Identity in Italy*, trans. Noor Giovanni Mazhar (Basingstoke: Palgrave Macmillan, 2014), p. 1, translating *Il Grande Dizionario della Lingua Italiana*.
37 F. L. Beaty, *Byron the Satirist* (DeKalb, Ill.: Northern Illinois University Press, 1985), p. 84.
38 See Bizzocchi, *A Lady's Man*, p. 10.
39 Byron also quoted lines 41–2 of Parini's ode 'La recita de' versi' (1783) in the dedication to *Childe Harold* IV, while Foscolo famously introduced Parini as a character in *Ultime lettere di Jacopo Ortis* (letter of 4 December 1798), which Byron read in 1813 and reread (in Teresa Guiccioli's copy) in 1820.
40 V. Alfieri, *Vita di Vittorio Alfieri da Asti scritta da esso* (Florence: Guglielmo Piatti, 1806).
41 See Bizzocchi, *A Lady's Man*, pp. 5–6.
42 See Bizzocchi, *A Lady's Man*, pp. 134–5; and M. Merlato, *Mariti e cavalier serventi nelle commedie del Goldoni* (Florence: Carnesecchi, 1906).

43 Cheeke, *Byron and Place*, p. 119.
44 Letter to Richard Belgrave Hoppner of 31 January 1820, in *BLJ*, vol. VII, p. 28.
45 On Byron and the *improvvisatore*, see G. Angeletti, '"I feel the improvisatore": Byron, improvisation, and Romantic poetics', in L. Bandiera and D. Saglia (eds.), *British Romanticism and Italian Literature: Translating, Reviewing, Rewriting* (Amsterdam: Rodopi, 2005), pp. 165–80.
46 *BLJ*, vol. VII, pp. 42–3.
47 'An Italian Carnival' is quoted from *CMP*. Page numbers follow quotations in the main text.
48 *CPW*, vol. V, p. 83. On this unpublished prose preface, see D. Saglia, *Byron and Spain: Itinerary in the Writing of Place* (Lampeter and Lewiston, NY: Edwin Mellen, 1996), pp. 178–80; and Graham, *Don Juan and Regency England*, pp. 46–7.
49 *CPW*, vol. V, p. 83.

Select bibliography

Agamben, G., *State of Exception*, trans. K. Attell (Chicago, Ill.: University of Chicago Press, 2005).
Alfieri, V., *Vita di Vittorio Alfieri da Asti scritta da esso* (Florence: Guglielmo Piatti, 1806).
——, *Vita*, ed. G. Cattaneo (Milan: Garzanti, 2000).
Angeletti, G., 'From "the heightening of the beau ideal" to "palpable things": Byron, Clough and the poetry of experience', *La Questione Romantica*, 5:1–2 (2016), 97–114.
——, 'From place to topos: Byron's Italy as exotic discourse; women and places of the mind', in L. M. Crisafulli (ed.), *Immaginando l'Italia: itinerari letterari del Romanticismo inglese* (Bologna: CLUEB, 2002), pp. 183–202.
——, '"I feel the improvisatore": Byron, improvisation, and Romantic poetics', in L. Bandiera and D. Saglia (eds.), *British Romanticism and Italian Literature: Translating, Reviewing, Rewriting* (Amsterdam: Rodopi, 2005), pp. 165–80.
——, *Lord Byron and Discourses of Otherness: Scotland, Italy, and Femininity* (Kilkerran: Humming Earth, 2012).
Bahktin, M., *Rabelais and His World*, trans. H. Iswolsky (Bloomington, Ind.: Indiana University Press, 1984).
Bandiera, L. and D. Saglia (eds.), *British Romanticism and Italian Literature: Translating, Reviewing, Rewriting* (Amsterdam: Rodopi, 2005).
Barton, A., '"A light to lesson ages": Byron's political plays', in J. D. Jump (ed.), *Byron: A Symposium* (London: Macmillan, 1975), pp. 138–62.
Beaton, R., *Byron's War: Romantic Rebellion, Greek Revolution* (Cambridge: Cambridge University Press, 2014).
Beatty, B., 'Continuities and discontinuities of language and voice', in A. Rutherford (ed.), *Byron: Augustan and Romantic* (London: Macmillan, 1990), pp. 117–35.

——, 'Determining unknown modes of being: a map of Byron's ghosts and spirits', in G. Hopps (ed.), *Byron's Ghosts: The Spectral, the Spiritual and the Supernatural* (Liverpool: Liverpool University Press, 2013), pp. 30–47.
Beaty, F. L., *Byron the Satirist* (DeKalb, Ill.: Northern Illinois University Press, 1985).
Behler, E., *Frühromantik* (Berlin: Walter de Gruyter, 1992).
Benzoni, G., *I Dogi* (Milan: Electa, 1982).
Bernard, H. R., *Research Methods in Anthropology: Qualitative and Quantitative Approaches* (Plymouth: AltaMira, 2011).
Beste, H. D., *Italy as It Is; or Narratives of an English Family's Residence for Three Years in That Country* (London: Henry Colburn, 1828).
Bizzocchi, R., *A Lady's Man: The Cicisbei, Private Morals and National Identity in Italy*, trans. N. G. Mazhar (Basingstoke: Palgrave Macmillan, 2014).
Black, J., *The Life of Torquato Tasso; with an Historical and Critical Account of His Writings*, 2 vols (London: John Murray, 1810).
Blessington, Lady, *A Journal of the Conversations of Lord Byron with the Countess of Blessington* (London: Richard Bentley & Son, 1893).
Bode, C., *Selbst-Begründungen: Diskursive Konstruktion von Identität in der Britischen Romantik* (Trier: WVT, 2008).
Bone, D., 'Tourists and lovers: *Beppo* and *Amours de Voyage*', *The Byron Journal*, 28 (2000), 13–28.
Bosco, U., 'Byronismo italiano', *La cultura*, 3:6 (1924), 252–64.
Bowers, W., 'Italian travel, English tourism, and Byron's poetry of exile', *Litteraria Pragensia*, 23:46 (2013), 86–102.
Brand, C. P., *Italy and the English Romantics: The Italianate Fashion in Early Nineteenth-Century England* (Cambridge: Cambridge University Press, 1957).
Brown, D., *God and Enchantment of Place: Reclaiming Human Experience* (Oxford: Oxford University Press, 2004).
Bruni, L., *Le vite di Dante, e del Petrarca* (Florence: All'insegna della stella, 1672).
Burwick, F. and P. Douglass (eds.), *Dante and Italy in British Romanticism* (Basingstoke: Palgrave Macmillan, 2011).
Butler, M., *Romantics, Rebels and Reactionaries: English Literature and Its Background, 1760–1830* (Oxford: Oxford University Press, 1981).
Buzard, J., *The Beaten Track: European Tourism, Literature, and the Ways to Culture, 1800–1918* (Oxford: Clarendon Press, 1993).
——, 'The uses of Romanticism: Byron and the Victorian Continental tour', *Victorian Studies*, 35:1 (1991), 29–49.
Byron, Lord, *Byron's Complete Miscellaneous Prose*, ed. A. Nicholson (Oxford: Clarendon Press, 1991).
——, *Byron's Letters and Journals*, ed. L. A. Marchand (London: John Murray, 1973–94).

——, *Byron's Letters and Journals: A New Selection*, ed. R. Lansdown (Oxford: Oxford University Press, 2015).
——, *The Complete Poetical Works*, ed. J. J. McGann (Oxford: Clarendon Press, 1980–93).
——, *Don Juan*, ed. T. G. Steffan, E. Steffan and W. W. Pratt (London: Penguin, 1996).
——, *His Very Self and Voice: Collected Conversations of Lord Byron*, ed. Ernest J. Lovell, Jr (New York: Macmillan, 1954).
——, *Lord Byron: The Major Works*, ed. J. J. McGann (Oxford: Oxford University Press, 1986).
——, *The Works of Lord Byron: Letters and Journals*, 6 vols, ed. R. E. Prothero (London: John Murray, 1902–4).
Callaghan, M., 'The struggle with language in Byron's *Cain*', *The Byron Journal*, 38:2 (2010), 125–34.
Cardinal, R., 'Romantic travel', in R. Porter (ed.), *Rewriting the Self: Histories from the Renaissance to the Present* (London and New York: Routledge, 1997), pp. 135–55.
Carlson, M., 'The Italian Romantic drama in its European context', in G. Gillespie (ed.), *Romantic Drama* (Amsterdam: John Benjamins, 1994), pp. 233–48.
——, 'Nationalism and the Romantic drama in Europe', in G. Gillespie (ed.), *Romantic Drama* (Amsterdam: John Benjamins, 1994), pp. 139–52.
Cash, A., *John Wilkes: The Scandalous Father of Civil Liberty* (New Haven, Conn.: Yale University Press, 2006).
Chandler, J., 'The Pope controversy: Romantic poetics and the English canon', *Critical Inquiry*, 10:3 (1984), 481–509.
Chard, C., *Pleasure and Guilt on the Grand Tour: Travel Writing and Imaginative Geography, 1600–1830* (Manchester: Manchester University Press, 1999).
Cheeke, S., *Byron and Place: History, Translation, Nostalgia* (Basingstoke: Palgrave Macmillan, 2003).
——, *Writing for Art: The Aesthetics of Ekphrasis* (Manchester: Manchester University Press, 2008).
Christensen, J., '*Marino Faliero* and the fault of Byron's satire', *Studies in Romanticism*, 24:3 (1985), 313–33.
Clifford, J., 'Introduction: partial truths', in J. Clifford and G. Marcus (eds.), *Writing Culture: The Poetics and Politics of Ethnography* (Berkeley, Calif.: University of California Press, 1986), pp. 1–26.
——, 'On ethnographic allegory', in J. Clifford and G. Marcus (eds.), *Writing Culture: The Poetics and Politics of Ethnography* (Berkeley, Calif.: University of California Press, 1986), pp. 98–121.
Clifford, J. and G. Marcus (eds.), *Writing Culture. The Poetics and Politics of Ethnography* (Berkeley, Calif.: University of California Press, 1986).

Clubbe, J., 'Byron and Scott', *Texas Studies in Literature and Language*, 15:1 (1973), 67–91.
Cochran, P., 'Byron, Alfieri, and the writing of plays', in P. Cochran (ed.), *Byron at the Theatre* (Newcastle: Cambridge Scholars, 2008), pp. 36–59.
——, 'Byron and Drury Lane', in P. Cochran (ed.), *Byron at the Theatre* (Newcastle: Cambridge Scholars, 2008), pp. 1–35.
——, *Byron and Italy* (Newcastle: Cambridge Scholars, 2012).
—— (ed.), *Byron and Latin Culture* (Newcastle: Cambridge Scholars, 2013).
Coleridge, S. T., *Complete Poetical Works*, ed. E. H. Coleridge (Oxford: Clarendon, 1912).
Colombo, A., *'I lunghi affanni ed il perduto regno': cultura letteraria, filologia e politica nella Milano della Restaurazione* (Besançon: Presses Universitaires de Franche-Comté, 2007).
Cooke, P. M. G., 'Byron, Pope and the Grand Tour', in A. Rutherford (ed.), *Byron: Augustan and Romantic* (London: Macmillan, 1990), pp. 165–80.
Coope, R. and P. Smith, *Newstead Abbey, a Nottinghamshire Country House: Its Owners and Architectural History, 1540–1931* (Nottingham: Thoroton Society of Nottinghamshire, 2014).
Cox, J. N., *Romanticism in the Shadow of War: Literary Culture in the Napoleonic War Years* (Cambridge: Cambridge University Press, 2014).
Crisafulli, L. (ed.), *Immaginando l'Italia: itinerari letterari del Romanticism inglese* (Bologna: CLUEB, 2002).
Cronin, R., *In Search of the Pure Commonwealth: The Politics of Romantic Poetry* (Basingstoke: Palgrave Macmillan, 2000).
Crook, K., 'Truth and sense on Italy: Byron's Guidebook', in L. M. Crisafulli (ed.), *Immaginando l'Italia: itinerari letterari del Romanticismo inglese* (Bologna: CLUEB, 2002), pp. 155–65.
Curley, M. J., *Alessandro Manzoni: Two Plays* (New York: Peter Lang, 2002).
Curreli, M., 'Golfo dei poeti, lapidi bugiarde e altri miti', *Soglie*, 6:2 (2004), 19–44.
Curtis, P., 'Byron and digression', in J. Stabler (ed.), *Palgrave Advances in Byron Studies* (Basingstoke: Palgrave Macmillan, 2007), pp. 60–80.
Dante, A., *Opere minori*, ed. D. de Robertis (Milan: Ricciardi, 1979–84).
Davis, J. A., *Italy in the Nineteenth Century* (Oxford: Oxford University Press, 2000).
De Man, P., 'The rhetoric of temporality', in C. S. Singleton (ed.), *Interpretation: Theory and Practice* (Baltimore, Md.: Johns Hopkins University Press, 1969), pp. 173–209.
Dear, M., J. Ketchum, S. Luria and D. Richardson (eds.), *Geohumanities: Art, History, Text at the Edge of Place* (Abingdon and New York: Routledge, 2011).
Deigan, F. D., 'Byron's, Shakespeare's, and Manzoni's Venice', in *Alessandro Manzoni's The Count of Carmagnola and Adelchis*, trans. F. D. Deigan (Baltimore, Md.: Johns Hopkins University Press, 2004), pp. 47–51.

Deliyannis, D. M., *Ravenna in Late Antiquity* (Cambridge: Cambridge University Press, 2010).

Duffy, C., *The Landscapes of the Sublime, 1700–1830* (Basingstoke: Palgrave Macmillan, 2013).

Duggan, C., *The Force of Destiny: A History of Italy since 1796* (London: Allen Lane, 2007).

Duncan, J. S. and N. S. Duncan, 'Roland Barthes and the secret histories of landscape', in T. J. Barnes and J. S. Duncan (eds.), *Writing Worlds: Discourse, Text and Metaphor in the Representation of Landscape* (London and New York: Routledge, 2001), pp. 18–37.

Eliot, C. W. J., 'Gennadeion Notes, III: Athens in the time of Lord Byron', *Hesperia*, 37:2 (1968), 134–58.

——, 'Lord Byron, Father Paul, and the artist William Page', *Hesperia*, 44:4 (1975), 409–25.

Eliot, T. S., 'Byron', in *On Poetry and Poets* (New York: Noonday Press, 1943), pp. 223–39.

Finlay, R., *Politics in Renaissance Venice* (New Brunswick: Rutgers University Press, 1980).

Fischer, D. D., and D. Reiman (eds.), *Shelley and His Circle, 1773–1822*, 8 vols (Cambridge, Mass.: Harvard University Press, 1961–2002).

Foscolo, U., *Opere*, ed. F. Gavazzeni (Milan: Ricciardi, 1981).

Franklin, C., 'Cosmopolitanism and Catholic culture: Byron, Italian poetry, and *The Liberal*', in L. Bandiera and D. Saglia (eds.), *British Romanticism and Italian Literature: Translating, Reviewing, Rewriting* (Amsterdam: Rodopi, 2005), pp. 255–68.

——, '"My hope was to bring forth heroes": *The Two Foscari* and the fostering of masculine *virtù* by [a] stoical heroine', in R. Gleckner and B. Beatty (eds.), *The Plays of Lord Byron: Critical Essays* (Liverpool: Liverpool University Press, 1997), pp. 163–80.

Garber, F., *Self, Text, and Romantic Irony: The Example of Byron* (Princeton, NJ: Princeton University Press, 1988).

Gifford, W., 'Lord Byron's *Dramas*', *The Quarterly Review*, 27 (July 1822), 476–524.

Gillespie, G., 'The past is prologue: the Romantic heritage in dramatic literature', in G. Gillespie (ed.), *Romantic Drama* (Amsterdam: John Benjamins, 1994), pp. 429–64.

Gilman, S., *The Jew's Body* (London and New York: Routledge, 1991).

Goethe, J. W., *The Flight to Italy: Diary and Selected Letters*, ed. and trans. T. J. Reed (Oxford: Oxford University Press, 1999).

——, *Italian Journey*, trans. W. H. Auden and E. Mayer (Harmondsworth: Penguin, 1970).

Goodden, A., *Madame de Staël: The Dangerous Exile* (Oxford: Oxford University Press, 2008).
Graham, P. W., 'Byron and the business of publishing', in J. D. Bone (ed.), *The Cambridge Companion to Byron* (Cambridge: Cambridge University Press, 2004), pp. 27–43.
——, *Don Juan and Regency England* (Charlottesville, Va.: University Press of Virginia, 1990).
Green, M. J. A. and P. Pal-Lapinski (eds.), *Byron and the Politics of Freedom and Terror* (Basingstoke: Palgrave Macmillan, 2011).
Gross, J., *Byron: The Erotic Liberal* (Lanham, Md.: Rowman & Littlefield, 2001).
Guiccioli, T., *Lord Byron's Life in Italy*, trans. M. Rees, ed. Peter Cochran (Newark, Del.: University of Delaware Press, 2005).
——, *My Recollections of Lord Byron and Those of Eye-Witnesses of His Life* (New York: Harper & Bros., 1869).
Hachmeister, G. L., *Italy in the German Literary Imagination: Goethe's 'Italian Journey' and Its Reception by Eichendorff, Platen, and Heine* (Rochester, NY: Camden House, 2002).
Hale, J., *England and the Italian Renaissance* (London: Fontana, 1996).
Haley, B., *Living Forms: Romantics and the Monumental Figure* (Albany, NY: State University of New York, 2003).
Halmi, N., 'Byron between Ariosto and Tasso', in F. Burwick and P. Douglass (eds.), *Dante and Italy in British Romanticism* (Basingstoke: Palgrave Macmillan, 2011), pp. 39–53.
——, 'The very model of a modern epic poem', *European Romantic Review*, 21:5 (2010), 589–600.
Hamilton, P., *Metaromanticism: Aesthetics, Literature, Theory* (Chicago, Ill.: University of Chicago Press, 2003).
——, *Realpoetik: European Romanticism and Literary Politics* (Oxford: Oxford University Press, 2013).
Havely, N., 'Francesca frustrated: new evidence about Hobhouse's and Byron's translation of Pellico's *Francesca da Rimini*', *Romanticism*, 1:1 (1995), 106–20.
Headland, T. N., K. Pike and M. Harris (eds.), *Emics and Etics: The Insider/Outsider Debate* (Newbury Park, Calif.: Sage, 1990).
Heffernan, J. A. W., *Museum of Words: The Poetics of Ekphrasis from Homer to Ashbery* (Chicago, Ill.: University of Chicago Press, 1996).
Hennig, J., 'Goethe and an English critic of Manzoni', *Monatshefte*, 39:1 (1947), 9–16.
Hewlett Koelb, J., *The Poetics of Description* (Basingstoke: Palgrave Macmillan, 2006).
Hobhouse, John Cam, *Historical Illustrations of the Fourth Canto of Childe Harold* (London: John Murray, 1818).

Holt, E., *The Making of Italy, 1815–1870* (New York: Athenaeum, 1971).
Hopps, G., 'Gaiety and grace: Byron and the tone of Catholicism', *The Byron Journal*, 40:1 (2013), 1–14.
Horová, M., 'The carnival of history: Byron's *Marino Faliero, Doge of Venice*', *Litteraria Pragensia*, 23:46 (2013), 53–69.
Huizinga, J., *Homo Ludens* (Bungay: Paladin, 1970).
Hunt, L., *Lord Byron and Some of His Contemporaries* (New York: AMS, 1966).
Hutcheon, L., *Irony's Edge: The Theory and Politics of Irony* (London and New York: Routledge, 1994).
Iamartino, G., 'Translations, biography, opera, film and literary criticism: Byron and Italy after 1870', in R. Cardwell (ed.), *The Reception of Byron in Europe*, 2 vols (London and New York: Thoemmes Continuum, 2004), vol. I, pp. 98–128.
Jakob, M., *Paesaggio e letteratura* (Florence: Olschki, 2005).
James, H., *Italian Hours*, ed. John Auchard (Harmondsworth: Penguin, 1995).
Jameson, A., *The Loves of the Poets* (London: Henry Colburn, 1829).
Jamison, K. R., *Touched with Fire: Manic-Depressive Illness and the Artistic Temperament* (New York: Free Press, 1996).
Jenkins, E., *Lady Caroline Lamb* (London: Victor Gollancz, 1932).
Jones, K., *A Passionate Sisterhood* (London: Virago, 1998).
Kayser, W., *The Grotesque in Art and Literature*, trans. U. Weisstein (New York and Toronto: McGraw-Hill, 1966).
Kelsall M., *Byron's Politics* (Brighton: Harvester Press, 1987).
Kelsall, M., 'Venice preserved', in R. Gleckner and B. Beatty (eds.), *The Plays of Lord Byron: Critical Essays* (Liverpool: Liverpool University Press, 1997), pp. 33–67.
Kenyon Jones, C., '"Of painting I know nothing": Byron's response to some European Art', *Newstead Abbey Review* (2016), 32–46.
King, M., 'Early Italian Romanticism and *The Giaour*', *Byron Journal*, 4 (1976), 7–21.
Kriegel, A. D., 'Liberty and Whiggery in early nineteenth-century England', *The Journal of Modern History*, 52:2 (1980), 253–78.
Langley Moore, D., *The Late Lord Byron* (London: John Murray, 1961).
——, *Lord Byron: Accounts Rendered* (London: John Murray, 1974).
Lansdown, R., *Byron's Historical Dramas* (Oxford: Oxford University Press, 1992).
Lauvergne, H., *Souvenirs de la Grèce, pendant la campagne de 1825* (Paris: Le Normand Fils, 1826).
Laven, D., 'Sex, self-fashioning, and spelling: (auto)biographical distortion, prostitution, and Byron's Venetian residence', *Literaria Pragensia*, 23:46 (2013), 38–52.
Lefebvre, H., *The Production of Space*, trans. D. Nicholson-Smith (Oxford: Blackwell, 1991).

Lockhart, J. G., *Memoirs of the Life of Sir Walter Scott*, 4 vols (Paris: Baudry's European Library, 1837).

Long Hoeveler, D., 'Germaine de Stael's *Corinne, or Italy* (1807) and the performance of Romanticism(s)', in F. Burwick and P. Douglass (eds.), *Dante and Italy in British Romanticism* (Basingstoke: Palgrave Macmillan, 2011), pp. 133–42.

Luther, M., *Luther's Works*, 55 vols, ed. J. Pelikan and H. T. Lehmann (St Louis, Miss.: Concordia, 1955–85).

Luzzi, J., *Romantic Europe and the Ghost of Italy* (New Haven, Conn.: Yale University Press, 2008).

Machiavelli, N., *Il principe: politica e questione morale*, ed. Marcella Vasconi (Bussolengo: Demetra, 1995).

Mack Smith, D., *The Making of Italy, 1796–1866* (Houndmills: Palgrave, 1988).

Makdisi, S., *Romantic Imperialism: Universal Empire and the Culture of Modernity* (Cambridge: Cambridge University Press, 1998).

Manzoni, A., *Tragedie*, ed. G. Bollati (Torino: Einaudi, 1965).

Marchand, L., *Byron: A Portrait* (London: John Murray, 1971).

Martin, P., *Byron: A Poet before His Public* (Cambridge: Cambridge University Press, 1982).

Mazzini, G., 'Byron e Goethe', in *Scritti editi ed inediti*, 106 vols (Imola: Galeate, 1915), vol. XXI, pp. 187–241.

McCue, M., *British Romanticism and the Reception of Italian Old Master Art, 1793–1840* (Farnham: Ashgate, 2014).

McFarland, T., *Romanticism and the Forms of Ruin: Wordsworth, Coleridge and Modalities of Fragmentation* (Princeton, NJ: Princeton University Press, 1988).

McGann, J. J., *The Beauty of Inflections: Literary Investigations in Historical Method and Theory* (Oxford: Oxford University Press, 1985).

McGann, J. J., 'Byron and "The Truth in Masquerade"', in R. Brinkley and K. Hanley (eds.), *Romantic Revisions* (Cambridge: Cambridge University Press, 1992), pp. 191–209.

——, *Fiery Dust: Byron's Poetic Development* (Chicago, Ill.: University of Chicago Press, 1968).

——, 'Hero with a thousand faces: the rhetoric of Byronism', *Studies in Romanticism*, 31:3 (1992), 295–313.

——, '"Mixed company": Byron's *Beppo* and the Italian medley', in D. D. Fischer and D. Reiman (eds.), *Shelley and His Circle, 1773–1822*, 8 vols (Cambridge, Mass.: Harvard University Press, 1961–2002), vol. VII, pp. 234–97.

——, *The Romantic Ideology: A Critical Investigation* (Chicago, Ill.: University of Chicago Press, 1985).

——, 'Rome and its Romantic significance', in *The Beauty of Inflections: Literary Investigations in Historical Method and Theory* (Oxford: Clarendon Press, 1985), pp. 313–33.

Medwin, T., *Medwin's Conversations of Lord Byron*, ed. E. J. Lovell, Jr (Princeton, NJ: Princeton University Press, 1966).

Melchiori, G., 'Byron and Italy: catalyst of the "Risorgimento"', in P. G. Trueblood (ed.), *Byron's Political and Cultural Influence in Nineteenth-Century Europe: A Symposium* (Basingstoke: Macmillan, 1981), pp. 108–21.

——, 'The influence of Byron's death on Italy', *The Byron Journal*, 5 (1977), 67–78.

——, 'L'Italia di Byron', *Lettere Italiane*, 10:2 (1958), 133–53.

——, 'L'Italia per Byron', *I poeti romantici inglesi e l'Italia: catalogo della mostra di Palazzo Braschi, 16.12.1980–31.1.1981* (Rome: Assessorato alla Cultura del Commune di Roma, Sovrintendenza Archivistica per il Lazio, British Council, Keats-Shelley Memorial Association, 1980), pp. 21–5.

Merlato, M., *Mariti e cavalier serventi nelle commedie del Goldoni* (Florence: Carnesecchi, 1906).

Mitchell, W. J. T., *Iconology: Image, Text, Ideology* (Chicago, Ill.: University of Chicago Press, 1986).

Montagu, Lady, *Letters Written during her Travels in Europe, Asia, and Africa to Persons of Distinction, Men of Letters &c. in different parts of Europe* (London: Thomas Martin, 1790).

Moore, T., *Life, Letters, and Journals of Lord Byron* (London: John Murray, 1838).

Mortenson, R., *Byron's Waterloo: The Reception of Cain, A Mystery* (Seattle, Wash.: Iron Press, 2015).

Muoni, G., *La fama del Byron e il Byronismo in Italia* (Milan: Società Editrice, 1906).

Muoni, G., *La leggenda del Byron in Italia* (Milan: Società Editrice Libraria, 1907).

Murray, J., *The Letters of John Murray to Lord Byron*, ed. A. Nicholson (Liverpool: Liverpool University Press, 2007).

Newey, V., 'Authoring the self: *Childe Harold* III and IV', in B. Beatty and V. Newey (eds.), *Byron and the Limits of Fiction* (Liverpool: Liverpool University Press, 1988), pp. 148–90.

Nietzsche, F., *The Birth of Tragedy and the Genealogy of Morals*, trans. F. Goffering (New York: Doubleday, 1956).

Nora, P., 'Between memory and history: *les lieux de mémoire*', *Representations*, 26 (1989), 7–24.

O'Neill, M., 'Realms without a name: Shelley and Italy's intenser day', in F. Burwick and P. Douglass (eds.), *Dante and Italy in British Romanticism* (Basingstoke: Palgrave Macmillan, 2011), pp. 77–91.
Ogden, D. S., 'Byron, Italy, and the poetics of liberal imperialism', *Keats-Shelley Journal*, 49 (2000), 114–37.
Origo, I., *Allegra* (London: L. and W. Woolf, 1935).
——, *The Last Attachment* (London: John Murray, 1949).
Page, N., *A Byron Chronology* (Basingstoke: Macmillan, 1988).
Pal-Lapinski, P., 'The politics of judicial torture in *The Foscari*: Byron and Verdi', *Litteraria Pragensia*, 23:46 (2013), 70–85.
Parker, M., *Literary Magazines and British Romanticism* (Cambridge: Cambridge University Press, 2000).
Petrarch, F., *Petrarch's Lyric Poems: The Rime Sparse and Other Lyrics*, trans. R. M. Durling (Cambridge, Mass.: Harvard University Press, 1976).
Pite, R., *The Circle of Our Vision: Dante's Presence in English Romantic Poetry* (Oxford: Clarendon Press, 1994).
Pittock, M., 'Byron's networks and Scottish Romanticism', *The Byron Journal*, 37:1 (2009), 5–14.
Pocock, J. G. A., *The Machiavellian Moment: Florentine Political Thought and the Atlantic Republican Tradition* (Princeton, NJ: Princeton University Press, 2003).
Pomarè, C., *Byron and the Discourses of History* (Farnham: Ashgate, 2013).
——, '"I am now an Italoquist": Byron's correspondence in Italian', *The Byron Journal*, 44:2 (2016), 97–108.
Poole, G., 'Byron's impact: English radicals, Italian brigands and the Byronic hero', *Litteraria Pragensia*, 23:46 (2013), 103–18.
Pope, A., *The Poems of Alexander Pope*, ed. John Butt (London: Methuen, 1963).
Porta, A., *Byronismo italiano* (Milan: Cogliati, 1923).
Procházka, M., 'Imaginative geographies disrupted: representing the other in English Romantic dramas', *European Journal of English Studies*, 6:2 (2002), 207–20.
Quennell, P., *Byron in Italy* (London: Collins, 1941).
Rae, W., *Records of a Route through France and Italy; with Sketches of Catholicism* (London: Longman, Rees, Orme, Brown, Green & Longman, 1835).
Rawes, A., 'Byron's confessional pilgrimage', in G. Hopps and J. Stabler (eds.), *Romanticism and Religion from William Cowper to Wallace Stevens* (Aldershot: Ashgate, 2006), pp. 121–36.
——, *Byron's Poetic Experimentation:* Childe Harold, *the Tales and the Quest for Comedy* (Aldershot: Ashgate, 2000).
——, 'Byron's Romantic Calvinism', *The Byron Journal*, 40:2 (2012), 129–42.
——, '"From the Italian": Byron's translation of Pulci's *Morgante Maggiore*', *Litteraria Pragensia*, 23:46 (2013), 6–22.

——, '*Marino Faliero*: escaping the aristocratic', in B. Beatty, T. Howe and C. Robinson (eds.), *Liberty and Poetic Licence: New Essays on Byron* (Liverpool: Liverpool University Press, 2008), pp. 88–102.

——, '"The very *poetry* of politics. Only think – a free Italy!!!": Byron and the liberation of Italy', in F. Dellarosa and A. Sportelli (eds.), *British Risorgimento: Temperie politica e rappresentazioni simboliche* (Naples: Liguori, 2013), pp. 187–203.

Rawes, A. and M. Horová, 'Introduction', *Tears, and Tortures, and the Touch of Joy: Byron in Italy, Litteraria Pragensia*, 23:46 (December 2013), 1–5.

Riall, L., *The Italian Risorgimento: State, Society and National Unification* (London and New York: Routledge, 1994).

Rizzuti, A., 'Viganò's "Giovanna D'arco" and Manzoni's "March 1821"', *Music and Letters*, 86:2 (2005), 186–201.

Roberts, C., *Edward Gibbon and the Shape of History* (Oxford: Oxford University Press, 2014).

Robinson, C. E., *Shelley and Byron: The Snake and the Eagle Wreathed in Fight* (Baltimore, Md.: Johns Hopkins University Press, 1976).

Roe, N., *Fiery Heart: The First Life of Leigh Hunt* (London: Pimlico, 2005).

Romano, D., *The Likeness of Venice: A Life of Doge Francesco Foscari, 1373–1457* (New Haven, Conn.: Yale University Press, 2007).

——, *Patricians and Popolani* (Baltimore, Md.: Johns Hopkins University Press, 1987).

Ruskin, J., *Praeterita: The Autobiography of John Ruskin (1885–89)* (Oxford: Oxford University Press, 1983).

——, *The Works of John Ruskin*, ed. E. T. Cook and A. Wedderburn, 39 vols (New York: Longmans, Green & Co., 1903–12).

Rutherford, A. (ed.), *Byron: The Critical Heritage* (London: Routledge & Kegan Paul, 1970).

Sachs, J., *Romantic Antiquity: Rome in the British Imagination, 1789–1832* (Oxford: Oxford University Press, 2010).

Saglia, D. (ed.), *Byron e il segno plurale* (Bologna: Bononia University Press, 2011).

——, 'Byron's Italy and Italy's Byron: codes of resistance and early Risorgimento literature', *Rivista di letterature moderne e comparate*, 56 (2003), 275–95.

——, *Byron and Spain: Itinerary in the Writing of Place* (Lampeter and Lewiston, NY: Edwin Mellen, 1996).

——, '"Don Alfonso" and the theatrical matrix of *Don Juan*, 1817–1821', in P. Cochran (ed.), *Aspects of Don Juan* (Newcastle: Cambridge Scholars, 2013), pp. 240–54.

——, 'From Gothic Italy to Italy as Gothic archive: Italian narratives and the late Romantic metrical tale', *Gothic Studies*, 8:1 (2006), 73–90.

——, 'Locating Byron: languages, voices, and displaced utterances', *Philological Quarterly*, 86:4 (2007), 393–414.

——, *Lord Byron e le maschere della scrittura* (Rome: Carocci, 2009).

——, 'Touching Byron: masculinity and the celebrity body in the Romantic period', in R. Emig and A. Rowland (eds.), *Performing Masculinity* (Basingstoke: Palgrave Macmillan, 2010), pp. 13–27.

Schaff, B., 'Italianised Byron – Byronised Italy', in M. Pfister and R. Hertel (eds.), *Performing National Identity: Anglo-Italian Cultural Transactions* (Amsterdam: Rodopi, 2008), pp. 103–21.

Schmidt, A. A., *Byron and the Rhetoric of Italian Nationalism* (Basingstoke: Palgrave Macmillan, 2010).

Schoina, M., 'Byron and *The Liberal*: a reassessment', *Litteraria Pragensia*, 23:46 (2013), 23–37.

——, 'Revisiting Byron's Italian style', *Byron Journal*, 36:1 (2008), 19–27.

——, *Romantic 'Anglo-Italians': Configurations of Identity in Byron, the Shelleys, and the Pisan Circle* (Farnham: Ashgate, 2009).

Schor, E., 'The "warm south"', in J. Chandler (ed.), *The Cambridge History of English Romantic Literature* (Cambridge: Cambridge University Press, 2009), pp. 224–45.

Scirocco, A., *L'Italia del Risorgimento 1800–1871* (Bologna: Il Mulino, 1993).

Scott, W., *A Legend of the Wars of Montrose*, ed. J. H. Alexander (Edinburgh: Edinburgh University Press, 1995).

——, *Rob Roy*, ed. D. Hewitt (Edinburgh: Edinburgh University Press, 2008).

——, *Waverley*, in *The Complete Works of Walter Scott, with a Biography and His Last Additions and Illustrations*, 7 vols (New York: Conner & Cooke, 1833), vol. II.

Sha, R. C., *Visual and Verbal Sketch in British Romanticism* (Philadelphia, Pa.: University of Pennsylvania Press, 1998).

Shelley, M., 'The English in Italy', *The Westminster Review*, 6 (October 1826), 325–41.

——, *The Letters of Mary Wollstonecraft Shelley*, ed. B. Bennett (Baltimore, Md.: Johns Hopkins University Press, 1991).

Shelley, P. B., *The Letters of Percy Bysshe Shelley*, 2 vols, ed. F. L. Jones (Oxford: Clarendon Press, 1964).

——, *Shelley's Poetry and Prose*, ed. D. H. Reiman and S. B. Powers (New York: Norton, 1977).

Smollett, T., *Travels through France and Italy*, 2 vols (Dublin: Robert Johnston, 1766).

Stabler, J., *The Artistry of Exile: Romantic and Victorian Writers in Italy* (Oxford: Oxford University Press, 2013).

——, *Byron, Poetics and History* (Cambridge: Cambridge University Press, 2009).

——, 'Byron, post-modernism, and intertextuality', in J. D. Bone (ed.), *The Cambridge Companion to Byron* (Cambridge: Cambridge University Press, 2004), pp. 265–6.
Staël, Madame de, *Corinne, or Italy*, trans. S. Raphael (Oxford: Oxford University Press, 1998).
Stagni, M. T. C., *Con Byron tra Bologna e Ravenna* (Bologna: Pendragon, 2001).
Steffan, T. G., *Lord Byron's Cain* (Austin, Tex.: University of Texas Press, 1968).
Stendhal, 'Stendhal's account of Byron at Milan', in Lord Byron, *The Works of Lord Byron: Letters and Journals*, 6 vols, ed. R. E. Prothero (London: John Murray, 1902–4), vol. III, pp. 438–45.
Tally, Jr, R. (ed.), *Geocritical Explorations: Space, Place, and Mapping in Literary and Cultural Studies* (Basingstoke: Palgrave Macmillan, 2011).
Tanner, T., *Venice Desired* (Oxford: Blackwell, 1992).
Tasso, T., *Opere di Torquato Tasso*, 2 vols, ed. B. T. Sozzi, 3rd edn (Turin: UTET, 1974).
Taylor, B., 'Byron's use of Dante in *The Prophecy of Dante*', *Keats-Shelley Journal*, 28 (1979), 102–19.
Theile, V. and L. Tredenick (eds.), *New Formalisms and Literary Theory* (Basingstoke: Palgrave Macmillan, 2013).
Tuite, C., *Lord Byron and Scandalous Celebrity* (Cambridge: Cambridge University Press, 2015).
Valery, M., *Historical, Literary, and Artistical Travels in Italy* (Paris: Baudry's European Library, 1842).
Vassallo, P., *Byron: The Italian Literary Influence* (London: Macmillan, 1984).
Visconti, E., 'Dialogo sulle unità drammatiche di luogo e di tempo', *Il Conciliatore: foglio scientifico-letterario* (Bologna: Arnaldo Forni Editore, 1981), pp. 165–72.
Walsh, R. A., *Ugo Foscolo's Tragic Vision in Italy and England* (Toronto: University of Toronto Press, 2014).
Watkins, D. P., 'The ideological dimensions of Byron's *The Deformed Transformed*', in R. Gleckner and B. Beatty (eds.), *The Plays of Lord Byron: Critical Essays* (Liverpool: Liverpool University Press, 1997), pp. 347–63.
Watkins, D. P., *A Materialist Critique of English Romantic Drama* (Gainesville, Fla.: University Press of Florida, 1993).
Webb, T., 'After Horsemonger Lane: Leigh Hunt's London letters to Byron (1815–16)', *Romanticism*, 16:3 (2010), 233–66.
——, 'Leigh Hunt's letters to Byron from Horsemonger Lane gaol: a commentary', *The Byron Journal*, 37:1 (2009), 21–32.
——, '"Soft bastard Latin": Byron and the attractions of Italian', *Journal of Anglo-Italian Studies*, 10 (2009), 73–100.

Westphal, B., 'Foreword', in R. Tally Jr (ed.), *Geocritical Explorations: Space, Place, and Mapping in Literary and Cultural Studies* (Basingstoke: Palgrave Macmillan, 2011), pp. ix–xv.
——, *Geocriticism: Real and Fictional Spaces*, trans. R. T. Tally (Basingstoke: Palgrave Macmillan, 2011).
Wiley, M., *Romantic Geography: Wordsworth and Anglo-European Spaces* (Basingstoke: Palgrave Macmillan, 1998).
——, *Romantic Migrations: Local, National, and Transnational Dispositions* (Basingstoke: Palgrave Macmillan, 2008).
Wilkes, J., *Lord Byron and Madame de Staël: Born for Opposition* (Aldershot: Ashgate, 1999).
Wilton, A. and I. Bignamini (eds.), *The Grand Tour: The Lure of Italy in the Eighteenth Century* (London: Tate, 1996).
Winckelmann, J. J., *Briefe*, 4 vols, ed. W. Rehm (Berlin: de Gruyter, 1952–7).
——, *Geschichte der Kunst des Alterthums* (Dresden: Walther, 1764).
Wolfson, S. J., '"*This* is *my* lightning"; or sparks in the air', *SEL*, 55 (autumn 2015), 751–86.
Woof, R. S., *Byron: A Dangerous Romantic?* (Grasmere: Wordsworth Museum, 2003).
Woolf, S., *History of Italy, 1700–1860* (London: Methuen, 1979).
Wortley Montagu, Lady M., *Letters Written During Her Travels in Europe, Asia, and Africa to Persons of Distinction, Men of Letters &c. in Different Parts of Europe* (London: Thomas Martin, 1790).
Yarrington, A., S. Villani and J. Kelly (eds.), *Travels and Translations: Anglo-Italian Cultural Transactions* (Amsterdam and New York: Rodopi, 2013).
Zuccato, E., 'The fortunes of Byron in Italy (1810–70)', in R. Cardwell (ed.), *Byron's Reception in Europe* (London: Thoemmes Continuum, 2004), pp. 80–97.
——, *Petrarch in Romantic England* (Basingstoke: Palgrave Macmillan, 2008).

Index

Abrams, M. H. 125
Addison, Joseph 77, 85
Alborghetti, Count Giuseppe 121
Albrizzi, Countess Isabella
    Teotochi 159
Alfieri, Count Vittorio 3, 8, 24, 36,
    67, 86, 130, 211, 219
Alighieri, Dante 3, 8, 14, 24, 25, 32,
    33, 35, 36, 38, 39, 86, 106, 114,
    116, 117, 152–3, 212–14
    Divina Commedia 8, 24, 32, 116,
    153, 213
Angeletti, Gioia 13, 14, 15, 64
Ariosto, Ludovico 8, 18, 24, 27, 30,
    32, 35, 40, 67, 212
    Orlando furioso 8, 24
Aristotle 130
Auden, W. H. 173
Austria 5, 6, 9, 37, 38, 130–3, 137, 138,
    143, 209, 222

Bachelard, Gaston 77
Bakhtin, Mikhail M. 193, 196–7
Barberi, Dominic 125
Baretti, Giuseppe 24
Barton, Anne 197
Batoni, Pompeo 23
Beatty, Bernard 15, 16, 99, 112,
    146, 157
Bembo, Cardinal Pietro 8, 51
Benini, Rosa 9
Benzon (Benzoni), Countess
    Marina 159
Berchet, Giovanni 131, 133
Berni, Francesco 216
Beste, Henry Digby 50
Bizzocchi, Roberto 219
Black, John 8
    Life of Tasso 8, 28, 29
Blake, William 24
Bloom, Harold 125
Boccaccio, Giovanni 18, 86, 212, 214
Bologna 10, 51–2
Bone, Drummond 47
Borgia, Lucrezia 51
Bosco, Umberto 3
Bossi, Giuseppe 35
Bowles, William Lisle 146
Brand, C. P. 10, 24
Breme, Ludovico di 131, 133
Brown, David 106
Browning, Elizabeth Barrett 122
Browning, Robert 122
Bruni, Leonardo 35
Buratti, Pietro 8, 215
Burton, Richard 61
Bussone, Francesco (da
    Carmagnola) 132, 134,
    136, 137–8
Butler, Marilyn 7
Buzard, James 49, 50
Byron, Allegra 116, 123, 124, 128

INDEX

Byron, George Gordon, Lord
  Age of Bronze, The 6
  Beppo 3, 6, 9, 18, 19, 26–7, 49, 51,
    53–4, 115, 116, 126, 155, 157, 158,
    159, 210, 216–21, 222–3
  Blues, The 6
  Bride of Abydos, The 156
  Cain 6, 15–16, 64, 94, 95, 97, 98,
    101–8, 123, 124
  Childe Harold's Pilgrimage 4–5, 6,
    14, 15, 17–18, 19, 25, 26, 27–8, 31,
    32–3, 35, 44, 62, 63, 64, 78–90,
    112, 113, 119, 120, 127, 131, 151,
    157, 166–9, 176–82, 190, 201,
    205, 211, 214, 225
  Corsair, The 2, 26
  Deformed Transformed, The 6, 18,
    65, 74, 188–90, 198–205
  'Detached Thoughts' 218
  Don Juan 6, 13, 18, 19, 39, 40, 51,
    67, 71, 72, 96–7, 106, 108–10,
    118, 119, 123, 125, 126–7, 146,
    150, 155, 157, 158, 159, 160, 163,
    208–15, 212, 213–14, 221, 222–3
  Giaour, The 26, 113, 114, 120, 131
  Heaven and Earth 6, 123
  Island, The 6, 123
  'An Italian Carnival' 18, 221–3
  Lament of Tasso, The 6, 14, 25, 27,
    28–32, 35, 67
  Lara 120
  Manfred 30, 97, 120, 215
  Marino Faliero 6, 18, 19, 38, 68,
    70–1, 99, 103, 143, 188–93,
    195–6, 205
  Mazeppa 6, 17, 123, 149–65
  Morgante Maggiore 6, 14, 25, 34,
    38–40, 115, 117–18, 212
  'Ode from the French' 66, 68
  'Ode on Venice' 157, 159
  Parisina 17, 113, 115, 149–65
  Prophecy of Dante, The 6, 14, 19, 25,
    27, 31, 32–9, 67, 115, 153, 211
  Sardanapalus 6, 99
  Siege of Corinth, The 26, 99, 114,
    123, 126, 151
  Two Foscari, The 6, 16, 67, 99, 103,
    130–46, 188–90, 192–8, 205
  Vision of Judgement, The 6, 123, 125
  Werner 6

Campbell, Thomas 24
Canova, Antonio 87
Carlson, Marvin 131, 133, 136
Casti, Giovanni Battista 3, 8, 10, 24,
  158, 216
Castlereagh, Robert Stewart,
  Viscount 209
Cellini, Benvenuto 200–1, 204
Cervantes, Miguel de 118
Chandler, James 146
Chateaubriand,
  François-René de 182
Chaucer, Geoffrey 116
Cheeke, Stephen 12, 38, 78, 88,
  149–50, 186, 200
Christensen, Jerome 124, 206
Clifford, James 44
Clubbe, John 64, 71, 72
Cochran, Peter 114, 146, 217
Coleridge, E. H. 39, 66
Coleridge, Samuel Taylor 24, 34,
  113, 122, 151, 160–1
Confalonieri, Federico 131, 133
Cooke, Michael 89
Cornwall, Barry 7
Coryat, Thomas 23
Crashaw, Richard 115
Croker, John Wilson 154
Cronin, Richard 197
Curley, Michael J. 132, 138
Curtis, Paul M. 210

Dacre, Charlotte 7
Dallas, Robert Charles 122, 124
Dante *see* Alighieri, Dante
Daru, Pierre 8
Dear, Michael 77

Deigan, Federica Brunori 131
De Man, Paul 209–10
De Quincey, Thomas 24
Dibdin, Thomas John 218
Dickens, Charles 3
D'Isreali, Isaac 47
D'Orsay, Count Alfred 56
Dryden, John 115, 154
Dunbar, William 70

Eliot, T. S. 25, 70
Eustace, John Chetwode 8

Faliero, Doge Marino 51
Ferrara 24–5, 37, 115, 133, 149, 157, 176
Fielding, Henry 40, 117–18
Filicaja, Vincenzo da 8, 14, 24, 27–8, 30, 31, 32
Florence 36, 38, 86–7, 95, 117, 176, 214
Forteguerri, Niccoló 8, 24, 216
Foscari, Francesco 137–8
Foscolo, Ugo 8, 24, 39, 86, 211, 219, 225
Franklin, Caroline 34
Frere, John Hookham 24, 34, 39, 211

Gallino, Vincenzo 133
Gamba, Count Ruggero 133, 143, 163
Gamba, Pietro 122, 133, 163
Garber, Frederick 215
Genoa 13, 15, 72, 74
Gibbon, Edward 7, 83, 113, 151
Gifford, William 34, 67, 143–4, 154
Gillespie, Gerald 131
Ginguené, Pierre-Louis 8, 211, 214
Giorgione (Giorgio da Castelfranco) 217
Giraud, Niccolò 120
Godwin, William 151
Goethe, Johann Wolfgang von 8, 31, 56, 122, 136, 166–9, 172–6, 178–9, 181–2, 183, 184–6

Italienische Reise 8, 17, 54, 166–8, 172–6, 178–9, 181–2, 184
Goldoni, Carlo 8, 24, 215, 217, 219–20, 223
Gooden, Angelica 183
Graham, Peter 17, 210
Gross, Jonathan 14, 15, 142–3, 176
Grotta Byron, Portovenere 2
Guicciardini, Francesco 137
Guiccioli, Countess Teresa 35, 70, 99, 118, 121, 122, 123, 128, 131, 133, 159, 163, 170, 220, 225

Haley, Bruce 95
Halmi, Nicholas 13–14, 212
Hamilton, Paul 209–10
Hartman, Geoffrey 125
Haslett, Moyra 119
Heffernan, James 95
Hegel, G. W. F. 90
Hemans, Felicia 24, 31, 182
Hennig, John 136
Hobhouse, John Cam 31, 36, 69, 142, 143, 216, 219
Hoeveler, Diane Long 184
Hopps, Gavin 99, 119, 177
Horová, Mirka 10, 18
Hunt, John 39
Hunt, Leigh 7, 12, 24, 34, 46, 143, 153–4, 165, 182
Story of Rimini, The 7, 46, 153

Jakob, Michael 77
James, Henry 100–1, 102–3
Jameson, Anna 28, 182
Jamison, Kay Redfield 61

Kayser, Wolfgang 193
Keats, John 7, 24, 143
Kelsall, Malcolm 190, 197, 208
Kenyon Jones, Christine 165
Kinnaird, Douglas 218
Knox, John 112
Kriegel, Abraham D. 142

Landor, Walter Savage 24
Langley Moore, Doris 10
Lansdown, Richard 195
Lega Zambelli, Antonio 121
Leghorn 9
Leigh, Augusta 50, 74, 152, 156
Leigh, Medora 156
Luzzi, Joseph 32, 136, 176

McCue, Maureen 7, 95
McGann, Jerome J. 28, 95, 119, 124, 152, 155, 158, 169, 183, 216, 224
Macerata 132
Machiavelli, Nicolò 24, 86, 134, 137
Mai, Angelo 211
Makdisi, Saree 82
Malatesta, Parisina 151
Manning, Peter 13
Manzoni, Alessandro 16, 130–46
  Il conte di Carmagnola 16, 130–46
  'Marzo 1821' 132
Markus, Julia 146
Martin, Philip 211
Maturin, Charles Robert 151
Mawman, J. 100
Mayer, Elizabeth 173
Mazzini, Giuseppe 25
Medwin, Thomas 12, 33, 184
Melchiori, Giorgio 11
Merivale, J. H. 39
Metastasio, Pietro 8, 24
Meyer, Patricia 83
Mezzofanti, Giuseppe 211
Michelangelo 36, 86
Milan 9, 11, 51, 130–1, 133, 134, 138, 140, 215
Milbanke, Annabella 45, 46, 151, 152, 163, 165
Milman, Henry Hart 7
Milton, John 23, 32, 98, 209, 213
Mitchell, W. J. T. 78
Moir, George 136
Molière (Jean-Baptiste Poquelin) 218

Montagu, Lady Mary Wortley 98
Monti, Vincenzo 8, 24, 48
Moore, Thomas 13, 24, 45, 50, 51, 55, 56, 67, 70, 97, 123, 163
Morgan, Sydney, Lady 8, 48
Murray, John 9, 19, 32, 39, 46, 47, 49, 51, 53, 54, 55, 56, 67, 72, 97, 151, 153, 160, 164, 165, 166, 210, 222

Naples 133, 146, 167
Napoleon Bonaparte 7, 68, 69, 135, 137, 158, 197, 222
Nietzsche, Friedrich 116

Origo, Iris 10
Orwell, George 196
Otway, Thomas 50, 82
Ovid 65

Pala, Mauro 15
Panini, Giovanni Paolo 24
Panizzi, Antonio 24
Parini, Giuseppe 8, 219, 225
Pellico, Silvio 131, 136
Perticari, Giulio 36
Petrarch (Francesco Petrarca) 8, 18, 24, 28, 32, 35, 86, 212–14
Pindemonte, Ippolito 211
Piozzi, Hester 8
Piranesi, Giovanni Battista 24, 88
Pisa 9, 11–12, 15, 64, 72, 74, 108, 122, 161
Pite, Ralph 214
Pius VII, Pope 121–2
Plutarch 142
Pomarè, Carla 32, 206
Pope, Alexander 131, 142, 154
Praz, Mario 10
Procházka, Martin 207
Pulci, Luigi 3, 18, 24, 67, 117–19, 125, 126, 159, 211, 212, 214, 216

Quennell, Peter 10

Radcliffe, Ann 50, 82, 114, 182
   Italian, The 7, 114
   Mysteries of Udolpho, The 7
Rae, William 124
Ravenna 1, 2, 9, 10, 15–16, 46,
   56, 62–3, 64, 67, 74, 94, 96,
   97–8, 99–108, 114, 123, 153, 161,
   163, 209
Rawes, Alan 10, 17–18, 88, 146
Reynolds, John Hamilton 7, 24
Reynolds, Sir Joshua 98
Richardson, Douglas 77
Rimini 153
Rizzuti, Alberto 132
Roberts, Charlotte 83
Roe, Nicholas 154
Rome 5, 17–18, 23, 53, 55, 86, 88–90,
   95, 98, 106, 120, 166–82, 188,
   190, 198–205
Roscoe, William 7–8
Rose, William Stewart 34
Rousseau, Jean-Jacques 77, 113
Ruskin, John 53, 54

Sachs, Jonathan 95, 184, 186
Saglia, Diego 18–19, 146, 149, 155
Schelling, Friedrich 90
Schiller, Friedrich von 50, 82,
   88, 136
Schmidt, Arnold Anthony 15,
   16, 205
Schoenfield, Mark 146
Schoina, Maria 12, 46, 150
Schor, Esther 7
Scott, Sir Walter 15, 24, 32, 40, 61,
   64, 67, 69, 72–4, 113, 117–18,
   120, 160
   A Legend of Montrose 15, 64–5, 66,
      67, 72–3, 74
   Rob Roy 61, 65, 69, 73
Segati, Marianna 55, 216
Segati, Pietro 216
Sforza, Francesco 134
Shakespeare, William 50, 66, 71,
   72, 82, 88, 105, 114, 135, 136,
   202, 217
Sheil, Richard Lalor 7
Shelley, Mary 3, 7, 12, 24, 48–9, 100,
   108, 113, 160, 182
Shelley, Percy Bysshe 7, 12, 24, 32,
   34, 55, 98, 99, 100, 102, 103, 104,
   108, 113, 115, 122, 161, 173, 182
Sicily 133, 167
Simmel, Georg 82–3
Sismondi, J. C. L. Simonde de 8,
   214, 219
Smollett, Tobias 98, 103
Stabler, Jane 15–16, 61, 150, 157, 187,
   208, 214
Staël, Madame de (Anne-Louise
   Germaine Necker, baronne de
   Staël-Holstein) 7, 50, 61, 136,
   166–72, 173, 175, 176, 177–9,
   181–2, 183, 184, 214
   Corinne, ou l'Italie 7, 15, 17, 61–4,
      74, 166–7, 169–72, 176, 177–9,
      181–2, 214
Steffan, Truman Guy 103, 108
Stendhal (Henri Beyle) 7, 8, 182,
   183, 215
Southey, Robert 13, 24

Tasso, Torquato 8, 14, 24, 25, 28–9,
   30, 31, 32, 35, 39, 40, 67, 114,
   116, 117, 212
   Gerusalemme liberata 8, 24, 30
Turin 124

Vasari, Giorgio 98
Vasi, Giuseppe 24
Vassallo, Peter 10, 35, 39
Venice 1, 3, 5, 8, 9, 10, 15, 17, 46,
   48–9, 51, 52, 53–4, 55, 65, 67,
   74, 80–2, 84, 86, 90, 94, 95,
   100, 101, 107, 114, 116, 130, 134,
   137, 138, 140, 141, 145–6, 148,
   157, 161–2, 176, 186, 188–98,
   205, 215–21

Verona 50–1
Vico, Giambattista 79
Virgil 97
Visconti, Ermes 131, 135, 143
Voltaire (François Marie Arouet) 159

Watkins, Daniel P. 204
Webb, Timothy 164–5

Wellington, Arthur Wellesley, Duke of 152
Westphal, Bertrand 77
Wiley, Michael 62
Wilkes, Joanna 170, 184
Winckelmann, Johann Joachim 23, 167
Wordsworth, William 24, 98

EU authorised representative for GPSR:
Easy Access System Europe, Mustamäe tee 50,
10621 Tallinn, Estonia
gpsr.requests@easproject.com

www.ingramcontent.com/pod-product-compliance
Lightning Source LLC
Chambersburg PA
CBHW030120240426
43673CB00041B/1344